M000214633

Freelance writer **DAVID ABRAM** was born and brought up in south Wales. His first foray into the Corsican mountains came in 1986 during the sabbatical year of a French degree, when he stumbled upon some waymarks and followed them blindly for two days until wild pigs polished off his supplies. Since then, as a guide book writer and photographer, he's walked extensively in the Himalayas, Europe, Morocco and North America but still regards Corsica as a benchmark trekking destination.

Regular opportunities to indulge his passion for the island's mountains are provided by annual updating trips for his other guidebook to the island, *The Rough Guide to Corsica*. David lives and works in Frome, Somerset.

Corsica Trekking – GR20
First edition 2008

Publisher
Trailblazer Publications
The Old Manse, Tower Rd, Hindhead, Surrey, GU26 6SU, UK
Fax (+44) 01428-607571
info@trailblazer-guides.com
www.trailblazer-guides.com

British Library Cataloguing in Publication Data
A catalogue record for this book is available from the British Library

ISBN 978-1-873756-98-0

GR® et PR® sont des marques déposées de la FFRP
(Fédération Française de Randonnée Pédestre)

Editor: Anna Jacomb-Hood
Series editor: Patricia Major
Layout: Anna Jacomb-Hood
Maps: Jane Thomas (trail maps); Nick Hill (town plans and illustrations on pp61-2)
Index: Jane Thomas

Warning: mountain walking can be dangerous
Please read the notes on when to go (p21) and on mountain safety (pp37-9). Every
effort has been made by the author and publisher to ensure that the information
contained herein is as accurate and up to date as possible. However, they are unable
to accept responsibility for any inconvenience, loss or injury sustained by anyone
as a result of the advice and information given in this guide.

Printed on chlorine-free paper from farmed forests by
D2Print (☎ +65-6295 5598)

CORSICA TREKKING

GR20

DAVID ABRAM

TRAILBLAZER PUBLICATIONS

Acknowledgements

A big thank you to everyone at Trailblazer for getting this book off the ground, especially Anna Jacomb-Hood who gave the text a thorough going-over and laid it out, Jane Thomas who updated the maps, and Corinne Sinclair and Laura Stone for last-minute additional research. Thanks, too, to Rorie Fulton for road-testing the route descriptions, Peter Gorecki for photos opposite p33 and p128, and – last but by no means least – Bryn Thomas, without whom this book, and its chunkier forerunner, would never have seen the light of day.

A word of thanks is also due to all those readers of the original *Trekking in Corsica* who took the trouble to write in with feedback, especially: Hilary Sharp, Justin Murphy, Andrew Pemberton, Jiska De Wit, François Parent, Neil Courtis, Dave Fitzgerald & Tim Billington, Renato Losio, Owen McGowan, Elise McManus, Fiona Gillett, Alan O'Shea, George Tonks, Mark & Carolyn Sanders and NC Walker.

A request

The author and publisher have tried to ensure that this guide is as accurate and up to date as possible. Nevertheless things change. If you notice any changes or omissions that should be included in the next edition of this book, please write to David Abram at Trailblazer (address on p2) or email him at david.abram@trailblazer-guides.com. A free copy of the next edition will be sent to persons making a significant contribution.

Updated information will shortly be available on the Internet at
www.trailblazer-guides.com

Cover photo: Crossing an early summer névé on the GR20
© David Abram

CONTENTS

INTRODUCTION

'Une montagne dans la mer' is how Corsica is often described, but 'a *range* of mountains in the sea' would be a more accurate tag. Rising to 2706m (8876ft) at its highest point (more than double the height of Ben Nevis) the island's interior comprises a vast jumble of snow-streaked peaks and deep, forested valleys reminiscent of continental Europe at its most rugged. Imagine such a wilderness surrounded by a vivid blue sea and a string of shell-sand beaches, with views that on clear days extend to the distant Alps and Tuscany, and you'll understand why many regard Corsica's landscapes to be quite simply the most astounding in all the Mediterranean.

Stringing together the scenic highlights of the island's mountainous core, the GR20 is the most illustrious of all France's long-distance waymarked routes. Around 18,000 mountain enthusiasts attempt it each year. Barely half, however, manage all 16 stages between Calenzana in the north and Conca in the south, a total distance of around 170km. The first three days alone, which involve a relentless series of ascents and descents of over 1250m, claim a dropout rate rivalling that of the French Foreign Legion.

Physical challenges aside, the essence of the 'big GR's' appeal lies in the fact that, perhaps more than any other comparable walk in Europe, it takes you to places normally only accessible with ropes. Wriggling along the island's jagged watershed, it links ancient transhumant paths between valleys with a series of astonishing ridge-top traverses from where the full beauty of the Corsican interior is revealed. That these high, exposed sections over bare rock are rarely more taxing than an easy scramble is testament largely to the ingenuity of one man, the alpinist Michel Fabrikant, who devised the GR20 in the 1970s. These days, under the stewardship of Corsica's Parc Naturel Regional (PNRC), Fabrikant's red-and-white waymarked route is as well set up as it was conceived. Between each of its *étapes* stand staffed refuges offering basic shelter, water, toilets, washing facilities and bivouac areas. Most also stock supplies of food and drink, and helicopters are on hand to remove rubbish left behind.

Trekkers used to wilder mountain routes where you have to rely on your own maps, compass skills and equipment, may find this level of infrastructure (not to mention the volume of pedestrian traffic in summer) somewhat intrusive. But the regular waymarking and accommodation does allow you to trek with a lighter pack – a godsend given the 19,000m or so of total altitude gain and loss on the route. Wander away from the marks and you'll quickly appreciate how helpful they are, especially in bad weather.

Any foray into mountains at this altitude has to be undertaken with a certain degree of caution, but don't be intimidated by the GR20's reputation. The severity of the route definitely tends to be exaggerated (not least by the Corsicans themselves, few of whom ever actually attempt it). The main reason for this reputation, ironically enough, is the very infrastructure that renders it so safe. Being without technical obstacles, the GR20 – which can be neatly slotted into a two-week holiday with time to spare for a break on the beach at the end – attracts a large number of trekkers for whom it is the first real taste of high mountain terrain. Ill-prepared for the physical effort involved and carrying far too much kit, many fall by the wayside. Others tackle the route as if it were some kind of competition or army assault course to be completed as quickly as possible; they too like to talk up the trail's rigours.

The reality is that if you're moderately well equipped, keep your eye on the weather and are up to walking six to seven hours a day over steep gradients, the GR – or 'Jay-Er' as it's referred to in French – should pose no insurmountable problems.

In fact it is hard to think of another long-distance route in Europe that crams such a diversity of landscape into a route traversable in under a fortnight. And as if that weren't incentive enough, the GR20 also finishes within easy reach of some of the most idyllic beaches in the world.

The Moor's Head

Flown everywhere from refuge rooftops on the GR20 to the masts of fishing boats in Bastia harbour, Corsica's quirky flag features an emblem whose emotive resonance is as strong as its roots are obscure. The **Tête de Maure**, or 'Moor's Head' – a profile of a black boy sporting a white bandanna – is known to have been imported to the island by the kings of Aragon in the 13th century.

The image, which in Spanish heraldry appears with the head scarf covering the eyes, probably symbolized the crusades against the North African occupiers of the Iberian peninsula. But quite why 'King' Theodore von Neuhof and, later, Pascal Paoli adopted it as an icon of Corsican independence is a subject of much speculation.

One theory is that the Moor's Head harks back to an old legend in which a local peasant youth travelled to Granada to liberate his lover from the clutches of the king of Andalucia after she'd been abducted from her village by pirates. Having somehow sprung her from slavery he returned to the island with her, hotly pursued by a Moorish army led by General Mansour bin Ismail. Wreaking havoc on the journey between Porto and Aléria, the invaders were eventually met and routed by a Corsican force who promptly impaled the defeated general's head on a pike and paraded it in triumph around the island – whence, some maintain, the source 'Tête de Maure' image.

Whatever the emblem's origins it has, over the past three decades, gained considerable potency as a symbol of nationalist defiance and identity. Hung as a backdrop at paramilitary press conferences, you'll see it outside municipal buildings, on hunting knives and wherever a French Tricoleur is raised.

JE SUIS CORSE J'EN SUIS FIER

Using the guide

The aim of this book is to help you get the most out of your GR20 trek: to make the planning easier, avoid wasting time and energy once you're on the trail and interpret the country you'll walk through. It's split into four main sections. The first part tells you everything you'll need to know before leaving home.

Part 2 introduces Corsica itself, setting out background on the island's history, culture, society and wildlife, as well as giving advice on more down-to-earth matters such as making phone calls and booking accommodation.

Featured in Part 3 are practical accounts of Corsica's main towns, at least one of which you're bound to have to pass through en route to or from the hills.

Part 4 goes on to describe the GR20 route itself. The account is broken down into stages, or *étapes*, sketching out the terrain you'll cross on any given day and giving practical information you might need along the way, notably where to eat, sleep and find water, and how to reach other parts of the island by public transport.

Trail maps

Accompanying each stage in Part 4, our sketch maps are designed to be used in conjunction with the large-scale topographical maps published by IGN (the Institut Géographique National) – not to replace them. However, they include detail you won't find on other maps, such as **walking times**, **accommodation** (marked as a black square), **view points**, **water sources** and **complicated junctions**. Everywhere to stay within easy reach of the route is also marked, be it a hotel or unstaffed hut. Further details on each place can be found in the text.

Up or down? The trail is shown as a dotted line. Many stretches cover noteworthy gradients. One arrow indicates a steep slope; two arrows indicate a very steep slope. Note that the arrow points towards the higher part of the trail.

If, for example, you were walking from A (at 900m) to B (at 1100m) and the trail between the two were short and very steep, it would be shown thus: A - - - **>>** - - - B.

Walking times None of the stage timings listed in the guide includes rests, so you'll need to **add on another 20-30 per cent for breaks** over the course of any étape. Inevitably, you may find yourself covering distances more quickly or slowly than we did, but after a few days you'll gauge how different your pace is and be able to adjust the estimates accordingly.

PART 1: PLANNING YOUR TREK

This section is designed to help you plan your trek: to make travel arrangements, calculate how much the trip will cost, and decide both when to go and what to take with you. It also sets out basic advice on mountain safety and what to do in emergencies.

Of course, how you approach a trekking trip is ultimately a matter of personal choice and there's no replacement for hard-won experience in the hills. However, forewarned is forearmed, and time spent reading up and planning ahead will pay dividends. Decisions that may seem trivial from the comfort of your armchair at home – such as what kind of sleeping bag to take or whether you'll be staying in the hotel or refuge – can take on great significance when you're miles from anywhere.

Independently or with a group?

The GR20 is backed up by a trekking infrastructure that's second to none. With the help of this book, the use of a phone or Internet connection and a smattering of French it's perfectly possible to organize your entire trip yourself, from purchasing your plane ticket to reserving a dorm bed in the *gîte d'étape* at the end.

If, on the other hand, time is tighter than your budget, you might prefer someone else to make all the arrangements. **Organized tours** come in a variety of forms: larger operators tend to offer a choice between **group tours**, where you join a guided party for the duration of the trip, and **self-guided itineraries**, where you walk at your own pace along a selected route using a written guide. In both cases transport, accommodation, meals and luggage transfer are standard. All you have to do is pay the bill, pack the equipment on the company's recommended gear list, walk and eat the hot meals dished up on your arrival at the end of each étape.

Apart from sparing you a lot of hassle, the best thing about being pampered on an organized tour is that it allows you to walk unencumbered by a heavy pack. This can make a huge difference to your overall experience of the GR20, where it may allow you to attain altitudes otherwise beyond your fitness level. However, the luxury of *sac allegé* (literally 'lightened bag') is an expensive one: your kit will have to be carried by jeep and mule up to the refuges, which explains why the cost of tours is high. The other drawback with organized holidays, of course, is that you're tied to a fixed itinerary with little scope for detours, which can be frustrating. Depending on the people in your party, the group atmosphere can also get claustrophobic.

What you end up paying for your trek depends on a wide range of factors: the quality of the food and accommodation, the size of the group, duration of the walk, qualifications of the guide, and the time of year. The only way to ensure a company's product is right for you is to read through its brochure carefully. Make comparisons between as many operators as you can (see below for a list of all those currently working in Corsica) and scrutinize the itinerary breakdowns and small print.

TREKKING AGENCIES

The prices quoted by agencies for organized treks do not usually cover the flight, though larger operators are only to happy to arrange air tickets for you (slapping on a hefty mark-up in the process). Nor will the listed price include visa fees, insurance, the cost of drinks, phone calls or tips. Solo travellers should also watch out for so-called **single-person supplements**; these apply mostly to tours involving stays in hotels and can add as much as 25% to the cost.

In the UK
● **Sherpa Expeditions** (☎ 020-8577 2717, 💻 www.sherpa-walking-holidays .co.uk) Established trekking operator offering the GR20 (accompanied) as far as Bavella for £799 (or £999 with flights). Be warned, however, that you'll have to carry your gear and a share of the group provisions for most of the route as Sherpa doesn't use local mule contractors, which makes this a less-enticing deal than those offered by the Corsican competition (see below). Note also, the price does not include meals or refuge fees.

● **Walks Worldwide** (☎ 01524-242000, 💻 www.walksworldwide.com) Challenging 15-day guided trek from Bavella to Asco along the GR20, including an optional ascent of Paglia Alba and finishing with the Cirque de la Solitude. The cost, £1375, includes flights, transfers, meals and guides. They also set up tailor-made treks on request.

● **KE Adventure Travel** (☎ 017687-73966, 💻 www.keadventure.com) offers a ten-night guided trip covering the GR20 from south to north starting at Bavella. It's semi-supported, you only carry a sleeping bag and overnight clothes, and costs from £1145 plus flights. For £725 plus flights they also offer a four-night foray over the northern portion of the GR20 from Vizzavona featuring side trips to Paglia Orba and Monte Cinto.

In Corsica
● **Jean-Paul Quilici** (☎ 04.95.78.64.33, 💻 www.jpquilicimontagne.com; 20122 Quenza) Seven-day treks along the southern GR20, or the whole route over a fortnight, guided by one of Corsica's few fully qualified high-mountain guides, Jean-Paul Quilici. No luggage transfer or any other services: this is basically old-fashioned guiding. For rates, consult Jean-Paul's website.

● **Compagnie des Guides et Accompagnateurs de Montagne** (☎ 04.95.48.05 .22, 💻 www.asniolu.com; 20224 Calacuccia, Niolu) Worth contacting if you wish to book a mountain guide independently.

● **Couleur Corse** (☎ 04.95.10.52.83, 🖳 www.couleur-corse.com; 13 Bd
François Salini, 2000 Ajaccio) Self-guided or fully supported GR20 tours. You
can do either the north or southern halves of the route (from around 600€).

● **Objectif Nature** (☎ 04.95.32.54.34, 🖳 www.objectif-nature-corse.com; 3 rue
Notre Dame de Lourdes, 20200 Bastia) Seven days of the GR20 for 650€, or
the full route in two weeks for 1200€.

● **Montagne Corse en Liberté** (☎ 04.95.20.53.14, 🖳 www.montagne-cor
se.com; 7 rue Meditérranée, 20090 Ajaccio) Corsica's largest trekking operator
has five options for the GR20 alone, ranging from seven-day self-guided trips
of the north, central and southern sections to fully supported sac allégé tours of
the entire route. Prices from 595€ to 1278€.

● **Tour Adventure** (☎ 04.95.50.72.75, 🖳 www.tour-aventure.com/gb/; 1 rue du
Général Fiorella, 2000 Ajaccio) Anglo-Corsican outfit, based on the island,
who offer fully supported, 'self-guided' tours of the GR20. You can do part of
the northern portion (eight days with guide; 1042€), or southern section (6
days; 535€), or the whole route with a qualified guide (for 1646€). Prices
include transfers, luggage relay, meals etc, but not flights.

● **Vallecime** (☎ 04.95.48.69.33, 🖳 www.vallecime.com; Casa Vanella, 20224
Casamaccioli) Once again, a choice of GR20 options and various transverse
routes led by experienced mountaineers from the Niolu Valley. One of them,
Jean-François Luciani, holds the speed record for the GR20 (37 hours) and does
a special fell-running tour for the absurdly fit. Wherever possible they use local
B&B accommodation and family restaurants rather than hotels, and bivouac in
working *bergeries*. English spoken.

In Continental Europe
● **France** Trekking in the Alps (☎ 04.50.54.62.09, 🖳 www.trekkinginthe
alps.com; Chemin des Biolles, Vallorcine 74660) Alps-based outfit run by a
British mountaineer, Hilary Sharp, who offers two annual six- or seven-day
trips to Corsica (one of spring walks, the other taking in the summits you can
see from the GR20), both out of Calvi, costing around 1050€ (without flights).
Cairn (☎ 04.50.34.48.03, 🖳 www.cairn-fr.com; 74300 Les Carrozu-Flaine) run
a variety of trips on the GR20 ranging in cost from 490€ to 1304€.

● **Netherlands** La Ligne Verte (☎ 31-30-296 5272, 🖳 www.valac.nl;
Cervantesiaan 35, 3533 HS Utrecht) The complete GR20 (from 1320€) or
southern (695€), or northern (650€) sections, fully supported by a Dutch-
French firm.

In the USA and Canada
● **France Active Travel** (☎ 830-868-2502, 🖳 www.franceactivetravel.com/
tour-corsica.com; 3005 S Lamar Blvd D-109 #355, Austin, Texas 78704) Fully
supported two-week GR20 tours from a French mountain specialist, with luggage transfer on most stages. The cost (around US$2180) includes food and
accommodation, but not flights.

● **Mountain Travel Sobek** (☎ 1-510-594-6000, 🖳 www.mtsobek.com; 1266
66th St, Suite 4, Emeryville CA, 94608) This company sometimes includes a

guided trek covering a section of the GR20 on its European tours. Check the website for the latest information.

● **KE Adventure Travel** (toll free ☎ 1-800-497-9675, ☎ 1-970-384-0001, 🖳 www.keadventure.com), 3300 East 1st Ave, Suite 250, Denver, Colorado 80206-5806) offers a ten-night guided trip covering the GR20 from south to north starting at Bavella. It's semi-supported, you only carry a sleeping bag and overnight clothes, and costs from US$2590 plus flights. For US$1650 plus flights they also offer a four-night foray over the northern portion of the GR20 from Vizzavona featuring side trips to Paglia Orba and Monte Cinto. Note: these prices do not include flights.

Getting to Corsica

FROM THE UK AND IRELAND

Since the advent of charter and low-cost flights, the cheapest and fastest way to get to Corsica from the UK has been by air. Overland travel, involving two ferry crossings and a long rail or road journey via Paris and one of the Riviera ports, is a commendable option only for those wishing to take their time and see a bit of France en route.

By plane
From the UK Corsica is roughly two hours flying time from Britain, depending on which airport you use. The only **direct scheduled flights** to the island are with **easyJet** which took over the route from BA's low-cost subsidiary, GB Airways, at the start of 2008. Schedules may change but are currently: from London-Gatwick to Bastia three times weekly (Tue, Thur and Sun) and to Ajaccio on Sundays. All the flights arrive at civilized times of day, though they leave the UK very early in the morning. Fares fluctuate according to demand, the date of your journey and how far in advance you book, but they're usually

---

❏ Which airport in Corsica?
Corsica boasts four international airports and you can fly to any of them from the UK. The fare and point of departure will probably be your main priorities initially but it's also worth bearing in mind which direction you intend to walk the GR20 in. For anyone intending to tackle the route from north to south, **Calvi** is the most convenient option; Calvi Sainte-Catherine airport lies so close to the trailhead at Calenzana that with a well-timed flight you can arrive and have the first étape under your belt by nightfall. Calvi is well connected to both Ajaccio and Bastia by rail but the journey from either takes half a day.

Arrive at **Figari** airport (in the far south; see box p105) and you'll either have a long bus or train ride ahead of you, or have to do the walk in the reverse direction from that described in this book.

cheaper than charter flights, typically costing between £125 and £225 return. Now that the route is run by easyJet, however, the bargain fares sometimes available to other destinations on this airline may also become available here. Currently, the lowest tariffs are available for Tuesday and Thursday departures so it pays if you can be flexible with dates. Fares and availability can be most easily checked on the easyJet website (🖳 www.easyjet.com). Note that the

❏ TRAVELLING INDEPENDENTLY FROM THE UK AND IRELAND

The following summary should prove useful if you intend to make your own travel arrangements. Of all the companies listed, Holiday Options is probably the single most useful for anyone wishing to fly to Corsica by charter.

Charter agents and tour companies

With the exception of Holiday Options, which actually charter their own flights, the following are package-tour companies and sell flight-only tickets only when they have a surplus. Few advertise the fact, however, and you'll have to ring each one close to your intended date of departure to dig up the best bargains.

● **Corsican Affair** (☎ 020-7385 8438, 🖳 www.corsicanaffair.co.uk)
● **Corsican Places** (☎ 0845-330 2059, 🖳 www.corsica.co.uk)
● **Cresta Holidays** (☎ 0871-664 7963, 🖳 www.crestaholidays.co.uk)
● **Holiday Options** (☎ 0844-477 0451, 🖳 www.holidayoptions.co.uk)
● **Simply Travel** (☎ 0870-166 4979, 🖳 www.simplytravel.co.uk)
● **VFB Holidays** (☎ 01452-716830, 🖳 www.vfbholidays.co.uk)
● **Voyages Ilena** (☎ 0845-330 2048, 🖳 www. voyagesilena.co.uk)

Airlines

● **Air France** (☎ 0870-142 4343, 🖳 www.airfrance.co.uk) The widest choice of scheduled routes with the fastest connections through Paris
● **BMI Baby** (☎ 0871-224 0224, 🖳 www.bmibaby.com) Low-cost flights direct from London to Nice
● **British Midland** (☎ 0870-607 0555; 🖳 www.flybmi.com) Non-stop flights to Nice, and regular direct charters through the summer to Corsica
● **easyJet** (🖳 www.easyjet.com) Low-cost scheduled flights from London Gatwick to Ajaccio and Bastia. Bargain fares to Nice from Gatwick, Luton, Bristol, Liverpool and several other UK cities; and to Marseille from Gatwick
● **Ryanair** (🖳 www.ryanair.com) Daily flights from Stansted to Toulon, Alghero (Sardinia) and Pisa; also rock-bottom fares from Dublin, Cork and Shannon to the UK for connections
● **Aer Lingus** (☎ 0818-365000 or ☎ 0870-876 5000, 🖳 www.aerlingus.ie) Daily flights to Paris and Nice from Dublin, Belfast and Cork

Useful websites

The following websites are worth checking for discounted flights to Corsica:
🖳 www.cheapflights.com; www.cheapflights.co.uk
🖳 www.expedia.co.uk
🖳 www.flights4less.co.uk
🖳 www.lastminute.com.

prices you're quoted on the website do not initially include **airport taxes** (£65 return) – these appear only after you've selected your flights.

Direct charter flights operate from early April until mid-October and nearly all leave on Sundays. Most of their seats tend to be block-booked by package-holiday operators but you can often pick up unsold tickets through a travel agent, by contacting an operator direct, or – most conveniently of all – through Holiday Options (see box opposite), which runs its own charters and consolidates seats for other companies. Tickets cost from around £250-300 in peak season down to £100 for last-minute deals.

Basically, the later you leave booking a charter seat the cheaper it is likely to be, although this obviously means you might end up losing out on a ticket altogether. Charters fly out of regional airports (Manchester, Birmingham, Bristol, East Midlands, Teeside and Edinburgh) as well as London (Gatwick, Heathrow and Stansted).

If you don't manage to pick up an easyJet ticket, or a charter fare, one option would be **flying indirectly** to Corsica, with a change of plane either at Paris or Lyon or one of the ports on the Côte d'Azur. With Air France you can travel to any of Corsica's four civilian airports from several airports in Britain, including London Heathrow, but fares tend to be top whack (from £200 to £400 return). Journey times are also considerably greater than with charter carriers as you have to wait for at least a couple of hours before picking up your connecting flight (which may even leave from a different airport if you fly through Paris). The best way to unravel the various permutations of flying schedules is to ask a travel agent. They'll take your dates of travel and work out the best options and fares.

Your third option is to travel **to Marseille or Nice**, with easyJet and pick up onward transport from there. EasyJet's fares to Nice (from Gatwick, Luton, Bristol or Liverpool) can be as low as £20 one-way but may involve departing or arriving at an awkward time of day. To find the cheapest deals you have to spend time trawling the airlines' websites (which advertise cheaper tickets than you'll be offered over the phone); again it helps if you can be flexible with your travel dates.

How much money you save in the long run, however, will depend primarily on the cost of your **onward ticket from the Côte d'Azur** to Corsica. Air France and its domestic subsidiary, Compagnie Corse Mediterranée (CCM), fly from Nice and Marseille but their lowest fares start at around £80 return. Add this to the cost of your other ticket and it's unlikely you'll end up with a cheaper deal than that offered by the charter agents.

Finally, if you can't get a bargain easyJet ticket direct, the other **low cost** way to reach Corsica would be to buy one of easyJet's cheapest tickets to Nice or a Ryanair flight to Genoa and catch the ferry to Corsica – which in theory is possible for as little as £100 return all-in. However, to do this you'd have to be sure that a boat was leaving from the same city on the same day as you arrive (far from a certainty). Otherwise you could well find yourself having to blow your net savings on a hotel room or a train ticket to whichever port the next scheduled ferry sailed from. Timetables are posted on the ferry company websites listed in the box opposite, but be warned: locating ferries that link up with cheap flights bought on the Internet can require the patience and mental dexterity of a brain surgeon. You're better off giving their London agents a ring.

From the Republic of Ireland You can fly with Aer Lingus (see box p14) from Belfast, Cork or Dublin to Paris or Nice from around 100€, and from there pick up a connection to Corsica with Air France or CCM. The cheapest option, though, would be to book a cheap Ryanair flight to London, Manchester or Birmingham and hook up with easyJet or a charter.

By train and ferry

With the wealth of cheap flights to Corsica on offer these days you'd need a good reason *not* to want to fly there. Travelling by land and sea takes considerably longer (more than ten times longer even if you time your connections well) and rarely saves you money. It is, however, a more environmentally friendly way to reach the island and can be a lot of fun if you're not in a hurry.

Thanks to the Channel Tunnel, the first leg of the journey from London (St Pancras) to Paris can now be covered quickly and usually painlessly on **Eurostar** (see box below) trains. Tickets for the $2^1/_2$- to 3-hour trip cost as little as £60 return when you book at least 14 days in advance.

From Paris **SNCF** (see below) offers a choice of services down to the Côte d'Azur. The one to go for is the flagship **TGV** (*train à grande vitesse*) **Méditerranée**, which zips to Marseille in about 3 hours 10 minutes. The cheapest fare is around £45 return and has to be booked at least two weeks in advance. The regular service, which takes $10^1/_2$hrs to cover the route, costs the same so it's worth booking ahead to secure a seat on the TGV.

Nice lies three hours beyond Marseille by rail but you might want to travel the extra so as to pick up the super-fast Corsica Ferries NGV (*navire à grande vitesse*) hydrofoil to Corsica (which doesn't operate out of Marseille), thereby saving nine hours or more on the crossing (see opposite).

By taking Eurostar and the TGV it's possible to reach Nice in only 10 hours from London (excluding the hour or so you'll need to change stations in Paris)

❏ **Rail booking agencies**
In the UK the best booking agency and source of advice on passes for all French rail services, including Eurostar, is the SNCF subsidiary **Rail Europe** (☎ 0870-584 8848, 🖥 www.raileurope.co.uk). You can also make reservations direct with **SNCF** through their website (🖥 www.sncf.com).

   For details about Eurostar services phone **Eurostar** (☎ 0870-518 6186), or go to 🖥 www.eurostar.com for online booking and timetable information.

for around £125. There is, however, a catch: to be eligible you have to book within 65 days of the date of your *return* journey. Nor are **rail passes** valid with these rock-bottom fares. But if you're travelling on another kind of rail ticket it may be worth investing in a pass if you're under 26 or over 60.

Ferries to Corsica Ferries run year-round from Marseille and Nice to Corsica, and from Toulon between April and September. You can also get to the island via the Italian ports of Genoa, Savona, La Spezia, Livorno (Leghorn), Piombo, Naples, and Santa Teresa di Gallura in Sardinia during the summer (June-Sep). However, finding out exactly which port the various companies sail to, and on what days, can be difficult via the Internet. Thankfully the ferry companies have agents in the UK who can fathom the complexities of the various schedules on your behalf (see box below).

The fastest route is **via Nice**, from where Corsica Ferries' **NGV** hydrofoils sail to Calvi, Ile Rousse, Bastia and Ajaccio. This service only takes around 2 hours 45 minutes as against 6-12 hours on the ferry and is no more expensive. It runs more or less daily from Nice (but not from Marseille or Toulon, which are only served by slow boats). Fares for foot passengers range from 45€ to 60€ one-way depending on the time of year.

The cheapest crossings from Italy are **from Livorno** (16-24€) but they're less frequent, with two to four departures per week to Bastia in the summer.

Whichever ferry you choose, **advance booking** is essential. Don't just turn up at the port expecting to get a ticket. Places are limited by the number of reclining chairs in economy class, and even the big boats can be fully booked from mid-May onwards.

Also worth taking into consideration before you buy your ticket is which port you'll arrive at: Calvi, only a short taxi ride from the trailhead of the GR20, is the one to aim for, or failing that, Bastia.

❏ FERRY COMPANIES

Listed below are the ferry options from France and Italy to Corsica. For more precise timetable information go to the companies' websites or contact their agents: Via Mare (UK ☎ 0870-410 6040, 🖳 www.viamare.com) for Corsica Ferries, Med Mar and Moby Lines, and Southern Ferries (UK ☎ 0844-815 7785, 🖳 www.southernferries.co.uk) for SNCM.

Tickets can be purchased online through the companies' websites or, for identical prices, through their agents.

From France
● **Corsica Ferries** (🖳 www.corsicaferries.com) From Nice to Bastia and L'Ile Rousse
● **SNCM Ferrytérranée** (🖳 www.sncm.fr) From Marseille to Ajaccio, Bastia, Ile Rousse, Porto-Vecchio and Propriano; from Nice to Ajaccio, Calvi, Bastia and Ile Rousse and from Toulon to Ajaccio and Bastia

From Italy
● **Med Mar** (🖳 www.medmargroup.it) From Naples to Porto-Vecchio, via Palau (Sardinia)
● **Moby Lines** (🖳 www.mobylines.com) From Genoa and Livorno to Bastia

PLANNING YOUR TREK

FROM CONTINENTAL EUROPE

In addition to Air France, most European airlines – including Lufthansa, KLM and Scandinavian Airlines – can sell a through ticket to Corsica with a change of plane in Paris, Marseille or Nice. The cheapest fares will be available online or through a travel agent, who will also be able to advise you about direct **charter** flights to Corsica. These operate from Germany, the Netherlands, Belgium, Sweden, Norway, Denmark and Switzerland between the end of March and mid-October, and offer the most cost-effective and convenient route to the island, with fares that are usually well below those offered by scheduled airlines.

Alternatively, book a cheap flight to Nice or Marseille and then jump on a connecting flight (with CCM; see box opposite) or a ferry (see box p17). Low-cost airlines flying to the Côte d'Azur from continental Europe include Virgin Express (🖳 www.virgin express.com; from Brussels) and easyJet (🖳 www.easyjet.com; from Amsterdam). Depending on which country you're travelling from you might also consider heading to France to link up with one of the many charter flights from Paris Orly or regional airports such as Strasbourg, Lille, Metz and Lyon. Fares range from around 175€ to 275€ according to the season; your travel agent will have access to these flights, run by charter companies such as Nouvelles Frontières (see box above) and Ollandini Voyages (🖳 www.ollandini-voyages.fr).

> ## ❑ FROM MAINLAND FRANCE
>
> ### Travel agents and tour operators
> Any of the following can book you onto flights to Corsica from the Côte d'Azur, although they may ask you to fax a photocopy of your credit or debit card before going ahead with any transaction.
> ● Go Voyages (☎ 01.53.40.44.29)
> ● Nice Voyages (☎ 04.93.13.36.86)
> ● Nouvelles Frontières (☎ 08.25.00.08.25)
> ● Tropical Voyages (☎ 04.93.55.02.02)
> ● Connect Voyages (☎ 01.42.44.14.00)
>
> ### Airlines
> ● Air France (☎ 08.20.82.08.20, 🖳 www .airfrance.fr) Return fares to Corsica start at around 71€ from Nice, or 167€ from Paris
> ● Compagnie Corse Mediterranée (☎ 04 95.29.05.00, 🖳 www.aircorsica.com) Three to six flights daily from Nice and Marseille to Ajaccio and Bastia costing from 80€ return depending on the season

Travelling overland from most of northern Europe, the quickest route to Corsica is usually via Bavaria to one of the north Italian ferry ports such as Genoa, La Spezia or Livorno (Leghorn), from where ferries depart regularly throughout the summer (April-Oct) – see box on p17. The only year-round sea link shuttles from Santa Teresa di Gallura in Sardinia to Bonifacio.

For **train** travellers, the website 🖳 www.railfaneurope.net has hotlinks to all of Europe's national rail companies, where you can access up-to-the-minute timetable information and fares for trans-continental routes.

FROM USA AND CANADA

There are no direct flights from either the USA or Canada to Corsica. You have to either pick up a connection in Paris, or fly down to Nice or Marseille and change planes there. Tickets to the latter two cities tend to cost around US$150 more than you'd pay to fly to the French capital but you'll save most of that on the cost of the onward leg from the Côte d'Azur.

Published **fares** for a return flight to Ajaccio during the trekking season are about US$1800 from New York (via Paris), US$2000 from LA/San Francisco, and C$1500 from Montreal and Toronto. Good first stops for quotes in North America are STA (US ☎ 1-800-781-4040; 🖳 www .statravel.com); and Travel CUTS (US ☎ 1-800-592-2887; Canada ☎ 1-866-246-9762, 🖳 www.travel-cuts.com).

FROM AUSTRALIA AND NEW ZEALAND

Flying from Australasia, Paris will be the gateway as there are no direct flights to the Côte d'Azur. Any of the dozen or so long-haul airlines who fly to France will be able to add on the domestic leg to Corsica. Alternatively you could catch the TGV down to Nice or Marseille and take the ferry, which would allow you to see a bit more of France en route (see p17 for details).

Return **fares** during the summer shoulder and peak seasons (including the cost of the add-on to Ajaccio or Bastia) start at around A$1750-2150 from Sydney, or NZ$3000-4000 from Auckland. Budget-flight specialist STA Travel (🖳 www.statravel.com) has branches in Sydney (☎ 134 782) and Auckland (☎ 0800-474400).

Visas

Citizens of all **EU countries**, **Norway**, the **USA**, **Canada**, **Australia** and **New Zealand** do not need a visa to enter France. Most other nationalities do.

Obtaining a visa from your nearest French embassy consulate is fairly straightforward, but check their opening hours before turning up and allow plenty of time, especially in the summer.

EU nationals who stay in France longer than 30 days are supposed to apply for a *carte de séjour*, a residency permit for which you need proof of earnings at least comparable with the French minimum wage (*le SMIG*). In practice, however, EU passports are no longer stamped so there is no proof of how long you've been in the country.

Budgeting

A trekking holiday in Corsica needn't make a big hole in your wallet, at least if you can resist the temptations of the island's *cafés terrasses* and mountain cuisine. At lower altitudes even those on a flexible budget will probably have to keep tabs on their expenses but the higher you hike the cheaper life tends to get. Apart from a handful of ski stations, where it's possible to splash out on four-course meals and draught beer, your only noteworthy expenses are likely to be provisions, which are sold at premium prices in the shops and refuges along the route. **For rates of exchange see box p79**.

COSTS ON THE GR20

If you camp or bivouac outside refuges, stay out of cafés and restaurants alto-gether, re-stock only at road-level shops rather than at the *gardiens'* stores and cover the entire route in 10 days or less, the GR20 will be a relatively cheap trek by European standards. With a modest daily food allowance of, say, 17.50€/£12.50/US$25, plus camping/bivouac fees of 6.50€/£4.50/US$9 per night, you could spend as little as 250€/£180/US$360. Only a handful of diehards, however, get by on so little. You're more than likely to succumb to various temptations along the way that'll inflate your budget: hot meals, cold beers, a night or two inside a hut in bad weather, and a celebratory splurge at Conca. Add in transport to and from the trailheads, a night or two in a hotel en route plus a few days' camping on the beach to round things off, and you'll be looking at a minimum 500€/£360/US$720 spending money for the fortnight. Plenty of people, however, manage to get through double that – usually by tak-ing time out at villages off the main route, ordering slap-up meals and rounds of beers at every possible opportunity and sleeping in comfortable hotels.

There's also a host of other expenses that are worth taking into account when working out exactly how much cash you'll need. A chunk of them are likely to be incurred travelling through the gateway towns – Ajaccio, Bastia, Calvi or Porto-Vecchio – where money can disappear very quickly indeed. Hotels on the coast tend to be pricier, as does eating out; and you might also have bus tickets, stamps, camera film and batteries (for digital cameras) and medical bits and bobs to buy. The most reliable way to estimate a figure is to calculate how much money you think you'll need altogether, then add at least 50%, just to be on the safe side.

GETTING CASH

At none of the refuges or villages along the GR20 will you find an ATM so take enough cash to get you through. Only at those places where the path dips down to road level (namely Asco Stagnu, Castel di Verghio, Vizzavona, Bergeries d'E Capannelle, Bocca di Verdi and Conca) are debit or credit cards accepted. It's worth noting, however, that some hoteliers may agree to a cash-back bill – ie, add an amount on top of what you owe them which is then paid to you as cash.

If you need to visit a bank to change or withdraw money while on the GR20, Corte (an hour-long train ride north from Vizzavona) is likely to be the nearest place to do it.

Finally, before leaving home, consider what you'd do if your card went missing: it's always a good idea to take a second one as a back-up, keep some emergency cash or travellers' cheques in your passport or money belt, and write the telephone number of your bank or credit card company somewhere you'll be able to find it if anything does go wrong.

When to go

The text in this guide applies uniquely to the summer months, from early June until late October. During the **winter**, when its waymarks become buried under snow and ice, the GR20 is transformed into an extreme alpine route requiring crampons, ropes, ice-axes and, above all, the necessary level of expertise to survive and navigate in sub-zero conditions. It is only practicable for non-specialist trekkers after the spring snow melt. Large névés still cloak the approaches to some of the higher passes well into July, but by then safe routes across them are well trodden and easy to follow.

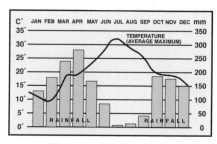

Temperature and rainfall

The main climatic problems in **high summer** are the **heat**, which can be intense, particularly at lower altitudes (the last stage to Conca is notorious for claiming sunstroke victims) and electrical **storms.** Lightning (see box p39) poses a constant threat from mid-July until early September, and is most common around mid-August, when a pre-dawn start is advisable so as to reach the end of the étape before the clouds bubble up around mid-day.

Apart from the weather, the key factor when planning your GR20 expedition is the **crowds.** At the beginning of the season, just after the refuges open in June, and from mid-September until the first dusting of snow in late October, numbers are manageable. Camping space around the huts during these periods is adequate and the atmosphere along the trail relaxed. Once summer is in full swing, however, the GR20 becomes inundated. The past five or six seasons (since a French hit comedy film, *Les Randonneurs*, brought the route to the attention of a mass public) have seen the refuges swarming with trekkers. In addition to overburdening the very rudimentary facilities they offer, such congestion seriously detracts from the locations' natural beauty. The PNRC recently announced plans to revamp several huts to accommodate the upsurge in popularity but this is only likely to attract still greater numbers and will do little to alleviate congestion at notable bottle-neck sections – all the more reason to avoid July and August if at all possible.

PLANNING YOUR TREK

GR20: Route options

TREKKING STYLES AND ROUTE OPTIONS

One of the curious things about the GR is that seemingly everyone – whether they're doing the route in five days or sixteen, with or without a tent, from the north or the south, alone or in a group – thinks their style is the way to go. Ultimately, of course, the best way is the way which most suits *you* and it pays to find out what that is early on.

To a large extent fitness will determine how much you can take on each day. Don't overstretch yourself. If your schedule means you have to double up days, ensure you combine easy, short ones rather than long étapes involving tough climbs. Above all, try not to be swept along by others walking at a faster pace than you're comfortable with, merely to arrive at Conca a day or two ahead of time.

One thing lots of trekkers regret after they've finished the route is that they didn't attempt one or more of the hugely rewarding **side trips**. Some of these, notably the waymarked trails up the big summits flanking the GR, take you into truly awesome landscapes that are a step up in every sense from what you experience along the main path. Bear in mind that some optional routings, such as the *Variante* over Monte Renoso (see p168), are far more inspiring than their lower-level equivalents (which were originally envisaged only as poor-weather alternatives).

The majority of those who complete all 16 stages do so in 10 to 12 days. Do it any quicker and you'd have to be doubling or tripling up lengthy étapes. Take any longer and you'll have plenty of time for detours and for lazing around on the high spots. It's amazing how many people race off at dawn to arrive at the refuge by lunchtime when they could be enjoying sublime scenery up on the trail.

Also worth considering are itineraries that tie together sections of the GR20 with sections of the other long-distance routes. Two of these – the Mare a Mare Nord (and its *variant*) and the Tra Mare e Monti – intersect the GR, giving access to radically different coastal or valley scenery and villages. Following

---

Variants (and *Variantes* ...)

Throughout this book you'll come across outlines of waymarked alternatives to the main routes called *Variants* or *Variantes* (the extra 'e' denotes a feminine noun: GR is short for *la Grande Randonnée*, whereas the other routes, *sentiers*, are nominally masculine). These may be liaison paths to villages, easier or more strenuous side options avoiding weather-prone obstacles, or just plain alternatives. In each case we sketch out their relative merits, under a separate heading, and provide route maps with trekking times and other useful information to help you navigate them.

❏ WAYMARKING

In order to ensure walkers don't get lost on the GR20, the whole route, in both directions, has been painstakingly waymarked with flashes of distinctive red-and-white paint. Dabbed on rocks at regular intervals of between 10m and 20m, the *balisage* (or *flèchage*) allows you to follow the path without constantly having to refer to a map. Up in the mountains, where the route may otherwise not be clearly defined, it's a godsend, especially in bad weather.

GR20 ROUTE

WRONG WAY

The marks come in different forms. A pair of parallel lines or spots means 'carry on'. If the lines have a stem beneath them, forming a 'flag', expect a turning ahead (in the direction of the flag). A red-and-white cross shows that you've gone the wrong way and should turn back. There are other variations but they are self-evident: a pair of lines which clearly bend left or right mean that you should follow the path around a corner, for example.

Yellow paint marks show alternative (ie *Variante*) routes of the GR20, usually more challenging ones via summits or high ridges. They tend

OR

TURN LEFT AHEAD

to be simple spots rather than lines. At those points where the route intersects lower altitude coast-to-coast paths, you'll also cross **orange** waymarks. Single **red** or **green** ones (without white ones next to them) are to be found only on approaches to a few prominent 2500m+ peaks, such as Punta Minuta next to Monte Cinto.

Cairns

Little piles of rocks, or simply two or three rocks balanced together, are used to mark mountain ascent routes that get covered in snow (where paint waymarks would be useless for much of the year). The big drawback with them is that they often trace different routes of varying grades and can therefore lead you off-track onto steeper rock than you might be comfortable with.

them, even if only for a few stages, will give you a far more rounded picture of the island than you'd get from just the GR20.

With less time, say around one week, you might opt to cover certain **sections of the GR20**. From Calenzana, Castel di Verghio is easily reachable in five days. With six to seven days you could press on to Corte via the Mare a Mare Nord via the Tavignano Gorge. This would take you through the most rugged and toughest stretches of the GR20 route, where the landscape is at its most spectacular. Alternatively, pick up the trail at Vizzavona, from where you can cover the more restrained (and correspondingly easier) southern section to Conca in six days.

NORTH OR SOUTH?

Many trekkers follow the Grande Randonnée from south to north, ie in the reverse direction to that described in this book. The advantage is that you begin with the least strenuous étapes and build up to the more gruelling ones. On the other hand, walking northwards will present you with the more subdued, sun-blasted south faces of the massifs rather than the eternal snows and darker crags of their northern slopes. The waymarking is equally dependable in both directions. Ultimately you might end up following the trail from south to north just because your flight landed at Figari Airport, from where Conca is far more accessible than Calenzana. To avoid confusion, stage timings on our maps are given only from north to south.

What to take

It's hard to overstate the importance of getting your choice of kit right. If you don't you could well spend your entire trek regretting it. Little things – like an ill-fitting boot, a sleeping bag that's a bit too thin or a rucksack that rubs – can not only make life uncomfortable but could bring your holiday to a premature end. Of those who fail to finish the GR20, the vast majority do so because of foot problems rather than lack of fitness – problems that could well have been avoided with a little advance preparation.

What you should take ultimately depends on how high and far you hope to walk; the time of year; how you sleep and eat along the route. The overriding principle to keep in mind, however, should be the **weight** of your rucksack: keep it as light as possible. On the GR20 you'll have to contend with some lengthy ascents and lugging a heavy pack uphill for hours can be a grind, especially in the heat. So, before you set off, weigh everything you're taking. Men shouldn't carry much more than 15kg, or a quarter of their body weight; women will generally feel overburdened with more than 10-12kg. Take into account the weight of any water and food you'll be trekking with; if the load is still too much think again about what you could live without.

There are all sorts of ways to keep the weight of a pack down to a minimum (Nicholas Crane, the well-known British walking writer, famously chops the ends off his toothbrushes and drills holes in what's left, and only takes three socks which he wears in strict rotation). For most people, though, getting a full bag to a manageable weight will mean spending money. Light, strong, good-quality trekking equipment doesn't come cheap but once you're on the trail the investment will feel worthwhile.

FOOTWEAR AND FOOT CARE

Your top priority should be your **boots**. These days, outdoor equipment stores stock a bewildering array of technical footwear, ranging from stiff plastic winter boots for use with crampons to ultra-lightweight trainer-style shoes that wouldn't look out of place on a tennis court.

Corsica's trails require something in between. For the **GR20** a good, solid, two- or three-season boot with plenty of ankle support and a durable Vibram-style sole is the ideal choice. Bear in mind you'll be walking over rough, sharp granite most of the time and will have to negotiate patches of loose scree, smooth and wet rock, névés of snow or ice and the odd scramble up very steep slabs. So your footwear should be supportive without being too rigid, water-proof and have a sole that grips well even in wet conditions. Leather boots have for generations been regarded as unbeatable but these days synthetic 'breath-able' fibres, such as Gore-Tex, in combination with water-resistant Nubuck leather, keep your feet just as dry and cool in hot weather, though many people find they overheat inside them.

One definite advantage of these new versatile shoes is that they take a lot less **wearing in**. At the other extreme, stiff leather boots need at least a couple of weeks' use before they become supple. This inevitably involves some dis-comfort (until the leather molds to the shape of your foot) and should always be done gradually, *before* your trek. Leave the breaking in of new boots until you're on a long-distance route and you'll almost certainly suffer for it.

Finding the correct combination of **socks** for your boots is another way of avoiding blisters (see box below). Since the introduction of synthetic fibres that

---

 ### Blisters – prevention and cure

Blisters are the bane of every trekker. Caused by friction between boot and foot, which produces a protective layer of liquid or pus to build up beneath the skin, they can completely ruin any long-distance walk. Bad ones sometimes take four or five days to heal – enough to curtail your trek.

As with most equipment-related problems, prevention is better than cure and you can do a lot to avoid getting blisters. Firstly, always wear your boots in well. Secondly, never walk with wet feet; if your socks get soaked in perspiration or water, take your boots off and dry them out each time you stop for a breather. The old wives' tale says to rub surgical spirit (alcohol) into your feet each evening for at least a week before you trek, to toughen them up. This will certainly harden the skin but it won't necessarily prevent blisters. In fact it can cause worse ones to form between the hard-er external layer and the softer skin beneath.

Never ignore discomfort. At the first sign of rubbing, either cover the affected area of the foot with zinc-oxide tape or plaster, or – best of all – apply a hydrocol-loid blister pad such as Compeed. This acts like an additional layer of skin and once stuck on your foot should stay there for a couple of days. Although quite expensive they're extremely effective if you catch the blister early enough. Ordinary plasters can fold and rub against your skin, actually causing blisters rather than preventing them.

The only way to deal with a blister once it's become unbearable is to burst it and to rest up. Use a hypodermic syringe (an essential component of your trekking medical kit, see p32, which most pharmacists will give you for nothing) or, if you don't have one, a needle (which you can sterilize by burning its tip until it turns black). Allow the blister to dry out afterwards, then apply antiseptic and some kind of dressing.

The worst-case scenario would be if your blister became infected, which hap-pens when bacteria enter the wound. If this happens a few days' rest with your feet up and repeated bathing with antiseptic might sort you out; if not, limp to the near-est doctor.

wick-out perspiration, man-made blends have tended to supersede pure wool and cotton as the benchmark materials. For Corsica a very thin inner layer together with one thicker technical outer sock (ideally with extra woven padding on the toes and heels) should suffice. The inner layer protects you from rubbing while the outer sock provides insulation.

Quality modern boots all have state-of-the-art padding and should be extremely comfortable from the outset but you can increase their shock-absorbability with **insoles** made of rubber-like materials such as Sorbothane. Good ones are expensive but they can be an invaluable aid for anyone who suffers from foot ache or knee problems.

During the summer trekking season there's too little snow on the GR20 to warrant **crampons**. However, you might be glad of a pair of **trekking poles** (see p32) when crossing névés and short **gaiters** ('*stop-tout*' in French) are good for keeping ice, water and annoying pieces of grit out of your boots.

Finally, one item of footwear you'll be glad of in the evenings to give your feet a break from boots after a day's trekking, is a pair of flip-flops or **slippers**. Better still, invest in a pair of Teva-style **outdoor sandals**, which are very light, comfortable and have grippy soles. They'll also come in useful if you take time out on the beach.

RUCKSACK

As with boots, comfort is the key when choosing a rucksack. After you've found one that fits well, then and only then compare capacities and features. External frames are best avoided (internal ones tend not to stick into your back and are less rigid); pockets are always handy; and you might be glad of buckles and elastic webbing for roll mats, and easily accessible compartments for things like water bottles, maps and guide books. To accommodate the fluctuations in volume as you work through your food, an extendable lid is also a good idea.

Rucksacks come in all sizes, from slim climbing bags to bulky backpacks. For the GR20 a medium-sized one will probably suit you best. Make sure the straps can be adjusted: when walking uphill it's better to take the weight on your shoulders; descending tends to be more comfortable if you loosen shoulder straps and tighten the waistband.

Finding out the most efficient way of **packing your sack** usually takes a day or two of experimentation but it always helps to store your things in plastic carrier bags or stuff sacks. These not only divide gear into more manageable sections but also prevent essentials such as down kit, clothing, books and maps getting damp. Remember, no rucksack will be 100% waterproof in a torrential downpour, despite what the manufacturer may imply in its blurb.

SLEEPING BAG AND MAT

Whether you bed down in gîtes d'étape, refuges, or on open mountainsides, a good sleeping bag is a must. Even in mid-summer, night temperatures on the GR20 can be quite chilly at altitude.

When choosing a bag it's always a trade-off between weight and warmth. Ounce for ounce, **down** insulates best but loses its efficiency when damp and is difficult to dry out. Artificial fillings, on the other hand, don't lose their loft so dramatically when wet and are much cheaper, but are a lot less compressible; they're also a little bit heavier (typically 150g for a full-length two-season plus bag).

All things considered, the top choice for the GR20 would have to be a pricey goose-down sleeping bag offering two- to three-season comfort in temperatures of -5° to -10°C. For maximum flexibility you might consider fortifying it with a lightweight outer shell, or **bivouac sack**, made from a breathable, waterproof fabric such as Gore-Tex; this would allow you to sleep outside without the worry of the feathers getting damp. Bottom-of-the-range bivvy sacks tend to be waterproof enough but not all that breathable; this means your body heat will condense on cool nights to form a liquid layer inside the shell which can then soak into your sleeping bag – a nuisance if it's made of down.

In refuges and anywhere at lower attitudes, a lightweight summer sleeping bag should suffice. But if you're aiming to bivouac, consider taking an outer sack too. Some kind of **liner**, made from fleece fabric or a cotton or silk **sheet-sleeping bag**, might also be a good idea; apart from adding extra warmth if you need it they're ideal for clammy or hot summer weather down at sea level.

A **sleeping mat** is essential if you intend to camp or bivouac but would be a waste of space in refuges or gîtes d'étape. Self-inflating Thermarest pads are ideal for sleeping in tents. However, they tend to pierce easily and are thus less suited to bivvying than foam mats; of the latter, the so-called Z-Rest is the most compact (it also unfolds and lies flat straightaway unlike its rolled counterparts).

TENT

With refuges punctuating the whole of the GR20 at convenient intervals you can easily make do without a tent. A good sleeping bag should provide enough warmth, and on those rare nights when it rains you can always seek shelter inside a hut. That said, the privacy and security offered by a tent can be very welcome, especially on the GR20 where bivouackers tend to be corralled together into enclosures, and you'd also be glad of one if you spend time on the beach at any point. Of course, the extra kilos are a lot less onerous if you can split the tent between two or more people. For solo trekkers the benefit versus weight equation comes down firmly against camping unless you have an ultra-light one-man tent that compacts well.

CLOTHING

If the weather's on your side shorts and T-shirts, and maybe a sunhat and glasses, are probably all you'll need on the GR20. Between June and October the weather is generally warm and dry and you'll work up a constant sweat even at altitude. To be equipped for the sudden changes of weather the island can be prone to, however, you'll also need some clothes for wet and cold conditions, and something snug for those fresh evenings in the hills.

Once again it pays to invest in purpose-made outdoor gear if you can. Cotton and wool will certainly do the job but hi-tech wicking textiles, which transfer moisture from the inside to the outside of the garment, will keep you much drier and more comfortable on the trail, while fleeces provide considerably more warmth for less weight than a woollen jumper.

The following tips apply only to the late spring to early autumn trekking season. If you're planning to tackle snow and ice at altitude during the winter in Corsica and aren't sure what kit you'll need, nor how to use it, consider signing up for a winter mountain-skills course or changing your plans.

Base layer

Cotton may be soft on the skin but it's no longer the most comfortable base layer to trek in. Once it gets wet it stays that way, which means you're soaked in perspiration most of the day. For Corsica, **T-shirts** made of light wicking fibres are the ideal thing to wear next to your skin. They literally dry in minutes, are ultra-light, warm and can be washed with little or no soap (which means you can get by with only two). Unfortunately they fray easily when caught in brambles and thus fare badly in the *maquis*; and they're expensive.

As far as **underwear** goes, women will do fine with three pairs of whatever they normally wear. Men, however, should bear in mind the potential horrors of 'crotch rash', an ailment that's nowhere near as amusing as it sounds if it strikes when you're hours away from the nearest hut. Aside from regularly using talcum powder one of the most effective ways of preventing the rubbing that sets it off is to wear close-fitting lycra 'shorts-style' briefs instead of boxers (which can bunch up inside your shorts). Sports shops even sell them impregnated with an anti-microbial compound that kills the offending fungi or bacteria before they can take hold. You should also change your underwear daily and ensure that the tops of your legs get a chance to dry out periodically in hot weather. If you do develop a rash, hydrocortisone cream, available over the counter at most pharmacies, is the most effective treatment.

For the GR20 an additional **thermal base layer** will come in useful for anyone intending to bivouac or camp. A close-fitting suit of ultra-fine Polartec-type fleece material will keep you cosy at night, or you could go for an all-in-one outfit with a long zip up the front (these have the advantage of not riding up to leave a gap between your trousers and top).

Mid-layer

The job of a mid-layer is to provide insulation: to keep out the chill that quickly sets in if you sit around in a sweaty shirt on top of a hill and, in cold or wet weather, to generate a warm buffer between your inner garment and outer shell. **Fleece** long ago succeeded wool as the benchmark fabric because it's light, wind-resistant and fast drying. Nowadays, pricier fleeces also boast a degree of water-resistance (although this may reduce breathability). Other features you'll need in any mid-layer are a long body so your lower back won't be exposed when you stretch while scrambling or bending forwards. Large chest pockets for storing maps are another plus, and you may be glad of a long front zip so you can cool off more quickly after exercise. Finally, check out the weight of the fleece before you buy it: 500-600g will be ample for trekking in Corsica. Any heavier than that and you'll probably find it too warm.

As for **trousers**, a pair of running shorts or anything made of four-way-stretch fabric (such as Lycra) that gives complete freedom of movement is all you're likely to need during the day. If the weather turns chilly, track pants (jogging trousers) or some other kind of lightweight long trousers are a good idea. Outdoor shops stock a range of technical ones with natty features such as microfleece lining, articulated knees, lower leg zippers (to make them easy to take on and off while wearing boots) and cargo pockets. But the most important thing is that they should be light and tough. When trekking at lower altitudes (at the start and end of the GR20) a pair of long trousers made of rip-stop fabric will prevent your legs getting badly scratched in the maquis.

Outer layer

One thing you shouldn't ever scrimp on, especially on the GR20, is a **jacket**. At altitude, a good one can literally mean the difference between life and death.

These days, the only jackets worth bothering with are those made from the new generation of lightweight, waterproof and highly breathable fabrics such as Gore-Tex, Triplepoint Ceramic and Sympatex. Sometimes called 'shells', they're essentially just that. Worn over a mid-layer fleece, breathable outer layers keep out the wind, rain and snow while preventing the build-up of moisture that can form a life-threatening layer of ice in extreme cold, and even in moderate conditions will quickly drain away body heat.

The important criteria to consider when choosing a coat are its overall fit and comfort and the durability of the fabric (the heavier and stiffer it is, the longer it's likely to last). The pricier ones tend to have lots of knobs and bells you probably won't need, such as complicated zip configurations giving adjustable ventilation, velcro flaps and jazzy elastic drawcords. They also have a maze of different pockets; ones in the chest are easily accessible places to store maps, though be warned that the more gear you stuff into them the less breathable your coat's expensive fabric will be.

Even on the GR20 the summer heat can seem Saharan at times, making some kind of **sunhat** indispensable. Apart from stopping your face and neck from burning, it'll also prevent your head from overheating (sunstroke) and reduce the risk of heat-induced fatigue and dehydration.

After the sun disappears it can soon get surprisingly cool and you'll be glad of a **warm hat**, especially at night. An additional layer inside your hood will also come in very useful in windy weather, which is common on the high ridges of the watershed.

Pack a pair of thin thermal **gloves** if you intend to trek at altitude around the beginning or end of the season when the risk of cold snaps increases. In wet weather you'd be glad of ones with a waterproof and breathable outer layer and preferably some kind of grippy material lining the palms and fingers. Another feature that will make life that little bit more comfortable are elastic, close-fitting wrist bands; these ensure your gloves fit snugly inside the sleeves of your jacket.

COOKING GEAR

Every refuge should in principle have gas hobs but a portable stove allows you to cook up hot meals and boil water for tea wherever you are and whenever you want. This can be a real advantage on the GR20 where queues for the gas rings are par for the course in peak season. On those occasions where you find yourself having to camp or bivouac in the middle of nowhere, it's also nice to be able to cook for yourself rather than make do with a cheerless cheese roll for an evening meal.

As ever, weight is the crucial factor when deciding **which kind of stove** to take. For ultimate efficiency and flexibility, MSR-style multi-fuel burners – which are feather-light, run on virtually every kind of inflammable liquid and operate reliably even in extreme cold – are unbeatable. They are, however, very expensive. Most people make do with some kind of cheaper cartridge-based stove system, where you screw a flame burner onto a small, pressurized gas container. The catch here, of course, is that you're not allowed to take compressed gas onto aircraft and thus have to rely on what's available locally, which in the case of Corsica means very little indeed. The only kind of cartridges routinely

---

Water

On a typical GR20 day you should aim to carry a minimum of three litres of water and drink as much as you can before you set off. On the trail itself, top up whenever you pass a spring and remember the old axiom that 'little and often is better than lots in one go'.

As with most parts of the world, stream water should not be considered safe to drink unless you purify it first (with either chlorine-, silver-nitrate- or iodine-based tablets, or a filter). Animals drink from and defecate in streams up to source altitudes, while in summer thousands of trekkers on the GR20 wash and bathe in streams every day.

Although it's always a good idea to take some kind of water **purification tablets** as a back up, springs (safe to drink from without purifying the water) are numerous enough for you not to need them. Throughout this book we highlight where the most convenient water sources are and how much liquid you're likely to need to get by.

Wherever possible, avoid buying mineral water. Although the 1.5-litre bottles it comes in make good-sized containers, the empties create unnecessary refuse. Lightweight aluminium ones, such as those made by Swiss manufacturers Sigg, are a more environmentally friendly and durable alternative, as are **Platypus Hoser**-type reservoirs. Made from durable plastic laminate that doesn't adversely flavour liquids, these come in a variety of shapes and sizes, from one to four litres, and can be stored in rucksack pockets or inside jackets. You drink from them by sucking on a hose that's normally attached to your shoulder strap, which not only saves you having to stop and remove your pack to drink but also frees up your hands and encourages you to consume more.

sold in village shops and supermarkets on the island are old-fashioned Bleuet Camping Gaz ones. These are very light and cheap (as are their burners) but don't work all that well in cold weather, nor when they're running out (which can take a frustratingly long time). A more convenient option would be some kind of stove fuelled by resealable cartridges. These are hard to get hold of in Corsica but you can buy adapters that convert standard Camping Gaz canisters into resealable units at any good outdoor equipment shop.

For Trangia owners, and anyone with a MSR-type stove, methylated spirits is the most readily available fuel in Corsica, where it's sold as *alcool à brûler* (Corsican housewives use it to clean windows).

PHOTOGRAPHIC EQUIPMENT

Compact digital cameras have rapidly taken over as the mountain enthusiasts' tool of choice. They're lightweight, reasonably tough and don't require film. The main drawback with them when it comes to the GR20 is battery life (or lack of it). You won't be able to re-charge at refuges (even those with good solar panels). Hotels and bar owners, at places such as Asco Stagnu (Haut' Asco), Col de Verghio, Vizzavona and Col de Verde, on the other hand, are quite happy for walkers to plug in to their supply, provided they patronize their establishments. Just be sure to remember to bring a three-to-two-pin **adapter**, and a memory card large enough to see you through your trip.

While compact digitals will provide a perfectly adequate record of your walk, an SLR plus a few lenses – digital or otherwise – will give a lot more scope to be creative and capture some of the subtle light effects you experience in the mountains. On the other hand, a heavy camera and its peripherals will seem a burden if you don't get a lot of use out of them.

Anyone serious enough about photography to consider an SLR worth the additional kilo or two should also consider taking a powerful **zoom lens**, ideally 28-250mm; this will give maximum compositional flexibility for minimum weight. Smaller essentials to pack in your camera bag would be a **lens hood** for reducing glare and a **UV filter** for cutting through the high-altitude haze that envelops the Corsican mountains for much of the summer. A **polarizer** will do the same job and deepen the blue of skies. Take along a sturdy, well-padded **carrying case** that you can sling around your neck or attach to your pack; stash your camera in your rucksack and you'll probably find yourself less inclined to use it. Finally, for those essential self-timer shots, a small, lightweight **tripod** is very handy indeed; these days you can get tiny ones that perch on rocks. If you use one of these, don't forget to pack a **shutter release cable**.

Landscape colours and contours are at their richest in the early morning and late evening; snap away in the middle of the day and you'll find the results drained and flat-looking. And be aware of the havoc snow can play with your exposure meter. When photographing névés, it's always a good idea to bracket up a half or one stop.

Kodak and Fuji print **film**, and Fuji-Sensia slide film, are available everywhere, but professional-quality slide film (*pellicule diapositive*) is harder to come by. It's also much more expensive in Corsica than in the UK, mainland France, Holland or USA, so stock up before you come.

MEDICAL KIT

The best kind of medical kit is the one you never use but even healthy, fit trekkers usually have to dip into theirs a couple of times to deal with the kind of everyday aches, pains and minor ailments thrown up by punishing routes such as the GR20. What follows is a list of basic bits and pieces you shouldn't trek without. Finally, don't forget to bring an adequate supply of any **prescription drugs** you might need while you're away.

● Hydrocolloid **blister pads**: always good to have even if you don't use them. In Corsican pharmacies they're known by their brand name, Compeed
● **Zinc-oxide tape** with strong adhesive: just the stuff for fixing dressings that might otherwise get rubbed off by the movement of your boots or clothes
● **Sterilized gauze**: soaks up blood and pus, and keeps wounds clean
● **Antiseptic cream** or spray: for preventing minor infections
● **Plasters**: ditto
● Anti-inflammatory, Ibroprufen-based **pain killers**, such as Nurofen: these effectively suppress the discomfort of sprains, bruises and toothache
● **Mosquito repellent**: DEET-based ones are the most effective but they're also considered by many to be harmful; Citronella is a natural alternative
● **Deep-heat spray** or balm: eases minor sprains and pulled muscles
● **Hydrocortisone cream**: for treating heat rash ('crotch rash')
● **Hypodermic needles**: for piercing blisters; most pharmacists in Corsica will give you some for nothing if you explain you want them to '*percer des ampoules*'
● **High-factor sun cream**: simply essential, whichever trek you do
● **Knee support**: a good strong elastic support can greatly strengthen weak or injured knees, particularly on long descents
● **Nail scissors** or file: to prevent painful in-growing toenails
● **Spare pair of glasses** or contact lenses if you wear them

ODDS AND ENDS

Here's a checklist for those little things that are all too easily forgotten but which could well prove indispensable:
● **Compass** or GPS: no trip into the Corsican mountains should be undertaken without a compass or GPS but bear in mind that neither will get you out of a scrape if you don't know how to use it
● **Trekking poles**: up to half your combined body and pack weight can be shifted from legs to arms with a properly adjusted pair of poles (long for descents and short for climbs); this can take a lot of the stress off your knees and generally increase your speed and efficiency over gradients

---

(Opposite) Top: South face of Capu Ladroncellu. **Bottom**: Approaching the Bocca Palmenti (see p162). Note the red-and-white GR20 waymarks painted on the rocks. (Photos © David Abram).

● **Body wallet**: the best place to stow away your passport, money, air ticket and other paper valuables; slip them inside a plastic bag first, to stop them being soaked through by perspiration

● **Penknife**: no self-respecting Frenchman takes to the hills without his trusty Opinel to slice baguettes, cheese and charcuterie; but Swiss Army or Leatherman multi-purpose knives, with corkscrews, bottle openers, scissors, files and all kinds of other useful tools, are much more versatile

● **Sunglasses**: ideally with some kind of strap to stop them falling off if you take a tumble

● **Head torch**: much better than a normal pocket lamp because it allows you the use of both hands. When buying one, compare how long batteries last and take along a spare set. The new generation of LED-diode lamps are far lighter and last far longer than standard ones, although the beam they produce is more diffuse

● **Plastic map case**: useful for protecting guidebooks as well as maps; don't put it around your neck, where it will flap uncontrollably in the wind, but attach the cord to one of your zip pullers and store it inside a chest pocket

● Piece of **tent fabric** and **glue**: for emergency repairs if you're camping

● **Liquid soap** for washing clothes: most Corsican shops stock stuff called Génie, which works well but should never be used in streams; more biodegradable brands are available through large camping stores in northern Europe and the US (but not Corsica)

● **Puritabs**: chlorine-based tablets kill all water-borne bacteria and viruses, and are healthier over long periods than iodine solution. Silver-nitrate tablets (such as Micropur) taste better than either of these, but take a long time to work

● A long piece of **string** and some **clothes pegs** for drying washing

● **Gaiters**: especially useful in early summer for crossing melting névés

● **Mobile phone**: coverage is very patchy on high ground but a mobile could be useful to call the mountain rescue service (☎ 112); see p38

● Half-litre aluminium **bottle**: the ideal container for cooking oil. **Film canisters** are perfect for storing small quantities of salt, spices and stock powder or cubes.

● **Towel**: outdoor shops sell special low-bulk, highly absorbent ones specially designed for trekking

● **Swim suit**: handy for those tempting mountain streams, pools and Corsican beaches

● Spare pair of **bootlaces**

● **Toothpaste** but only as much as you'll need; squeeze the rest out to save weight

● **Snorkel and face mask**: you'll be glad you carried one if you end up on the beach as the seas around Corsica are unbelievably clear

● **Toilet paper**

(Opposite) Top: Ortu di u Piobbu (see p114) – one of eighteen huts punctuating the GR20. (Photo © David Abram). **Bottom**: Bunks at the Bergeries d'Asinau (see p188). Refuge facilities may be rustic but they are sufficient to allow for ultra-lightweight trekking. (Photo © Peter Gorecki).

RECOMMENDED READING

Background

At some stage of your trip you could well find yourself pinned down by bad weather or killing time waiting for a bus, in which case a good paperback will prove worth its weight. Unfortunately there are few Corsica-related titles still in circulation.

One explanation for this is the monolithic reputation of Dorothy Carrington's *Granite Island* (Penguin). Since it was first published (in French) in the 1960s, *Île de Granite* has been regarded as the definitive introduction to the island and its people. Part history, part travelogue, it roves engagingly over Corsica's past, with fascinating digressions into some of the more arcane facets of island life such as banditry, vendetta, religious brotherhoods and the occult. Although a touch dated now, it still deserves to be top of your reading list.

Dorothy Carrington subsequently wrote a string of erudite books on Corsica, including *Napoleon and his Parents on the Threshold of History* (Viking), the definitive work on the early years of France's future emperor. Anyone interested in matters more occult than historic might enjoy her most recent offering, *Dream Hunters of the Soul* (Phoenix), where she lifts the lid on the hidden worlds of Evil Eye healing, vampires, witchcraft and pagan sects.

James Boswell, posing here in Corsican dress, visited the island in 1765 and wrote a best-selling account of the trip, entitled *An Account of Corsica*.

The book that first defined the island in the minds of English readers, however, was written two centuries before Dorothy Carrington's. *An Account of Corsica* by James Boswell, a 25-year-old dilettante adventurer who would later become famous as Dr Samuel Johnson's biographer, is a quirky travelogue describing the author's quest to meet the rebel leader Pascal Paoli in 1765. Clutching a letter of introduction from no less than Jean-Jacques Rousseau, Boswell lands in Cap Corse from where he sets off on a journey across the island that will leave him enraptured by its mountains, forests and wild inhabitants. *An Account of Corsica* was a best seller in its day, playing a seminal part in Britain's later military alliance with the rebels against France. But it's very much a product of its times and non-specialist, modern-day readers tend to find Boswell's style and philosophical pretensions less than riveting.

General guidebooks

For those who intend to explore Corsica by road or rail as well as via its footpaths, two English-language guidebooks stand out. The *Rough Guide to Corsica* (by the same author as this book) includes dozens of walks and treks, plus a wealth of historical and cultural background. In addition to full coverage of places to stay and eat, you also get lots of interesting background on the island and its people. Lonely Planet's *Corsica* covers much the same ground, albeit more thinly.

Specialist guidebooks

For technical advice on climbing the island's lesser-known peaks get hold of Robin Colomb's *Corsica Mountains*. Written more for rock climbers than trekkers, it covers the main routes and summits and plenty more besides, backed up with helpful line drawings.

Field guides

The most comprehensive guide to the region's flora is *Mediterranean Wild Flowers* by Grey-Wilson and Blamey (HarperCollins). Comprising 560 pages of species descriptions and wonderful colour illustrations, it includes most of the trees, shrubs and flowers you're likely to come across between sea level and 1000m. Apart from its comparatively high price its only shortcoming is its weight, which makes it impractical for trekking. A lighter-weight, more modern alternative is *Wild Flowers of Southern Europe* by Davies and Gibbons (The Crowood Press), over 200 pages shorter but still more than adequate as an identification aid. Well designed and concise, it uses photographs rather than paintings.

Bertel Brun's classic *Birds of Britain and Europe* (Hamlyn) covers most of the avian species you'll spot on the island but for a more Corsica-focused rundown, try to get hold of Jacquie Grozier's *A Birdwatching Guide to France South of the Loire* (Arlequin Press), which includes a site guide to Corsica's birding hot-spots. Few non-specialist bookstores stock it but you can order it direct from the publisher (UK ☎ 0870-010 9700, 💻 www.arlequinpress.co.uk/birdwsg.htm). Although too cumbersome to serve as a field guide, the definitive *Birds of Corsica* (BOU), by local ornithologists Thibault and Bonnacorsi, is the academic's choice, placing the island's birdlife in the wider context of the Mediterranean region. It lists all 323 species ever recorded and contains a hefty bibliography.

Other commendable titles you're unlikely to want to trek with but which provide excellent reference sources are Burton, Arnold and Ovenden's *Field Guide to the Reptiles and Amphibians of Britain and Europe* (HarperCollins), great for identifying those scuttling creatures encountered on Corsica's trails, and Higgins and Riley's *Butterflies of Britain and Europe* (HarperCollins).

MAPS

The maps in this guide should be adequate for navigating the GR20. But when exploring off-track areas, or for a fine-grain picture of outlying terrain, you might want to invest in a set of **IGN** (*Institut Géographique National*) **TOP25**

❏ WHERE TO BUY MAPS OF CORSICA

IGN maps are available in Corsica but shops on the island may not always have the ones you want in stock (this is especially true of the TOP25s covering the GR20, which tend to sell out early in the season).

The only way to be sure of obtaining the maps you need is to buy them in advance in your home country. Below is a list of specialist map shops from whom it is possible to purchase both the TOP25 and Michelin series. You can order by phone or over the Internet but, before parting with any money, compare prices and check the retailer's shipping costs and typical delivery times as these vary greatly.

In the UK
Maps Worldwide (☎ 08451-220559, 🖳 www.mapsworldwide.co.uk)
Stanfords (☎ 020-7836 1321, 🖳 www.stanfords.co.uk)
The Map Shop (☎ 0800-085 4080, 🖳 www.themapshop.co.uk)

In Continental Europe
● **France: Institut National Géographique (IGN)** (☎ 01.43.98.80.00, 🖳 www.ign.fr)
● **Denmark: Nordisk Korthandel** (☎ 3338 2638, 🖳 www.scanmaps.com)

In the USA
Distant Lands (☎ 626-449-3220, 🖳 www.distantlands.com)
Maplink (☎ 805-692-6777, 🖳 www.maplink.com)
Omnimap (☎ 800-742-2677, 🖳 www.omnimap.com)

In Canada
World of Maps (☎ 800-214-8524, 🖳 www.worldofmaps.com)
World Wide Books and Maps (☎ 604-879-3621, 🖳 www.itmb.com)

In Australasia
● **Australia: Map Land** (☎ 03-9670 4383, 🖳 www.mapland.com.au)
  The Map Shop (☎ 08-8231 2033, 🖳 www.mapshop.net.au)
● **New Zealand: Mapworld** (☎ 0800-627967, 🖳 www.mapworld.co.nz)

Séries Bleue maps. Published in distinctive blue covers, these range over the island in 19 overlapping maps at a scale of 1:25,000 (1cm=250m). Their level of detail and accuracy is of the highest standard and they're beautifully drawn, with 10m contour lines and helpful shading to emphasize the topography. Every footpath is clearly highlighted, along with refuges, gîtes d'étape, springs, different kinds of woodland, standing stones, caves and anything else that could possibly be of interest to trekkers. They're also GPS friendly. The catch is the cost: at 9.70€ each (around £7) you'd need to spend 58.20€ (£41.90) for the full set of six covering the whole GR20. In Corsica the Euro price is almost double what you would pay ordering online from IGN.

The standard-issue map for motorists is the cheaper **yellow** 1:200,000 (1cm=2km) **Michelin No 90**, which covers the whole of Corsica on a single sheet. Again, it's clear, impeccably accurate and attractively styled. A neat feature of Michelin maps is the green shading which indicates roads offering outstanding scenery or views.

Mountain safety

When walking Corsica's waymarked trails it's easy to be lulled into a false sense of security. But accidents do happen, especially on exposed and remote stretches of the GR20. Nearly all are the result of inexperience, of underestimating potential dangers or being inadequately prepared for a sudden deterioration in the weather.

The key to avoiding trouble in the mountains is to **plan ahead**. Carefully assess the physical challenges of your route and the impending weather conditions, and make sure you've enough warm, dry clothing, food and water to cope if things take an unexpected turn for the worse. It's also important to know your own limits: knee, ankle and foot injuries are particularly common over the first few days of a trek, before your body has fully acclimatized; and navigation is an altogether more difficult and serious business in poor visibility.

The majority of accidents happen when trekkers wander off the trail. Corsican waymarks, especially those along the GR, follow ingeniously simple routes that often mask the potentially treacherous nature of the terrain. Allow your concentration to lapse for a few minutes and you'll soon see how much steeper, more slippery and awkward the rock tends to become off the path. So if you lose the paint blobs, retrace your steps until you find them and start again rather than press on in the hope of rejoining the trail later. This is particularly important in fog or mist when you're scrambling over high ridge-tops.

Trekkers with experience of wilder, non-waymarked routes will find plenty of incentive to explore areas off the main paths. We've highlighted some of the most rewarding detours in our route guides but bear in mind that help is less likely to be at hand if you do venture off-trail and that you should thus redouble your safety precautions: keep a vigilant eye on the weather, take along a map and compass, and make sure you don't go up anything you wouldn't feel happy descending afterwards. Also, take time to view your route in reverse as you progress, memorizing key landmarks in case you have to retrace your steps.

TREKKING ALONE

One of the golden rules of mountain safety is, 'never trek alone'. Without company you're considerably more vulnerable if anything should go wrong. Break a leg or ankle and you could have a very long wait or crawl to reach help. In practice, however, trekkers are rarely alone for long on Corsica's routes and many people do choose to walk solo. In this case, a few extra safety precautions are advisable. Firstly, always leave your name with a gardien if you leave the main path (eg, to climb a side peak or follow a rarely frequented *Variant* route) and remember to let them know you've arrived safely afterwards. Secondly, wear bright clothing and carry a torch and a whistle for attracting attention if need be. The international **distress signal** in the mountains is to hold your arms above your head in a 'Y' shape; with a whistle, blow six short bursts at one-minute intervals. A **mobile phone** might also be a piece of precautionary kit worth considering.

In the event of accident or injury, **dehydration** is a serious risk. If you're immobilized and unable to reach help you probably won't be able to get to a water source either. It is therefore essential to carry extra water if you trek alone. On the GR20 solo walkers should also bear in mind where they are in relation to other people following the étape. Fall asleep on a rock somewhere off the main trail after lunch and you could easily find yourself detached from the main body of trekkers, which could mean a night without shelter if you injure yourself.

MOUNTAIN RESCUE

Corsica boasts a first-class, professional mountain rescue service operated by a special division of the police force (*gendarmerie*) based at Corte (☎ 04.95.61 13.95). Throughout the summer their red-and-white helicopters patrol the mountains, airlifting out injured trekkers and climbers. If you're ever in the unfortunate position of needing to summon their help, make sure you know as exactly as possible where you are (and can ideally quote map coordinates).

Staffed refuges all have radio links with the gendarmerie. Otherwise, the liaison routes outlined in the guide indicate the quickest way to a telephone. When the chopper or rescue team appears, alert the crew by raising both your arms above your head.

> ❑ **Emergency help**
> ● **By phone** In the event of a serious accident, phone ☎ **17** (police) or ☎ **18** (fire brigade). If you're unable to get through to either of these try the Peloton de Gendarmerie de Haute Montagne (PGHM) on ☎ 04.95.61.13.95.
> ● **At a refuge** Emergency services may be summoned from any refuge.
> ● **By mobile phone** In principle, even in areas without coverage, you should be able to reach the emergency services by dialling ☎ **112**.

Try to get the victim onto open ground from where they may be most easily recovered. Finally, bear in mind our advice on insurance (see opposite). The gendarmerie don't always charge for their services but are entitled to do so (they will if they think you've been imprudent), in which case your rescue could set you back a huge amount of money.

WEATHER FORECASTS

The latest weather bulletins for the Corsican mountains are posted (in French) twice daily on ☎ 08.36.68.02.20 and on the Internet at 🖥 www.meteofrance .com. However, they tend to offer only a general picture of expected conditions over the interior massifs. The most reliable sources of localized weather information, particularly high in the mountains, are the refuge gardiens, who are familiar with conditions typical of the route you'll be covering.

Lightning

The proximity of Corsica's mountains to the sea ensures a steady succession of violent electric storms in the summer. Lightning thus poses a very real risk to trekkers, especially those on the GR20. Over the past decade it has been the cause of more fatalities than anything else along the route. The way to work out if a storm is heading in your direction is to count the gap between the 'flash' and the 'bang'. Light travels around one mile (1.6km) in five seconds, so if you hear the thunder ten seconds after you see the lightning, it means the storm is only two miles away. You should then check repeatedly to see if this gap is increasing or decreasing.

To avoid being struck:
● Avoid open water (streams and lakes)
● Jettison anything metal you may be carrying, such as carabiners or trekking poles
● Move off high, exposed ground as quickly as possible
● Do not shelter under solitary trees
● Avoid close contact with other trekkers; if you're in a group, spread out
● Avoid places where elements meet (such as stream banks, boulder edges and the bottom of trees)
● Never shelter under boulders (dry crevices in rocks are OK); other relatively safe places to hide include shrubs, ground beneath trees of uniform height and dry trenches
● Crouch with your feet together and your head tucked over your knees if possible
● Remain vigilant for 30 minutes after the storm has passed

Health and insurance

Citizens of all EU and EEA countries are entitled to free or reduced cost treatment (for anything that becomes necessary during the trip) on production of an European Health Insurance Card (**EHIC**); in the UK these are available online or by post (get an application form from a post office). An EHIC won't, however, cover the cost of a routine doctor's consultation, nor of medicine or dental treatment (in principle you can claim a proportion of these expenses back from your home health service by sending off the receipts on your return). More importantly, EHICs don't cover mountain rescue, which can cost a small fortune in Corsica. For this reason some kind of private **insurance** cover is essential. Most companies will include trekking in their standard travel policies as long as it doesn't involve the use of ropes, but you should always check beforehand.

In addition to meeting medical and emergency expenses, typical travel policies also insure your equipment, money and air ticket against theft or damage and will make good costs incurred through loss of luggage, or journey curtailment. However, the level of cover varies considerably between companies, which is why you should carefully read and compare benefit tables before you purchase any insurance.

PART 2: CORSICA

Facts about the island

HISTORICAL OUTLINE

Corsica has been continuously inhabited for at least 9000 years, since settlers first crossed the Tyrrhenian Sea from what we now know as the Tuscan coast. Based on hunter-gathering and simple forms of settled agriculture, their society, whose enigmatic standing stones and burial chambers still litter the Corsican *maquis*, was perennially under threat from more technologically advanced invaders. When these first Megalithic peoples were finally forced into the mountains by warlike settlers known as the Torréeans, a pattern was established that would be repeated throughout Corsica's troubled history. Time and again, waves of conquerors have poured onto the flat east coast, sweeping aside its previous colonizers to seize the region's lucrative sea lanes. Yet their subjugation of the indigenous inhabitants was rarely absolute. Greeks, Romans, Vandals, Pisans, Genoans, and most recently the British and French have all counted Corsica as theirs, but none successfully quashed the spirit of rebellion that has always defined the island psyche.

Prehistoric Corsica

Archaeologists are agreed that the first permanent settlers arrived in Corsica in the seventh millennium BC, probably from northern Italy, and that they lived as hunter-gatherers in walled-up rock shelters and caves. The oldest human remains so far discovered – a 9000-year-old skeleton of a woman known as the 'Dame de Bonifacio' – dates from this period. (The skeleton is now housed in the museum at Levie, capital of the Alta Rocca region of southern Corsica.) Rudimentary agriculture and knowledge of animal husbandry arrived a thousand years later with other incomers, establishing a pattern of transhumant life that has survived in the mountains until the present day.

The first structures – dolmens and standing stones (menhirs) – were erected in the fourth millennium. Some were carved with faces, ribs and daggers, or with helmets that when viewed from behind were unmistakably phallic. Among the oldest figurative sculpture ever found in the western Mediterranean, they are thought to have been representations of enemy warriors rather than funerary stones. The basis of this theory was the tempestuous arrival, shortly after the period when carved menhirs started to appear (around 1500BC), of a new society on the island. The **Torréeans**, named after the huge dry-stone towers (*torri*) they piled over the remains of the megalithic peoples they vanquished, are believed to have migrated from Asia Minor. They brought with them iron-working skills – hence the daggers and helmets – and an altogether more sophisticated ritual life.

Greeks and Romans

The patterns of settlement and stone building established by the Torréeans lasted until in-fighting between various sub-groups precipitated what seems to have been a large-scale migration across the straits to Sardinia, where another bumper crop of torri sprang up over succeeding centuries. In Corsica, meanwhile, the east coast saw the first arrival of the **Greeks**. Fleeing Persian persecution and attracted by the island's position within easy reach of the Italian and French coasts, the **Phocaeans**, based at an outpost they called Alalia (now Aléria), introduced viticulture and olive trees. They also instigated a prosperous trade in grain and in copper, lead and iron ore mined in Cap Corse. The colony's success, however, did not go unnoticed by the Phocaeans' rivals in the Mediterranean and within 30 years Alalia found itself overwhelmed first by the **Etruscans** and later by the **Carthaginians**, with the former colonizers pushed north-west to their new capital at Massiglia (now Marseille).

Hot on their heels was the **Roman** general Lucius Cornelius Scipio, who invaded in 259BC, renaming the settlement **Aléria**. A systematic programme of building and territorial expansion ensued, but it took another 40 years to subdue the Corsican tribes of the east, who had teamed up with the Carthaginians to fight the occupiers, and a full hundred years before the interior could be brought to heel.

Bolstered by thriving trade in luxury goods such as jewellery, ceramics, honey and clothes – and by the presence in the largest of the east coast's lagoons of a major naval base – Corsica's Pax Romanica endured for five centuries, during which time **Christianity** gained its first toe-hold on the island. Aléria's downfall was ushered in by the devastating fire of AD410 which laid waste to most of its civic buildings and much of its population.

Weakened by constant malaria epidemics, the dwindling Roman settlement that survived was further depleted by attacks from the **Vandals**, who occupied much of the island in the late fifth century. They, in turn, were ousted by a succession of regional powers: Byzantines, Ostrogoths and, in AD725, the Lombard kings from Italy. By this time, however, Corsica was beginning to reel from repeated incursions by **Saracen** raiders from the Barbary states of North Africa. What began as essentially a campaign of piracy, mounted to take slaves and plunder, gathered momentum until permanent settlements crept inland.

Saracen raid, ninth century
(Lithograph from *Histoire Illustrée de la Corse*, Galletti)

CORSICA

Papal rule

Meanwhile, a promise had been made in 754 by Pépin le Bref, king of the Franks, by which he agreed to hand over the island to the **Papacy** in exchange for help defeating his arch-enemies, the Lombards – a contract eventually honoured two decades later by King Charlemagne (781-810), Pépin's heir. But, despite mounting punitive missions to the Maghreb coast, the Papacy found it impossible to repulse the Saracen raids, which were draining the coastal settlements of their lifeblood and destroying the island's already lame economy.

Forced to take refuge in the interior, the islanders regrouped in the mountains as the Papacy in alliance with the Pisans and Genoese attempted to curb the Saracen onslaught. In their fortified *castelli*, the Corsicans gradually evolved their own system of loose feudal government, dominated by local overlords (*signori*) known as the **Cinarchesi** who, opposing or conciliating the Papacy, Pisa and Genoa as circumstances required, ruled their respective territories. Although elected chiefdoms initially, many were able to consolidate their power by taxing their subjects and establishing hereditary clans. Some of these dynasties, such as the Colonna d'Istrias and Della Roccas, continue to dominate the island's political life to this day.

Ruthlessly individualistic, jealous and unprincipled, the Cinarchesi dissipated their power by constant feuding; they failed to mount a unified challenge against either the Saracens or their Italian rulers. However, they were increasingly able to assert their authority as the Saracen threat subsided, beaten back by retributive attacks mounted from Pisa and Genoa.

Pisans and Genoans

By 1077 Pope Gregory VII had given up attempting to administer Corsica and its troublesome nobles and, in recognition of Pisa's support for the Papacy's war against the Saracens, dispatched the Pisan Bishop Landolph to whip the island's church into shape. Full administrative control was handed over 14 years later by Gregory's successor, Urban V.

The most eloquent and enduring symbols of **Pisan rule**, and of the ambitious ecclesiastical mission the Pisans mounted in Corsica in the eleventh and twelfth centuries, are the exquisite Romanesque **chapels** dotted all over the island. Made of immaculately dressed yellow granite, these churches were marvels of medieval mathematical precision. Unostentatious yet quietly impressive, they were built first on the ruins of the old Roman cities and later at major intersections of mule paths at the centre of traditional *pieves*, or parishes.

Pope Urban's decision to make Corsica a Pisan protectorate only served to intensify Genoan claims to the island. In 1133 the Papacy was finally forced to appease the two warring Italian superpowers, dividing the bishoprics between them. The fighting, however, continued unabated, with Genoa capturing Bonifacio in 1187 and Calvi in 1208 before decisively defeating the Pisan navy in the battle of Meloria in 1284.

Taking advantage of the ongoing struggle, the Corsican leader **Sinucello della Rocca** marshalled popular resentment against the increasingly rapacious local Cinarchesi signori and declared Corsica an autonomous principality, with himself as head. Through clever politicking he even mustered enough support to form a prototype national assembly, complete with its own rudimentary constitution, before the rout of the Pisan navy deprived him of his strongest ally. Stripped of his lands and betrayed by an illegitimate son, Sinucello was finally captured by the Genoans in his 90s and imprisoned on the mainland, where he died in 1306.

Only nine years earlier, Pope Bonifacio VIII had made a bold initiative to forestall Genoa's replacement of Pisa as Corsica's overlords by conferring sovereignty on the Spanish kings of **Aragon**. They, however, were unable to press their claim despite repeated attempts to do so in the 1330s. Their attacks were repulsed by the Genoans, whose own campaigns to break out of the coastal strongholds and extend power across the island were foiled by outbreaks of the Black Death.

The People's Revolt of 1358

With both Aragon and Genoa held at bay, a power vacuum formed in which the Cinarchesi warlords, whose influence had for decades been limited by Pisan domination and the unassailable supremacy of Sinucello della Rocca, were able once again to flex their feudal muscles, increasing taxes on the local population and making repeated calls to arms in pursuit of their territorial claims.

Popular indignation at such abuses of seigneurial power eventually erupted into a full-blown **people's revolt**, led in 1358 by **Sambocuccio d'Alando**. He and his army quickly seized control of the land north and east of the island's watershed – known as the Diqua dai Munti ('this side of the mountains') – driving the Cinarchesi signori from their castles and incorporating their ancestral lands into a region known henceforth as the Terra del Comune. Keen to consolidate these victories and form a buttress against any future Aragonese/Cinarchesi expansion, Sambocuccio invited the Genoans to send a governor for the province. Meanwhile, the wild south-west of the island, the Dila dai Munti ('beyond the mountains', also known as the Terra dai Signori), remained a Cinarchesi stronghold backed by the kings of Aragon.

The Terra del Comune regime instituted by Sambocuccio, which endured for nearly two hundred years, was an extraordinarily enlightened one for the times. Villages were governed democratically by *consulte*, assemblies made up of local people (some of them women), while agricultural land was owned and managed collectively.

Ensconced in their coastal fortresses, the trade-oriented Genoans were content to allow the Terra del Comune's rural population to rule itself. Over time, however, the visionary democratic system began to crumble as a new hereditary class of nobles – the so-called *caporali* – emerged and revived the old system of private land ownership. At around the same time the Aragonese-backed Cinarchesi started to mount vicious attacks on the Genoans' main strongholds, pitching the island into a period of great instability.

The most successful of the Cinarchesi warlords was the demonic **Vincentello d'Istria**, a lurid, charismatic figure with a wart on his face the size of a dislodged eyeball. Through exceptional military prowess and some inspired statesmanship he was able to extend his rule over nearly all the island and might have achieved total independence for Corsica had not his erstwhile supporters mounted a coup and handed him over to the Genoans for execution.

Unable to contain the mounting anarchy of the early fifteenth century, Genoa was compelled to transfer stewardship of Corsica to the **Office of St George**, a wealthy trade corporation with its own private army. It was the Office who erected the mighty citadels that still dominate many Corsican towns and strengthened coastal defences with a chain of watchtowers. Their forces managed to impose order, containing the perennial threat from the Cinarchesi warlords, whose repeated attempts to oust the Office eventually proved their downfall. By 1511 the last of them had been wiped out.

Sampiero Corso and the Genoan era

Meanwhile the struggle for power in Europe between Francis I of France and the Hapsburg Emperor Charles V was being continued by their sons, Henry II of France and Philip II of Spain. The Genoans – and involuntarily the Corsicans – were under alliance to the Hapsburgs so Henry II despatched an expeditionary fleet against them to take Corsica and its key Genoan ports. Dominated by a large Turkish contingent under the infamous corsair Dragut, this naval force was led by a Corsican mercenary, **Sampiero Corso**, who had forged an illustrious reputation as a captain in the French army.

Having quickly and easily taken Bastia, Ajaccio and Corte he mounted protracted sieges against the tougher nuts of Bonifacio and Calvi, which were bombarded by the Turkish galleons before being comprehensively pillaged. French rule, however, was short-lived. As part of the expedient and far-reaching Treaty of Cateau-Cambrésis of 1559, through which France allied itself with Genoa to fight the Austrian Hapsburgs, the Genoans were handed back the island. Furious at this betrayal, Sampiero responded by staging an insurrection of his own in 1564. He and his troops swiftly took control of the interior, but support for their cause began to wane following repeated failures to take the Genoan ports. He was finally ambushed and beheaded in 1567, not by his Italian arch-adversaries but by his former brothers-in-law, who claimed to be avenging the death of their sister (Sampiero had strangled her after she'd betrayed him to the Genoans and run off to France with his family fortune).

With the Cinarchesi defeated and the French neutralized, Genoan rule settled into a period of relative stability in the sixteenth century. The Italians tightened their economic grip on the island: punitive taxes, trade monopolies and artificially low grain prices were imposed on a disgruntled rural population.

Sampiero Corso

Nevertheless they gave Corsican agriculture a much-needed boost: vast forests of chestnut trees were planted to make good a shortfall in cereal on the continent, and extensive olive orchards and vineyards were established. The resulting prosperity, which gave rise over time to a new Corsican bourgeoisie, lasted for 170 years, until the educated, politicized class the boom had spawned turned on its Genoan rulers.

The wars of independence

The catalyst for the **uprising of 1729** was the refusal of villagers near Corte to pay taxes imposed in the wake of two failed harvests. Spurred on by their compatriots' example, other villages followed suit, leading to a formal declaration of national independence two years later. To help put down the rebellion, the Genoans petitioned their old allies, the Austrians. Hapsburg Emperor Charles VI of Austria agreed to send a force of 8000 troops in 1732, but the venture got off to a bad start when hundreds of them were massacred while trying to storm Calenzana (see pp108-10). Having licked their wounds, the Genoan and Austrian commanders made a much better job of the other Balange strongholds, eventually pounding the rebels into a surrender.

The insurrection flared up again as soon as the fleet had left, but the Corsicans were depleted and hopelessly short of finance. Help, however, was at hand in a most peculiar form: **Théodore Von Neuhof**, a wealthy Westphalian dandy who had been a page in the French court, saw in Corsica a golden opportunity to realize his fantasy of becoming a reigning monarch. Having secured finance from Jewish and Greek merchants in Tunis, he landed at Aléria dressed as a Turkish Sultan with a retinue of Italians and Moors. Desperate to get their hands on his money and guns, the Corsican rebels agreed to the bizarre preconditions the adventurer made for his support and proclaimed him King Théodore I of Corsica. But after a few half-hearted sieges and ineffectual war games with the Genoans, it became clear the island's first king was far more suited to swanning around his make-believe court than ousting the Italian oppressors, and eight months later in November 1736 he was forced to make an ignominious departure from the east coast disguised as a priest.

The ensuing stalemate was broken two years later when, in response to a Genoan appeal for aid in 1738, the **French** sent troops to subdue the uprising. They killed more than a thousand patriots and many more were forced to flee before the French pulled out three years later. But the tide seemed to turn in the rebels' favour when the British, Austrians and Sardinians, seeking strategic advantage against the Genoan-French-Spanish axis in the War of Austrian Succession, dispatched a fleet to reinforce the Corsican general **Gian'Pietru Gaffori**.

Hope that this support would prove decisive was dashed when the British signed a peace treaty with the French and withdrew, but the war of independence rumbled on. Gaffori proclaimed a national constitution in 1752, based on military rule with himself as de facto head of state. That same year he and his patriot army stormed the Genoan stronghold of Corte.

Pascal Paoli

Gaffori was assassinated by Genoan stooges the following year, but his death only strengthened the nationalists' hand. To replace him the *consulta* at Corte recalled from the continent the heir of one of his most trusted generals, Giacinto Paoli, who had fled the island during the French onslaught. By the time he had become leader of the nation in 1755, **Pascal Paoli**, only 29 years old, was already steeped in the egalitarian political philosophies of Montesquieu and Rousseau. His plan was explicit from the start: to expel the Genoans and French by force of arms and install a lasting, autonomous, democratic government on the island.

The **Constitution** he subsequently devised was built on the island's existing model of representative democracy. According the vote to every man over the age of 25 and requiring that every parish send an elected deputy to a National Assembly based at Corte, it embodied the political tenets of the Enlightenment (sovereignty of the people, subordination of church to state, and the suppression of hereditary privileges) and was a pioneering experiment for its time. Rousseau praised Paoli's achievement in the strongest terms (he even considered coming to live in Corte) and the Americans were clearly inspired by Corsica's blueprint when they drafted their own Constitution 15 years later.

Other trappings of state followed: a mint and printing press were established, along with schools and the island's first university, and an arms factory opened. Radical new laws were also passed to curb the appalling **vendettas** (see box p167) that had caused tens of thousands of deaths during the Genoan period.

A visionary and charismatic politician he may have been, but the man granted the honorific title 'U Babu di a Patria' (Father of the Nation) possessed a far from flawless military sense. Time and again during his 14-year generalship the forces under his command squandered opportunities to evict the Genoans from their six citadels. Weakened by the naval blockade, the patriot army was also grossly under-equipped to take on the French forces occupying the five main coastal towns.

The beginning of the end for Paoli's regime came in 1768, when the Genoans finally sold off their remaining claim to the island to the French, who promptly dispatched 9000 troops to bring the Corsicans to heel. Although outnumbered nearly two-to-one, Paoli's men held on by harrying their better-trained, better-equipped adversaries with guerrilla attacks. But when 15 more battalions were sent from the mainland, bolstering the invading force to 30,000, Paoli made the fatal error of committing his army to open combat.

Pascal Paoli

Drawn into a pitched battle at **Ponte Nuovo** on May 8, 1769, the Corsicans were massacred and their leader, who was not present at the final engagement, fled to England.

Fêted by London high society and granted a stipend of £12,000 a year, Paoli bided his time for two decades until the French monarchy was swept aside and

The Battle of Ponte Nuovo

the new revolutionary state announced an amnesty for political exiles. Seeing this as his cue, the former leader returned in a blaze of glory and was quickly installed as president. Corsica, however, had moved on. A whole new generation had grown up since Ponte Nuovo and its most promising members – among them a young Napoleon Bonaparte – had been creamed off into French military academies where any latent nationalism had been drummed out of them. Of the old guard that remained, few had any stomach for the fight envisaged by Paoli – a fight that was doomed from the start. On the very day he set foot on the island again the Corsican Assembly voted to become an integral part of the new French state.

The Anglo-Corsican interlude

Nevertheless, Paoli still boasted many supporters on the island and when he finally fell out of favour with the French (over their ill-conceived invasion of neighbouring Sardinia) the resurgent Paolists, led by the Assembly, rallied to prevent his arrest. Fearing a civil war, families loyal to Paris – including the Bonapartes – fled, leaving their homes to the rampaging nationalist mobs.

Paoli and his ageing generals, meanwhile, knew they would be hopelessly outgunned when the inevitable French backlash came and moved quickly to secure the support of their old British allies, who sent a fleet (in 1794) under **Sir Gilbert Elliot** to bail them out. Spurred on by a young **Horatio Nelson**, the expeditionary force laid siege to the French garrisons at Bastia, Saint-Florent and, finally, Calvi (where Nelson lost the sight in his right eye). But the price for this intervention would be a high one.

Rather than restoring Paoli as president, the British nominated Elliot as viceroy. The move provoked riots across Corsica, whereupon Paoli was forcibly exiled to London. When his humiliated soldiers started to join forces with the French to mount reprisals on the British, Sir Gilbert and his troops made a prudently swift exit.

The Napoleonic era and restoration of the French monarchy

In spite of this fleeting, expedient alliance, patriotic opposition to French rule continued unabated throughout the 1790s. However, the uprisings were given short shrift by Napoleon and his dictatorial generals, who mounted a succession of brutal crackdowns culminating in the imposition of direct military rule in 1801.

**Napoleon Bonaparte
as a young officer**

Although Napoleon never enjoyed the unanimous respect of his fellow islanders, his demise 14 years later marked the end of an era for Corsica. Impoverished by centuries of rebellion and vendetta, its population began towards the beginning of the nineteenth century to set aside aspirations of independence and accept that its best chance of advancement lay in a future with France. Along with French citizenship came new opportunities. The expanding trade empire in Africa and South America needed administrators, and thousands of Corsicans would carve out lucrative careers as *pieds noirs* (literally 'black feet'; expatriates) in the colonies. Still more left their ancestral land to emigrate to the great cities of metropolitan France.

Back on the island itself, development gathered pace. A network of new roads and a railway line between Bastia and Ajaccio improved connections between sides of Corsica which had for centuries been separated by high mountains. More schools were founded and mines opened to generate work. Even the bloody tradition of vendetta, which had resisted Paoli's attempts to stamp it out, went into decline. None of this, however, could stem the flood of **emigration**. The island remained in essence a peripheral, deprived and irredeemably poor part of France, and during the second half of the nineteenth century its population almost halved.

The impact of emigration on the traditional economy was devastating. Subsistence farming disappeared altogether, while in the mountains whole villages became deserted as their inhabitants gave up shepherding to seek wage labour elsewhere.

The early twentieth century

Considering its history of acrimonious opposition to French rule, the island responded with surprising commitment to the general mobilization of 1914.

Grouped into their own regiments, Corsican soldiers quickly earned a reputation for the ferocity of their hand-to-hand fighting, epitomized by their use in combat of the *rustaghja* (a kind of billhook meat-chopper designed for charcuterie). However, Corsican bravery on the battlefield was ill-suited to the brutal realities of machine-gun warfare. In all, around 20,000 islanders perished in the 1914-18 war – more per capita than from any other region of Europe.

If the effects of pre-war emigration had been dire, the loss of what amounted to an entire generation of men had catastrophic consequences for Corsica. With the economy in ruins, anyone who could do so sent their children to the continent where, if family contacts could not procure salaried jobs, they eked out a precarious living as pavement vendors or migrant labourers. Others slipped into the **underworld** and during the 1920s organized crime on the Côte d'Azur came to be dominated by Corsican gangsters.

For the first time, ordinary uneducated islanders started to become familiar with money. Even if they weren't living on the continent and earning much themselves, they would see what it could buy. One of the consequences of this shift from subsistence to a more cash-oriented economy was the emergence of a new kind of **banditry**. Forced to take to the maquis after committing a vendetta murder, the traditional Corsican *bandit d'honneur* (see box p167) was a tragi-heroic figure; a victim of deeply held honour codes who lived a life of poverty, dependent on the goodwill of his clansmen.

During the 1920s, however, Corsican outlaws, taking their cue from the continental *milieu* (underworld), began to turn to racketeering and armed robbery. The resulting levels of violence and intimidation became so bad by 1931 that in November of that year the gendarmerie sent a special expeditionary force to wipe out the *bandits percepteurs* ('tax-collecting bandits'). The crackdown was successful, but the way in which traditional vendetta-style violence had slipped into naked extortion had set a dangerous precedent for the future.

World War II

Concerns over Corsica's endemic poverty and crime problems were swept suddenly aside by the outbreak of war in 1939. The Italian dictator Benito Mussolini had long set his sights on Corsica, regarding the islanders as Italians in all but name, and took the opportunity to mount what he regarded as a 'Liberation'. The Corsicans, however, regarded the arrival of 80,000 Italian troops on their soil somewhat differently.

Penned up by the saturation force, they could do little to counter the occupation until the Free French command in Algiers, under the rival generals de Gaulle and Giraud, decided to set up a Resistance network on the island. This was achieved using a submarine,

Corsican Maquisards, 1943

CORSICA

Maquisard, 1943
Note British sten gun and
Tête de Maure symbol

CORSICA

American bombing of Bastia
This catastrophic attack took place
on the day after the city's liberation by Free French forces,
September 1943.

the *Casabianca,* which made daring missions to the Corsican coast from North
Africa to drop agents, radios, arms, muni-
tions and money. In all, seven landings were
completed between December 1942 and
September 1943, when the 12,000-strong
Resistance movement – known as the
Maquis because its members spent most of
the occupation hiding out in the bush – was
finally called into action.

The catalyst was the signing of the
Italian armistice. Mussolini's fall and
Germany's subsequent declaration of war on
its former ally had neutralized the Italian
troops stationed on the island. But it had also
unleashed a much more sinister force of
10,000 Germans dug into a bridgehead near
Bonifacio. As the Allies pressed northwards
from Sicily in the autumn of 1943, Marshal
Kesselring withdrew his Ninth Panzer
Division via Sardinia and Corsica's east coast, covered by the German rear-
guard. Together with special operations battalions from North Africa the
Maquis did their best to forestall the German retreat and there was fierce fighting around Levie and along the east coast.
However, with the bulk of the allies' air
forces tied up in Italy, Kesselring's general,
Von Senger und Etterlin, was able to evacu-
ate most of his division from Bastia to
Leghorn (Livorno) without significant loss.

Nonetheless, the departure of the
Germans was hailed as a **Liberation** – the
first of a metropolitan French *département*
– and Général de Gaulle moved swiftly to
claim credit for the victory (even though it
had been masterminded by his arch-adver-
sary, Giraud). Meanwhile the left-wing
leaders of the Maquis seized control of the
island's administration, much to the chagrin
of the right-wing Général, who went to
great lengths in the coming years to prevent
the same thing from happening again when
mainland France was liberated by the allies.

For the rest of the war Corsica served as
an advance base for 'Operation Anvil', the
invasion of southern France. American

forces were stationed on the east coast and Bastia's Poretta airport became an important base from which allied planes flew missions into occupied Italy. Among the many airmen who lost their lives while stationed there was the French novelist Antoine de St-Exupéry, who disappeared on a reconnaissance flight out of Bastia in 1944.

Liberation
(Contemporary illustration, 1943)

The post-war period

After 1945 thousands of demobilized Corsicans returned to find their homeland as poor as ever. The Americans had sprayed the eastern coastal plain with DDT to rid it of malarial mosquitos, but paid employment was still scarce and the rate of emigration continued to rise: port records from the 1960s show that there were 10,000 more departures than arrivals annually.

To reverse the effect of centuries of economic neglect, the French government launched a two-pronged regeneration programme aimed at reviving **agriculture** and **tourism** on the island. Fruit and wine-growing took off on the east coast and visitor numbers rose to more than half a million in the early 1970s, but few Corsicans felt any real benefit from the initiatives. On the contrary, de Gaulle seemed bent on penalizing the islanders, stripping away their long-standing tax exemptions and increasing duty on cigarettes, tobacco and public transport. The effect of such attempts to bring the Corsican economy in line with that of the mainland was a sharp downturn in the balance of payments and rampant inflation.

Repeated strikes by an increasingly militant workforce seemingly had no effect on de Gaulle, who enraged public opinion still further by announcing that the remote Balagne-Déserte area south-west of Calvi was to be used as a testing ground for atomic bombs. When peaceful public protests failed to reverse his decision, angry armed activists kidnapped a team of government surveyors and threatened to kill them if the Elysée Palace didn't back down. It did, though: at the last minute work on the project was suspended. The **Argentella episode**, as the controversy became known, was effectively the first time since the restoration of the monarchy that Corsicans had taken up arms against the French state. It was to prove a turning point in the island's history.

Nationalist violence and the FLNC

De Gaulle's short-sighted policies had stirred up considerable anti-French feeling, but it was under the presidency of Giscard d'Estaing that this resentment coalesced into a fully fledged **armed struggle**. Its prologue was the arrival in Corsica of around 15,000 *pieds noirs* refugees, repatriated to the island following the Algerian war. Hot on the heels of the Argentella débâcle, their appearance was seen as yet another example of the State using Corsica as a 'dumping ground'. When it emerged that some of the *pieds noirs* wine growers were adulterating their produce with sugar to bump up its alcohol content (thereby threatening the reputation of the island's *appellation contrôlée* vineyards) a group of radical nationalists decided to teach them and the Elysée Palace a lesson.

On August 21, 1975, a team of separatist commandos occupied the cellar of an offending grower in **Aléria** and a siege ensued in which two of the 1250-strong force of gendarmes dispatched by Paris to flush them out were shot dead. The gunmen eventually surrendered and were packed off to prison on the mainland but their action led to the creation soon after of the Fronte di Liberazione Nazionale di Corsica, or **FLNC**.

For the next four years the Front pursued its goal of total independence with bombing campaigns, assassinations and machine-gun attacks on State property, both in mainland France and on the island itself. Second homes became another popular target, as did drug dealers. Money for the Front's struggle was raised initially through racketeering, which over time became institutionalized as *impôt revolutionnaire,* or 'revolutionary tax'. Inevitably the system's potential for abuse proved too strong a temptation for Corsica's petty criminals, the so-called *petits truands*, who soon followed in the footsteps of their bandit forebears and began extorting money under the umbrella of FLNC legitimacy.

Attempts by successive French governments to crack down on the worrying levels of separatist-related crime on the island failed to have any impact. Less than a decade after Aléria, what had started out as an ideologically motivated campaign of violence directed primarily at the State had degenerated into a form of organized crime with its own momentum.

By the late 1980s fault lines had begun to appear in the heart of the movement. With the Mitterrand-Rocard administration adopting a more conciliatory approach to *le problème corse*, disagreement raged over how best to take the struggle forward. Personal rivalries within the Front also began to intensify, culminating in 1990 with the **division of the FLNC** (and its respective political wings) into two factions: the Canal-Habituel and Canal-Historique.

Far from resolving the old power struggles, the split came as a de facto declaration of war between opposing elements in the armed nationalist movement. A bloody feud erupted and by the mid-1990s Corsica seemed to have descended into the dark days of its vendetta-ridden past. Dozens of militants were gunned down or car bombed – 15 of them in the summer of 1995 alone.

In Paris, meanwhile, under the presidency of Jacques Chirac, Prime Minister Juppé's government was pursuing a double-handed policy, publicly claiming not to talk to terrorists while secretly meeting FLNC leaders. These clandestine negotiations bore dramatic fruit in 1996 when between 450 and 600 Canal-Historique militants, armed to the teeth with a terrifying array of modern weaponry, staged a nocturnal press conference (or *nuit bleue*) at **Tralonca** to announce a truce. But the publicity stunt backfired hopelessly on its participants. Confronted with this mass of balaclava-wearing gunmen – not to mention their awesome arsenal of AK-47s, Kalashnikovs, grenade launchers and anti-aircraft missiles – the French public was horrified. As a result, Juppé could neither be seen to be giving in to the Front's demands nor even fulfilling promises made covertly in the talks that preceded the show of force. A deadlock ensued that was broken in defiant style the following summer when the FLNC-Canal-Historique bombed Bordeaux's mairie (where Juppé had been mayor since 1995).

By far the most shocking recent FLNC atrocity was the murder in 1998 of Préfet **Claude Erignac**, the French State's most senior representative on the island; he was shot in the head while leaving the opera in Ajaccio with his wife. The murder provoked outrage in Corsica and a groundswell of opposition to the armed struggle among ordinary islanders. One of the telling statistics revealed by a public enquiry into the troubles that year was that Corsica accounted for around half of France's violent crime, despite having only 0.05% of its population.

Paris, however, left the moral high ground it briefly occupied in spectacular style when Erignac's hard-line successor, Préfet Bernard Bonnet, was arrested and imprisoned for having ordered police commandos to carry out an illegal arson attack on the business of an FLNC militant. The so-called **Affaire de la Paillote** (the beach-shack scandal) redrew the political map: soon after it thousands of indignant Corsicans marched through the streets of Ajaccio calling for greater autonomy.

Meanwhile, the war between paramilitary factions rumbled on. A compelling behind-the-scenes insight into the feud appeared in April 2000 with the publication of a book by two former leaders of the FLNC, Jean-Michel Rossi and François Santoni. In it the two exploded the culture of secrecy that had enshrouded the inner workings of the armed struggle since its inception, exposing the degree to which the FLNC had become corrupted by mafia-style organized crime. Rossi and Santoni must have known that by breaking the Front's cardinal code of silence, not to mention blowing the whistle on some very powerful players in the Corsican underworld, they were signing their own death warrants. Yet their eventual assassinations – Rossi's on an Ile Rousse café terrace in July 2000, and Santoni's at a family wedding a little over a year later – still shocked the island deeply.

The Matignon Plan

Santoni's murder had the side effect of intensifying hawkish opposition to the peace negotiations which Prime Minister Lionel Jospin had reinitiated in the spring of 2000. The crux of these talks between Paris and the nationalists had been the so-called **Matignon Plan**, a wide-ranging portfolio of proposals offering increased autonomy for Corsica in return for an end to separatist violence. But the worsening situation on the island, plus the dramatic resignation of Jospin's Interior Minister over the PM's Corsica policies, had forced a climbdown by the Elysée Palace. Crucial parts of the initiative were withdrawn or diluted and by the winter of 2000-2001 the Gaullist opponents of Matignon were claiming the peace process was dead in its bed.

The death blow for the proposals came with the dramatic defeat of Jospin's socialist government in the general **election of 2002**. Both the incoming president, Jacques Chirac and his new, hard-line home affairs minister, Nicolas Sarkozy, had long been staunch opponents of devolution in general and increased Corsican autonomy in particular. Nevertheless, the new administration immediately got stuck in to serious negotiations with nationalist leaders in Corsica, and within six months presented a package of proposed reforms which it announced the Corsican electorate would vote on in a referendum. Loosely based on Matignon, the proposals were to devolve control over the island's education, cultural affairs, trade and tax to a bigger, more powerful regional assembly.

The ensuing campaign gripped not just Corsica but the entire country. Overriding his own political instincts, Chirac argued passionately for a 'yes' vote, which he said was a golden opportunity for Corsicans to both demonstrate their desire to remain part of France and bring an end to separatist violence, once and for all. In the event, however, the islanders narrowly rejected the government's plan in the **referendum of July 2003**. Sarkozy, in particular, was furious at the result, throwing up his hands on TV the next day saying that now 'nothing more can be done for the place!'.

At the time, many people felt Paris had blown its chances of securing a 'yes' vote by arresting, only two days before the referendum, the man wanted for the murder of Préfet Claude Erignac in 1998. Although the Corsican public had been united in its condemnation of the atrocity, they felt the high-profile arrest – after the suspected murderer, Yvan Colonna, had spent nearly five years on the run – had been carefully timed by the government to influence the vote in its favour. If that was indeed Sarkozy's intention his ruse failed badly; and if it wasn't the government grossly underestimated the Corsican people's tendency to over-react in the face of a perceived threat, or if treated in a heavy-handed, patronizing manner.

Corsica today

Since the landmark vote there has been very little shift in the gridlock gripping Corsica's political situation. Having failed to obtain the constitutional settlement it wanted, the French government decided instead to tackle the separatist problem 'by its roots', mounting a crackdown on organized crime and corruption. A major fraud investigation into the affairs of Corsica's premiership football club, SCB, revealed the club had been used by its president and other prominent nationalist figures as a front for extortion rackets and money laundering. Some of its sponsors had been bombed and blackmailed by paramilitaries; one, a high street travel agent, paid £300,000 per year in protection money to individuals associated with the club. The funds generated were, it was alleged, then diverted both to the FLNC, and the personal pockets of some of its leaders.

A massive trial of 21 suspected ringleaders followed and in the summer of 2005, the gang – among them the president of SCB and another top FLNC commander, Charles Pieri – were imprisoned for 10 years each. The paramilitaries responded to the arrests and verdicts with a bombing campaign to rival any seen since the early 1990s.

Coming not all that long after a referendum that very nearly secured Corsican devolution, the renewed violence only served to point up the paradoxes of the nationalist issue. At the start of the armed struggle in the early 1970s the movement's agenda was clear, its objectives, and methods deployed by the FLNC in pursuit of them, largely supported by the majority of the population. But since then many of the root causes of resentment – under-investment, the treatment of political prisoners and the status of the Corsican language – have been addressed. France now pours € 1.07 billion (around £770 million) of subsidies each year into the island, which benefits from preferential tax laws and social security exemptions. Four international airports, eight maritime ports and a network of high-grade roads have also been built, and there have been two amnesties for paramilitary prisoners as well as the inauguration of a Corsican university at Corte.

Such concessions may not have entirely made good the damage done by years of government neglect, but they have rendered Corsicans far more sympathetic to the idea of being part of the Republic. Even hardliners these days concede that full independence is no longer a realistic or desirable objective. Without huge financial support from the French State Corsica could simply not hope to survive economically.

At the same time, what the traumas of the past three decades seem to have reaffirmed above all else is that the island's problems cannot be resolved by money alone. Underpinning the armed struggle is a traditional Mediterranean culture dominated by clan affiliations and a readiness to resort to violence as a means of solving disputes. No amount of cash is likely to eradicate such tendencies. On the contrary, the recent tourist boom and massive investment from Paris and Brussels seem only to have exposed just how deeply entrenched these old values remain. The vicious feud of the 1990s between FLNC factions may have been expressed in terms of nationalism, but it embodied precisely the same fault lines that have fractured Corsican society since medieval times, and probably long before.

GEOLOGY

Corsica is broadly composed of two contrasting types of rock: crystalline **granite** in the south, centre and west, and schist in the north-east. It cannot be coincidental that the ancient political divisions of the Diqua and Dila dai Munti (see p43) – not to mention the modern rivalry between the départements of Corse-du-Sud and Haute-Corse, and their respective capitals Ajaccio and Bastia – replicate this essential geological dichotomy, which has endowed Corsica with a distinctly dual nature.

The two kinds of rock were created by different processes. First to form was the **magmatic**, which emerged hot from the earth's crust and over time cooled to become granite (including rhyolite and gabbro), mica and quartz. Later, volcanic lava poured from the crater of what is now Monte Cinto, Corsica's highest mountain, to add dollops of multi-coloured alkaline granite – the source of Scandola's startling red porphyry and the green-tinged cliffs of the Spelunca Gorge.

While these crystalline rocks were being eroded into the convoluted mass they are today, newer sedimentary deposits were forming in the sea beside them. Compression, caused by heat and tectonic movement as the Alps were being formed in the Tertiary Period 30 million years ago, then compacted these deposits to form **metamorphic** schist, the dark-green, shiny, slate-like rock of the island's northern and eastern flanks.

It is thought that throughout this period the Sardo-Corsican land mass was still firmly attached to the continent. By matching up rock on Corsica's west coast with the granite of the Massif de l'Estérel in Provence, geologists have theorized it must at some point have broken away and rotated south and east through the Mediterranean towards Italy.

Successive submergings then sculpted this drifting land mass, eroding basins which over millennia became filled with further sedimentary deposits – the origin of the white chalk outcrops and plateaux of Saint-Florent and Bonifacio. Glaciation added the final touches: the U-shaped valleys of the Corsican interior, arêtes (sharp mountain ridges), cirques (giant bowl-shaped hollows at the head of valleys), moraines (colossal dumps of boulders) and suspended valleys that dominate the landscape along the GR20 were all formed by the movement of vast ice flows.

The retreat of the glaciers and massive fluctuation in sea levels as the earth passed through its various ice ages might also explain how animals first reached Corsica. It is believed that at some point in its distant geological past the island was lapped by a much lower sea and that some kind of land bridge must have existed with the Italian coast, across which the first mammals would have migrated.

TOPOGRAPHY

An extension of the southern Alps adrift in the Mediterranean, Corsica is essentially a mountain range marooned in the sea. Most of the island lies more than 320m above sea level, and half a dozen peaks rise to an altitude of more than 2300m, the highest of them Monte Cinto (2706m). These major summits are all grouped in the **north-west**, from where the mighty Corsican watershed wriggles in a south-easterly direction. Running off it is a twisting, herringbone mass of deep valleys that funnel countless streams and rivers down to the coast. Each of these 19 principal valley systems makes up a distinct micro-region, often with its own patterns of weather, flora and land use. Walking between them you'll get a strong sense of their contrasting characters as rock colours, forest constitutions and humidity levels change.

In the **west** the mountain spurs of the central range extend right into the sea in many places, creating a convoluted coastline of dramatic, fjord-like inlets separated by huge ridges. The most spectacular of these is the Golfe de Porto, where giant red porphyry cliffs soar vertically from the shoreline, rising to meet the nearby massif of Paglia Orba and its mantle of towering pinnacles. Strings of beautiful coves and shell-sand beaches also indent the west

---

❏ **Vital geo-statistics**
- Corsica is 183km long (including the 40km finger-shaped peninsula of Cap Corse) and 85km wide at its broadest point.
- Its total surface area is 8682 square kilometres (roughly the same size as Crete, or just under half the size of Wales). Its nearest neighbour, Sardinia, 12km to the south, is nearly three times bigger.
- The island boasts nearly 1000km of coastline.
- Monte Cinto (2706m) is the highest mountain, with Monte Rotondo (2622m) second and Paglia Orba (2525m) third.
- At a little over 90km from source to mouth, the Tavignano River is Corsica's longest, although the Golo, which rises on Paglia Orba and drains into the sea on the east coast, flows faster.

---

coast, whose dramatic topography continues underwater as the land mass plunges to abysses of 800m or more.

The **eastern side** of the island, by contrast, comprises a more restrained, gently shelving alluvial plain, narrow in the north but widening towards its middle before being squeezed out by the encroaching hinterland. Striped with vineyards and fruit orchards, the fertile plain – broken by large lagoons (*étangs*) and expanses of reed-choked wetlands – provides Corsica's most productive agricultural land. Along its shore an immense, largely featureless beach extends in a straight line along virtually the whole bulging length of the island.

In the far **south** the mountains tumble into a broad wedge of undulating scrubland, dotted with outcrops of granite. A belt of white chalk crowns the tip of this south-western edge, where the former Genoan stronghold of Bonifacio clings to an overhanging lip of grooved cliffs, the shadowy profile of Sardinia clearly visible across the straits.

The watershed
A watershed – *le partage des eaux* in French – is the dividing line between river systems. In Corsica's case it refers to the granite spine of the island, the central ridge down the sides of which water flows towards the different coasts. Forming a natural barrier between valley heads, the line of highest ground cleaves diagonally from the hinterland of Calvi in the north-west to Solenzara in the far south-east – the guiding principle of the GR20. The *partage des eaux* also forms the ancient frontier between the regions of Diqua and Dila dai Munti, the basis for the modern départemental division of the island.

Its name implies the presence of water, but the watershed – which remains above 1163m once clear of the coast and is crossed only three times by roads (at Col de Verghio, Vizzavona and Bocca di Verdi) – is actually bone-dry for most of its extent. Nowhere are you more aware of this than on the *haute-route* section of the GR20 between Pietra Piana and Monte d'Oro, where the path follows a parched, sharp-edged ridgeline from which the mountainside falls away steeply to the east coast on one side and the west coast on the other.

CORSICA

CLIMATE

Corsica enjoys a typical Mediterranean climate with comparatively short, mild winters and long, hot, dry summers when average maximum **temperatures** hover around 27°C/80°F. During heat waves in July and August it is not uncommon for the island to roast at 35°C/95°F for days on end. However, temperatures drop considerably at **altitude** (typically 5°C/9°F for every 1000m/ 3000ft gained). Above the 1000m mark the weather rarely gets unbearably hot, while at 1800m/6000ft or over night-time remains fresh even in mid-summer. Ascend above 2000m/6500ft and you'll be in the high mountains proper where weather conditions can change swiftly (see p38).

In spring (mid-March to May) and autumn (Oct-Nov) average maximum temperatures drop to a very pleasant 15-17°C/60-64°F at sea level, although these times of year can be prone to heavy rain. Corsica receives an impressive 800-900mm (30-35 inches) of **rainfall** annually (more than some parts of Ireland). Most of it, however, comes in dramatic downpours that rarely last longer than a couple of days. When it does rain, flooding is often a problem, especially in late autumn when dry river beds can suddenly be transformed into fast-flowing torrents full of upended trees and mud slicks (a good reason never to camp on one).

Freezing, snowy conditions prevail in the high mountains from January until mid-March, when the watershed and its adjacent peaks are at their whitest and most picturesque. But **frost** is a rarity down on the coast (Ajaccio gets around a dozen frosty mornings per year, and Bastia half that). Corsicans love to boast of being able to eat outdoors until Christmas – in which case old ladies will warn that '*Natale à u balcone, Pasqua à u fucone*' (Christmas on the verandah, Easter by the fire).

Dry and sunny the island may be for most of the year but there are few days without **wind**, particularly on the coast. Depending on the direction they blow from, Corsican winds have different names and characters. When chilly and coming from the north, it might be the biting winter *traumutanda* or the summer *mistral*, the result of temperature disparities between the continent and Mediterranean which force currents of cooler air down the Rhône Valley. From the south-west, the *libecciu* often brings storms and rain, as does the *gregale* which blows off the Italian coast to the north-east. A heavy swell is usually stirred up by the *livante*, the strong east wind, while mist and fog are often the by-products of the warm, humid *sciroccu*, which blows in from North Africa. The windiest places in Corsica are Bonifacio, whose straits are notoriously perilous, and the extremities of Cap Corse in the north where some of the hillsides are completely bare.

Up in the mountains you'll notice the effects of **convection**, as differences in temperatures between the land and sea build up. During the day the granite island warms more quickly that its surrounding water mass, generating thermals that suck in humid air from the sea, which then condenses to form cloud in the afternoon. In the evenings, the same phenomenon occurs in reverse as the island cools down more quickly than the sea, creating cool offshore breezes.

FLORA AND FAUNA

Following Corsica's footpaths you'll be constantly struck by how extraordinarily unspoilt the island is. Overgrazing, indiscriminate hunting and, most recently, devastating fires have all taken their toll but, if anything, the landscape shows less evidence of human encroachment today than it would have a century or more ago, when the villages were more populated and the pressure on forests, rivers and mountain vegetation correspondingly greater. That this remains the case, in spite of some 1.75 million visitors pouring into Corsica each year, is a tribute to the immense efforts of the Parc Naturel Régional Corse (PNRC; see box below) whose domain encompasses 38% of the island's surface as well as important marine reserves.

Rigorous environmental laws have also kept polluters and developers at bay, as have the activities of nationalist paramilitaries, whose bombings of unsympathetic constructions and second homes have protected the coast from the kind of abuse sustained by other beautiful corners of the Mediterranean.

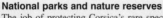

National parks and nature reserves

The job of protecting Corsica's rare species – including mouflon, osprey, red deer and bearded vulture – is the responsibility of the **Parc Naturel Régional Corse** (PNRC). Established in 1972, 'Le Parc', as it's usually referred to, encompasses 350,512 hectares of the island; 38% of Corsica's surface area. Conservation is just part of the work carried out by its 100-strong workforce, who are also charged with maintaining the 1500km network of waymarked paths. One of the premises behind the PNRC's creation of this impressive trekking infrastructure was the regeneration of the interior's flagging economy, and considerable resources have been deployed over the past three decades to renovate *bergeries*, restore remote chapels, support local artisans and generally preserve the traditional ways of life and occupations in the mountains.

Aside from its many refuges the PNRC's principal interface with the public is its **information offices** around the island, which offer advice and printed material on trekking-related matters; the best equipped is in Ajaccio (see p84). For a full rundown of the PNRC and its activities check out its website 🖥 www.parc-naturel-corse.com.

Corsica also boasts a string of smaller **coastal nature reserves** run by the Conservatoire de l'Espace Littoral et des Rivages Lacustres (Organization for the Conservation of Coastal and Lake Areas; 'Le Littoral' for short). Since its inauguration in 1975 this government-funded body has purchased around 15% of the island's shoreline and lagoons. A few of the reserves, notably the Littoral Sartènais in the far south-west of the island, have been opened up to the public by coastal paths. Plans to add more of these are also in the pipeline.

As a trekker the most conspicuous reminder that you're walking through a nature reserve or park will be the signboards and waymarks. Some indicate onward or liaison paths with villages; others are there to reinforce the **restrictions on camping and bivouacking** imposed in all protected areas. At notable beauty spots along the GR20, such as Lac de Nino, *gardiens* are employed to ensure no-one infringes the law, which also requires you to take litter out in your pack and refrain from lighting fires. For more on minimum impact trekking see p204.

Arguably the greatest threat to Corsica's pristine state today are plans currently being thrashed out between Paris, the island's politicians and militant nationalists over how far the powers of regional government should be increased. Environmentalists argue that if Corsica is granted the degree of autonomy its leaders are demanding, tough French environmental legislation might be overridden by the financial interests of unscrupulous local speculators, hastening the spread of concrete along the coast.

For the time being, however, Corsica remains exceptionally green and wild, and there's no better way of getting to grips with its wealth of flora and fauna than on foot. On the GR20 you'll traverse all three of its distinct **habitats**: from sea level the rich, quintessentially **Mediterranean Zone** – with palms, eucalyptus, oleander, wild cacti, olive and citrus trees standing out against the fragrant maquis scrub – extends to around 1000m. Above that, lush canopies of sweet chestnut give way to the slender pine, beech and spruce trees of the **Mountain Zone**. Rock and stream beds scattered with bushes of odorous alder and hardy flowering shrubs characterize the **Alpine Zone** above 2000m.

Birds

In common with many southern European countries, the local obsession with firearms has wrought havoc with the island's avian population, which seems to be regarded as fair game for target practice in the winter hunting season. Corsica may as a result offer a smaller number of birds than you'd expect for somewhere as wild but its diverse landscapes means a correspondingly broad spectrum of species is present. Some are rare enough to attract the attention of serious enthusiasts. But if you're not one of these, chances are you're unlikely to recognize a Corsican nuthatch, Sardinian warbler or Alpine accentor when you see one – all the more reason to sharpen up your bird-spotting knowledge before you come. The best way to do this is to get hold of one of the field guides recommended on p35; more committed birders might also surf the Web for the latest trip reports, which pinpoint the most promising spots for sighting specific species.

At the start of your trek, heading through the coastal maquis, **warblers** will continually flit across the path, sounding alarm calls from the tops of swaying bushes. Dozens of species live on the island, but the stars have to be the Marmara's warbler, which favours patches of low maquis, and the Sardinian and Dartford warblers, very rare in northern Europe but quite common in Corsica where they prefer high scrub. Listen out, too, for the distinctively explosive 'cheti-ti' cry of the buff-coloured Cetti warbler, another rare resident.

In the spring, overhead wires are where you're most likely to sight the viridescent **bee-eater**, the most colourful of Corsica's migrants. With its turquoise and emerald wings and red-brown breast, this exotic visitor presents a striking spectacle, especially when flashing in flocks across grassy meadows and around riverbanks.

At the shoreline, birdlife is less prolific than on comparable coasts in Britain and Ireland, with no large seabird colonies and surprisingly few gulls. However, exposed, rocky coasts such as those of the magnificent Scandola Nature Reserve (to the west of the island) are home to a small number of exciting species. Limited to a few small pockets in the islands of the western Mediterranean, the **Andouin's gull** is the rarest of these, recognizable by its slender wings and red-and-black striped beak. You'll almost certainly see it if you take one of the boat trips out into the Golfe de Porto, along with the **osprey**, or fish eagle, which builds enormous nests of twigs atop isolated rock pinnacles. There are thought to be only 10 pairs of this splendid bird of prey left in Corsica, but your chances of spotting one are good if you trek around the west coast where they dive to seize fish with their impressive talons. The Scandola region also harbours a thriving population of **Mediterranean shearwaters**, which skim at high speed across the waves.

The extensive interior **forests** are home to several endemics, the most famous of which is the **Corsican nuthatch**. Unique to the island, this tiny blue-grey bird was only identified as a separate species in 1883 by a British ornithologist (whence its misleading Latin name – *Sitta whiteheadi*). It's more often heard than seen – only an estimated 2000 nesting pairs survive – but in the forests of Aïtone, Asco and Ospédale you'd be unlucky not to glimpse one scurrying up a tree trunk.

Above the treeline the bird you'll get closest to will be the garrulous **yellow-billed chough**, which has carved a career for itself scrounging picnic scraps along the GR20. The ridge section at the head of the Restonica Valley, above the Capitellu and Melu lakes, is one of the many places where this normally shy bird will hop right up to you pecking for crumbs. Its much larger cousin, the **raven**, scours the same slopes but from a safer height, its gruff croak echoing off the granite cliffs.

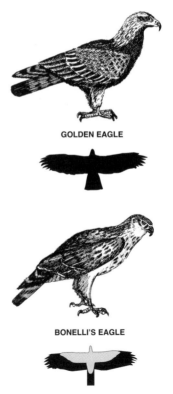

GOLDEN EAGLE

BONELLI'S EAGLE

Golden eagles rarely deign to descend to path level, preferring to ride the thermals high above the rocky ridges of the watershed. But they are a common-enough sight along the GR20 where they prey on smaller birds, rabbits and mice. Their distinguishing features are their dark-brown colour and the gold flecks that tinge the fronts of their head and wings, which broaden noticeably towards the tips. In flight the tail is long, wide and square-ended.

It is easy to distinguish from the smaller **Bonelli's eagle**, whose under-

LAMMERGEIER

sides are greyish white with a prominent black band running along the rear of the wings and over the tail.

The bird of prey every trekker wants to sight at least once in Corsica is the elusive **bearded vulture** or **lammergeier**. Their numbers have been reduced to only a handful of nesting pairs by centuries of persecution by shepherds, who mistakenly believed they took young lambs (whence the name which comes from the German, 'lamb-taker'). In fact, this majestic vulture, which boasts a wingspan of nearly three metres, survives off carrion left by hawks and eagles. Its nickname in French, *le casseur d'os*, derives from its habit of dropping bones to expose the nourishing marrow inside them. Lac de Nino is the place you're most likely to witness this extraordinary phenomenon; more background on Corsica's bearded vultures appears in the box on p136.

Finally, confirmed ornithologists should keep their binoculars handy in case one of the much smaller rarities of the island's mountains puts in a fleeting appearance. To sight the elusive **wallcreeper**, **snow finch** or **Alpine accentor** – the undisputed stars of the high-altitude zone – you'll need to hang around above 1900m for a few days and have a good deal of luck as they survive here only in perilously small numbers.

Reptiles

From spring until late autumn Corsican trails teem with **lizards**, although differentiating between the half a dozen or so species (and numerous subspecies) that inhabit the island can be tricky. The easiest to identify are the ubiquitous **Tyrrhenian wall lizards**, which sport two broad green dorsal stripes on their mottled brown backs. At higher altitudes you might also spot a **Bedriaga's wall lizard**, which lives between 600m and 2000m, usually on stones or rocks overhanging water. Their tails, bright blue in the case of juvenile males, can be half as long again as their bodies. Come across one with a blue throat and orange underbelly, on the other hand, and you can congratulate yourself on having seen the much rarer **Dalmatian algyroides**, which hangs out in shady wall crevices or under boulders during the hottest times of day. Splayed-toed **geckos** are far more common and often pop up inside houses where they cling to walls and ceilings waiting for flies and spiders.

Perhaps the most striking member of Corsica's lizard family, however, is the **fire salamander** (see photo opposite p65). Although not particularly rare, this slow-moving, slimy yellow-and-black creature is elusive, emerging from its hiding places only during wet weather, when it can often be seen skulking along the footpaths in search of baby frogs and newts. Traditionally collected for food, salamanders are also kept as pets and their numbers are thus declining in the wild.

Collectors, along with stray dogs and bush fires, have also been the principal scourge of the friendly **Hermann's tortoise**, which lumbers along the back roads and trekking trails of the coastal plain and lower-lying valleys in pursuit of its favourite foods: dandelion leaves and maquis berries. It's the only surviving species of tortoise still wild on the island.

Neither of the two kinds of **snake** resident in Corsica is poisonous but you should think twice before getting close as one of them, the **whip snake**, will probably take a swipe at you if you do. Known on the continent as *la coléreuse* ('the bad tempered one'), it will hiss loudly and bite if threatened. The subspecies of whip snake most often encountered amid dry maquis tends to be shiny black with yellow-green markings and a lighter, yellow-brown underbelly. **Grass snakes** are paler in colour and altogether less aggressive, although they'll secrete a nasty smelling odour from glands in the neck if picked up.

Mammals

Considering the great passion with which they continue to be hunted, it is a testament to the resilience and adaptability of the **wild boar** that so many – roughly 30,000 – still inhabit Corsica's dense forests. Distinguished from their semi-domesticated pig counterparts by their stocky stature and glossy black coats, the famously fierce *sanglier* subsists on acorns, chestnuts and wild fruit, which it supplements with juicy roots. The closest you're likely to get to one are the excavations they make in search of these, which cause considerable damage to ground cover in deciduous woodland. Constant pressure from humans has made boar highly secretive and you should count yourself fortunate if you see one, especially a full-grown male with tusks. These days they tend to be hunted in a most cowardly fashion: dogs are dispatched into the woods to flush the boar out onto a road where the camouflaged hunters wait with their rifles cocked. An estimated 10,000 are shot each year, making *la chasse au sanglier* (boar hunting) by far Corsica's most popular sport.

The island's own indigenous species of **deer**, *Cervus elaphus corsicanus*, is far less numerous. The smallest of Europe's red deer, it disappeared completely in the 1960s and would have remained absent had not a last-ditch PNRC breeding programme, which reintroduced animals from neighbouring Sardinia, revived the population. From high-fenced enclosures in the Alta Rocca region (in the far south of Corsica) a dozen or more young adults are released into the wild each year. Most are thought to fall victim to illegal hunting.

The only other mammalian subspecies believed to be unique to the island is the **Corsican dormouse** (*loir* in French). No-one knows for sure just how many of these shy, cute little creatures remain in the humid beech forests of the interior but they're often mistaken for squirrels due to their size (35cm) and the bushiness of their tails. Once again, hunting has been the cause of the animals' demise; men from the upper Taravo Valley (on the GR20), where they are most numerous, shoot them for their oily meat, prized both for its taste and its curative properties.

Yet another mammal hunted close to extinction, but which is now rigorously protected, is the **mouflon**, a reclusive sheep that inhabits remote mountain crags along the watershed. Corsica is one of its last strongholds. Only around 600 individuals survive in pockets high amid the central peaks, where you might be lucky enough to glimpse a flock grazing at sunrise or sunset. For more background on the mouflon, and tips on where to look for them see the box on p128 and also p189.

The maquis

At the start and end of the GR20 you'll encounter the infamous Corsican maquis, whose dense green carpet of spiny, aromatic scrub dominates the coastal zone below 1000m. The bane of walkers, it can form impenetrable walls of thorns and rough foliage that grow to a height of more than two metres if left unchecked. The maquis – from the Corsican *macchjhe* – also gives off a magnificently pungent aroma which you'll notice as soon as you set foot on the island, and probably never forget. Napoleon famously claimed he could smell it while imprisoned on Elba.

The heady fragrance derives from a mixture of plants. Most distinctive among them are members of the **cistus** (*cistre*) family, identifiable by their striking, wrinkled pink or white flower petals, which are shed each evening and their sticky resinous stems and leaves. This is the source of myrrh; Corsican shepherds used to collect it from the beards of their goats. Juniper (*genévrier*), lavender (*lavendre*), rosemary (*romarin*), myrtle (*myrte*), strawberry trees (or arbutus; *arbousier* in French), mastic (*mastique*), broom (*gênet*) bearing bright yellow flowers, and tree heather (*bruyère*) also add their perfumes to the great olfactory melting pot.

The subject of innumerable myths and legends, the maquis traditionally provided a rich source of sustenance for the islanders, yielding fire wood, fruit and medicinal herbs, and giving cover to wild boar and other game. The Corsican Resistance in WWII, who depended on the scrub for their survival, also named itself Le Maquis, and after the island's Liberation in 1943 the term *maquisard* was taken up as a moniker by Resistance fighters on the French mainland.

Cacti

The **Indian fig**, or **prickly pear** cactus, which grows in banks on roadsides and wasteland, was originally imported to Corsica from Mexico, although locals will tell you the Saracens brought it with them (whence its French name, *figue de Barbarie*). The pale red and orange fruit it throws out is fiendishly hard to pick (try and you'll probably end up with fingertips full of tiny needles) but Corsican villagers traditionally gathered them to make jam.

Another foreign import that thrives in the wild throughout the Mediterranean is the **Agave**, or 'century plant', a giant, Jurassic-looking cactus whose huge flowers sway on 4- to 6m-high stems. You'll see them sprouting from parched, south-facing slopes at sea level all over the island.

Flowers

Around 2500 different species of flowering plants are to be found in Corsica, 8% of them endemic to the island and its neighbour Sardinia. Which flowers you come across while trekking will depend on the altitude, soil, time of year and humidity but spring is the best period if you want to experience the amazing floral diversity at its peak. From early April until mid-June, the verges, meadows and woodlands, few of which have ever seen a drop of pesticide or fertilizer, are filled with wild flowers, and the maquis is at its most aromatic.

Our photographic field guide below identifies some of the flowers you're most likely to encounter on the footpaths described in this book. For a more comprehensive checklist seek out one of the specialist books featured on p35.

Cinquefoil
Potentilla

Hottentot fig
Carpobrutus edulis

Prickly pear flower
(Indian/Barbary fig)

Saxifrage

Yellow horned sea poppy
Glaucium flaum

Rock rose
Cistus saviaefolius

Helichrysum

Horse vetch
Hippocripis comosa

Star of Bethlehem
Ornithogalus

Corsican meadow
thistle

Periwinkle
Vinca

Corsican hellebore

Tassle hyacinth
Muscari comosum

French lavender
Lavandula stoechas

Foxglove
Digitalis

Spotted orchid

Wild garlic
Allium triquentum

Gentian
Gentiana lutea

Rampian
Phyteuma

Knapweed
Centaurea pullata

Peony

Water lotus

Devil's bit
Succia pratensis

Cyclamen

Thrift
Armeria maritima

Pink cistus, source of
ladanum gum myrrh

Granny's Bonnet
Aquilegia alpina

Trees

At sea level the trees best adapted to withstand the hot sun and parched, sandy soil of the shoreline are **pines** such as the Aleppo (*pin d'Alep*) and umbrella or stone pine (*pin parasol*), both of which grow in profusion behind the beaches of southern Corsica. **Eucalyptus** (*eucalypte*), originally introduced to help drain stagnant bodies of water and combat malaria, also do well on the coastal belt, notably around Porto, where some have reached awesome sizes.

More definitively Mediterranean, however, is the **olive** tree (*olivier*), which was first brought to Corsica by the ancient Greeks and has thrived ever since. You'll see swaths of them around Calenzana and around the villages of the Alta Rocca in the far south, which have witnessed a revival of oil production over the past decade. Equally ubiquitous are the slender-topped **cypress** (*cyprès*) sprouting from family tombs and graveyards on the margins of towns and villages.

Two species of **oak** (*chêne*) are indigenous to Corsica, the most distinctive of them cork oak, whose bark has for centuries been stripped to provide corks for wine bottles. The bare, red-brown trunks exposed afterwards are still a typical feature of the landscape around Porto-Vecchio, although the industry has all but died out in other parts of the island. With its spiny leaves and gnarled branches, evergreen **holm oak** (*chêne vert*) was never exploited commercially but it has been badly hit by fire in Corsica and few extensive woods of it remain. In remote corners of the west coast you'll also come across the rare kermes oak (*chêne kermès*) which forms bushes of small, holly-like leaves.

At higher altitudes the flaky red bark and huge 15cm cones of the **maritime pine** (*pin maritime*) litter the trails winding through forests exposed to coastal weather. When they die off the rotten trunks and branches become encrusted in fungus, often falling across footpaths.

The same is true of the poor old **sweet chestnut** (*châtaignier*), which in times past was integral to the rural economy but has since suffered from terminal neglect. In the fifteenth and sixteenth centuries the Genoans planted whole forests of them to provide flour for export. These days, however, very few nuts are collected and milled; the vast majority are eaten by semi-wild pigs who fatten on them before they are slaughtered in late November (one of the reasons why traditional Corsican sausages are so famously tasty). Aside from the region of Castagniccia, near Bastia – which is carpeted by one vast, unbroken sweet chestnut forest but not crossed by any long-distance footpaths – the places you'll see large numbers of chestnut trees are remote villages in central and western Corsica.

The most Corsican of Corsica's trees, however, has to be the lofty **Laricio pine** (*pin laricio*). These giants of the island's sub-alpine forests typically live for between 800 and 1000 years. Often sporting characteristic flat tops, the older specimens shed smaller (8-10cm) cones than those of the maritime pine and soar

Laricio pine
(From *Journal of a Landscape Painter in Corsica*, Edward Lear)

to a height of 50m. Their flexible, strong wood and great height made them highly prized by the Genoans, who gutted whole forests for ship masts and building timber during their rule. You'll cross forests of them on the GR20, notably around Vizzavona and while approaching Bocca di Verdi. The latter location also boasts the island's most impressive **fir** trees (*sapin*): until a few years back the stalwart Sapin de Marmaro, just below the plateau de Gialgone (see p170), was 56m high and reputedly the tallest tree in Europe until the top was lopped off by lightning.

Among the few trees adapted to the stark, extreme conditions of the alpine zone are **beeches** (*hêtres*), more often than not contorted into ghoulish shapes by the wind. The high ridges south of Bocca di Verdi, above Refuge d'Usciolu on the GR20, are renowned for these. Look out also for the beautiful woods of **silver birch** (*bouleaux blanc*) that line the stream beds around Refuge d'Ortu di u Piobbu.

The sap that dribbles from their eye-shaped bark knots used to be collected for use as a natural antiseptic; it also attracts ferocious red ants, so beware if you sit beneath one.

ECONOMY

From the wealth of luxury cars, designer outfits and super-bikes on the streets of Bastia and Ajaccio you could easily get the impression Corsica was booming. The islanders' love of ostentation, however, masks some harsh economic realities. For starters, **per capita income** languishes at three-quarters of the French average. **Unemployment** may be virtually nonexistent in the summer but in winter it rises to 10% – a figure that does not take into account the thousands who migrate to the continent in search of work at the end of the season.

Tourism and related service industries are by far the largest employers, accounting for 10-12% of gross domestic product (GDP). Nationalists, however, have consistently resisted attempts by the French government to promote tourism as the answer to all Corsica's economic woes, pointing to the fact that jobs in the sector tend to be poorly paid and seasonal.

Many Corsicans would like instead to see a revival of the island's **agriculture**, which currently earns only a paltry 1-2% of GDP. But with the paucity of cultivable land and poor profit margins, farming looks unlikely to take off in any big way. Most Corsicans living off the land today are only able to do so with the help of huge **subsidies**. Until 1999 the island enjoyed EU Objective 1 status, which entitled it to massive handouts from Brussels. Combined with the equally vast sums being poured in by Paris, these made Corsica for years the most subsidized region in the EU.

Another telling statistic is that over one-third of all those employed on the island work for the government or local councils. Add to this the tax and social security exemptions enjoyed by Corsica, not to mention the heavily subsidized transport links with the continent on which its economy rests, and you'll understand why only a few extremists these days consider total independence from France a realistic option.

If the island had any raw materials to export or if its manufacturing base were stronger the economic picture might be rosier. But **industry** remains only marginally more profitable than farming, generating 7% of GDP. Of the 1500 or so establishments registered, just under half are sole traders and only 1% employ more than 50 people.

PEOPLE, SOCIETY AND CONDUCT

Corsican culture remains as archetypally Mediterranean as its climate. Superficially more Italian than French, the islanders' style is ritzy by the standards of northern Europe. When it comes to cars and motorbikes size definitely matters and in the towns, designer labels, lap dogs and wrap-around shades are manifestly de rigueur.

Such overt demonstrations of affluence serve to reaffirm both the individual's status and that of his or her family. The **family** still forms the backbone of the island's society. When introduced for the first time, Corsicans don't ask each other where they're from but say 'de qui vous êtes?', literally 'whose are you?'. And the answer will have considerable resonance, situating the speaker within a clear network of clan allegiances.

The economic and cultural revolutions of the post-war period have done little to erode the pervasiveness of **clanism**, which continues to permeate most aspects of life. To get on – to secure better jobs, favourable planning decisions or smooth business affairs – it's not what you know that counts in Corsica so much as who you're related to. Every family at some point will have to call on the patronage of a highly placed relative, who in turn can depend on that family for his (they'll almost always be a man) political support in the future.

Suspicion of outsiders is also integral to the island mindset and Corsicans are often accused of being cool with visitors. It's certainly true that down on the coast, where decades of mass tourism have visibly jaded many of those in the service sector, people can seem taciturn and, all too often, just plain impolite. But engage people with respect and you'll soon find the surface frostiness lift, especially in the villages of the interior where traditions of hospitality are still strongly upheld. Of course, barriers are more easily broken down if you speak French but even without it you'll be surprised by how garrulous Corsicans can be.

❏ **Population pointers**
● The native population of Corsica currently stands at around 260,000, but swells to 750,000 in the summer.
● The 1884 high of 276,000 was reduced, following the two world wars and a century of emigration, to 170,000 by the mid-1950s.
● An estimated 800,000 Corsicans live on the continent, most of them in Paris, Marseille, Nice and the Bouches du Rhône region.
● Around 22,000 of the current population (just over 8%) is made up of immigrants, more than half of them Moroccan and Tunisian guest workers.
● Roughly 40% of the total population (108,000 people) live in Bastia and Ajaccio. By 2025 it is expected that two-thirds of the islanders will live on the coast. The interior, meanwhile, continues to empty; 15,000 people left their home villages in the last quarter of the 20th century. If you exclude the coastal belt, the island has an overall population density of just 10 inhabitants per square kilometre, comparable with some regions of the Sahara.
● Corsica has a rapidly ageing population, with one-quarter of its inhabitants over the age of 60; that figure is expected to rise to one-third by 2030.

Women

Gender roles in Corsica are not all that different from the prevailing norms across the water in Italy – or for that matter in most Catholic Mediterranean countries – but attitudes to women, in particular, are still quite conservative compared with northern Europe.

Corsican women are expected to look glamorous in public and to avoid bringing shame on their families through their relations with the opposite sex. After marriage a woman's role as mother and homemaker confers on her enormous prestige and respect but outside family life her influence tends to be limited. The proportion of women occupying political posts and top jobs in local government still lags well behind mainland France, despite the ever-growing female contribution to the island's economy.

The roots of Corsica's gender conservatism date back to traditional society when the treatment of women was frequently the cause of vendettas. Only a century ago the mere removal of a woman's headscarf on the church steps after Mass by a man outside her kin was enough to unleash a bloody feud. Adultery or even the suggestion of sex outside marriage could also have the direst of consequences: *vinditta* sometimes broke out if a girl so much as went for a walk with a sweetheart without the permission of her father. If a feud did erupt, however, it was often women who fanned the flames of vengeance by singing impassioned funerary dirges, known as *voceri*, over the corpses of dead relatives. Processing around the body in darkness, the female kinsfolk of the deceased would tear at their faces and hair as expressions of grief, urging the men seated outside to exact retribution and restore clan honour.

Women have tended to maintain a very low profile in the nationalist movement, though in the 1990s widows of paramilitaries and others killed in factional violence took to the streets to voice their opposition to the troubles. Set up in 1996, the organization **Manifest pour la Vie** (Demonstrate for Life) campaigned to great effect against the rule of terror in Corsica, despite constant intimidation and death threats.

Possible gaffes

When mixing with local people, even members of the younger generation, bear in mind that cultural differences do exist – albeit small ones – and that you might have to modify your behaviour in some situations. Above all **never discuss Corsican politics**. Even innocent questions about the troubles run the risk of causing offence; express an opinion and you could well find yourself at the wrong end of a gun barrel. Remember that some of the people you'll meet in mountain villages and refuges may have been, or still are, connected in some way to a paramilitary movement – either directly or indirectly through their family.

Minor **gaffes** that are unlikely to provoke a hostile reaction but which will do little to endear you to your hosts include: walking shirtless into a bar, restaurant, gîte d'étape or church (and most other public places except the beach); camping wild on the outskirts of villages without permission (see p71); entering family tombs; and complaining about prices. In fact, complaining about anything can be tricky. If you feel compelled to express dissatisfaction at any point, be sure to do it without appearing confrontational.

Also, don't assume it's OK to use **toilets** in a bar if you haven't ordered at least a coffee for the sake of form. The main reason there are so few public loos in Corsica is that, contrary to attitudes in most of northern Europe, locals tend to regard the offering of such facilities as a service rather than a duty to visitors.

There are a few less obvious *faux pas* to be aware of, most of them associated with the so-called **Evil Eye** or *occhju*. Many Corsicans – and not merely members of the older generation – believe that what might be termed 'bad luck' elsewhere, such as health problems and things going wrong generally, derives from malevolent spells. These are cast unintentionally by individuals who are jealous of you in some way, whether they know it or not. Corsicans will perceive jealously in a range of remarks that in northern Europe would be construed as mere politeness: complimenting someone's appearance or that of a pet, saying a baby is beautiful or merely smiling at someone you don't know. Do so and you could well find yourself the object of a defensive gesture known as *les cornes* ('the horns'), made by clenching the fist and pointing the index and little finger downwards.

If *les cornes* fails to ward off the Eye, or if a spell has been cast without your knowledge, a run of bad luck will ensue that can only be stopped by visiting a spell breaker, or *signatori* (literally 'sign-maker'). These are traditional healers who make the sign of the cross and intone secret prayers over a bowl of water containing three drops of oil (possibly with a lock of the victim's hair underneath it).

CORSICA

LANGUAGE

French is Corsica's lingua franca – the first language of the overwhelming majority of islanders and the primary medium for government, law, business and the press. The locals, especially those in the interior, tend to speak with a thick, Italian-like accent but only a relatively small number remain fluent in **Corsican**, which was methodically suppressed by successive French administrations.

Considerable debate surrounds the status of Corsican, whose close resemblance to Tuscan many claim makes it a dialect. Nevertheless, an official language it is, with a symbolic value that seems to grow in inverse proportion to the number of people who speak it. Revival of the Corsican tongue has always been one of the top priorities of the nationalist movement, which has succeeded in reintroducing it as an optional subject in schools and as the main medium of instruction at the University of Corte.

As a visitor you'll hear the distinctive rhythms and intonations of Corsican in villages along the trekking routes. However, polite attempts by outsiders to speak the language may not be greeted with the encouraging response you might expect. Many locals are understandably defensive about their native tongue and may interpret phrasebook-inspired renditions of it from foreigners as patronizing, as if the speaker doesn't expect them to be fluent in French. That said, only the dourest of nationalists will be offended by you saying *tiran-graze* (thank you) at the end of a meal or when you leave a gîte or refuge.

After French, **Italian** is the most widely understood language, both because of the huge numbers of tourists from across the Tyrrhenian Sea and because of its affinity with Corsican. Nearly everyone, young and old, understands it even if they can't speak it fluently. The same, however, doesn't apply to **English**, which you won't be able to rely on outside the tourist offices.

Practical information for the visitor

ACCOMMODATION

One important decision to make before leaving home is how you intend to sleep along the GR20. There are several options.

Refuges
The first is to bed down in a **refuge**. Corsica has a total of 16 mountain huts, established in the 1980s by the PNRC to service the island's famous haute route, since when a handful of additional privately run huts have sprung up to soak up the overspill.

Whether humble converted shepherds' shelters or spacious, state-of-the-art glass and aluminium structures, refuges offer very basic bunk-bed accommodation, along with simple self-catering facilities, cold-water showers and water sources. The dorms tend to be dingy, cramped and stuffy when packed with people and gear, which they are most of the time in the summer while the GR20 is fully open. How well you sleep will depend on the extent to which you can block out the smell of sweaty boots, snoring, the rustle of rip-stop Pertex and pre-dawn head-torch eruptions. If this sounds like your idea of hell consider bringing a tent or a thick-enough sleeping bag to bivouac in the specially demarcated areas outside, which often have a few dry-stone wind shelters to sleep beside.

The real appeal of refuges lies less in their dubious comforts than their locations, which are invariably superb. Hours away from the nearest road and at altitudes above 1300m, most enjoy wonderful views. If you trek the GR20 you'll doubtless while away lazy afternoons on the deep wooden decks that front the huts, or sprawled on the grass slopes surrounding them.

During the **summer** Corsican refuges are staffed by gardiens who collect the *nuitée* fees from trekkers on behalf of the PNRC and generally keep the huts clean and tidy. They don't receive wages but instead are allowed to sell provisions and cooked food with stocks replenished by regular mule trips down to road level. These little (but extremely lucrative) businesses mean it's possible nowadays to trek the GR20 without having to make time-consuming re-provisioning detours to villages, although you'll pay for the privilege as the prices of supplies in most refuges are extraordinarily high.

From October until late May Corsican refuges are not staffed but their dormitories, kitchens and dining areas remain unlocked for use by **winter** trekkers. Don't, however, count on there being supplies of gas if you turn up off season. It's more common to find a fire's worth of wood, which you can burn in the fireplace or wood-burner and then replace for the next visitors.

A night inside a hut typically **costs** around 9.50€ per head. The money raised from the nightly charge goes towards the maintenance of the refuges and the PNRC helicopter which is used to remove rubbish as well as provide a valuable search and rescue service. Beds are allocated on a first-come-first-served basis.

Camping and bivouacking

Both camping wild (*camping sauvage*) and bivouacking (*le bivouac*) are strictly forbidden throughout the Parc Naturel, which means across the entire GR20. You can, however, pitch a tent or bivvy next to the refuges along the route, in areas set aside expressly for the purpose (marked as 'Aire de Bivouac'). You'll be charged around 4€, but this doesn't buy you the right to use the interior facilities of the refuge itself (namely the kitchen utensils and cookers), although in bad weather the gardien usually allows anyone sleeping outside to bed down in the dining room.

Advice on equipment for camping and bivouacking along the GR20 appears on pp26-7.

Gîtes d'étape

Gîte d'étape **accommodation** is available at five points along the GR20. Gîtes are the French equivalent of hiker hostels, providing simple, good value for money bunk beds for walkers. Those punctuating the GR20 tend, alas, to lag well behind others on the island when it comes to standards of cleanliness and comfort, but they're luxurious compared with the refuges. The more modest of them (at Col de Verge, for example) hold a dozen or so bunks; others, such as the *station* at Asco Stagnu (Haut' Asco), have four or five times that number, along with a choice of larger and more private double and family rooms.

The *nuitée* (nightly) rate charged by gîtes d'étape, typically around 13€, includes a dormitory bed and the use of self-catering facilities if there are any. Increasingly, however, the owners are imposing obligatory half-board rates of around 30€, meaning you can't stay at their gîte unless you opt for breakfast and evening meal. For those who can afford it this is invariably a much better deal than you could expect by eating elsewhere. The food is generally copious and efforts are made to provide local specialities (although rarely vegetarian alternatives). Mealtimes tend also to be enjoyable occasions, fuelled by unlimited jugs of (rough) wine. A lot, of course, depends on the personality of the people who run the establishment and how much of a sense of vocation they bring to their work.

Their one real catch is the communal dormitories, or more specifically the attendant risk of nocturnal noise; if you think you may be kept awake by snoring, come armed with a supply of ear plugs.

If you do decide you want to stay in a gîte d'étape, try to book as far ahead as possible, especially in peak season, when demand far outstrips the number of available beds.

Hotels

There are only a few bona fide **hotels** along the GR20 (at Calenzana, Asco Stagnu/Haut' Asco, Col de Verghio, Vizzavona and Conca), but they're understandably popular and should, like gîtes d'étape, be reserved in advance. Reviews and contact details for all of them appear in the relevant section of the route guide.

Advance booking is particularly recommended if you intend to spend a night in one of the gateway towns, where beds of all description – especially at the bottom of the market – are in very short supply; on weekends in summer, you'll be hard pushed to find anything at all on spec.

When making a reservation, at least in more modest hotels, you'll probably be offered the choice of a room with or without a wash basin (*lavabo*), shower (*douches*) and toilet (*WC*, pronounced 'doode-vay-say'). Rooms without a bathroom are generally described as '*chambres avec douche-WC à l'étage*' (ie 'rooms with shower and toilet on the landing'). More hotel terminology appears in the list of useful words and phrases on p203.

An extra that can bump up your bill is **breakfast** as it may not be included in the room rate: if it isn't, count on anything between 6€ and 11.50€, or else head for a café (where it will cost around the same).

It's nearly always possible these days to settle up with a credit card but if this is your only means of paying make sure the hotel will accept your card when you check in. Finally, bear in mind that most places in Corsica, particularly those in the resorts and hills, open only during the summer. Wherever possible we've listed the opening period but it's always advisable to phone ahead, especially if you're around at the start or end of the season, as precise dates can fluctuate with demand.

LOCAL TRANSPORT

Except for trains, public transport in Corsica is privately operated, which means few skeleton services, few routes to really out-of-the-way places and a sharp drop in departure frequencies outside the tourist season. Getting to and from the trailheads of the GR20 is feasible throughout the year with a little advance planning although on Sundays (when most of the flights from the UK arrive) it can be trickier than you might expect.

Specific information on reaching Calenzana appears on p98.

Trains

Crossing the watershed between Ajaccio and Bastia via Corte, with a branch line peeling north-west to Calvi, Corsica's heavily subsidized train line – the Chemin de Fer de la Corse, or CFC – provides a year-round link between the island's major towns. Although somewhat slower and more rattly than the buses, the Micheline diesels offer a memorable way to travel. In fact, during the summer the line becomes a tourist attraction in its own right; of the 800,000 or so people who use it each year, more than half are visitors.

Unlike in mainland France, **fares** do not vary according to the day of the week or time of year. You pay for your ticket in advance at the station and present it to the conductor (*contrôleur*) during the journey. Special luggage areas provide ample space for rucksacks. It's also possible to store gear at the stations (ask at the ticket hatch for the *consigne*) but you have to pay between 5€ and 6€ (per working day or part thereof) for the privilege, and are pinned to the opening and closing hours of the station (which should always be checked before leaving your luggage).

The line has two separate **timetables** (*horaires*) for summer and winter, changing in late September and late June; the exact dates vary from year to year. The main difference is an increased number of services on Sundays and public holidays during the summer. On the Bastia–Corte–Vizzavona–Ajaccio line at least four trains operate Monday to Saturday, with two on Sundays. Only one or two, however, run daily from the junction at Ponte-Leccia to Calvi.

To check departure times you can phone the tourist office in Ajaccio, Bastia or Calvi; the staff all speak English. Better still, if your French is up to it, ring the CFC direct on ☎ 04.95.23.11.03 or visit 🖥 www.corsicabus.com.

Background information on Corsica's quirky narrow-gauge train line appears in the box on p160.

Buses

Getting hold of dependable information can be complicated when it comes to buses. With the exception of Ajaccio, no town has a dedicated bus station, while each route is served by a different company with its own seasons and headquarters. To compound the problem, tourist offices rarely have up-to-date timetables and when they do they often misread them. The only sure-fire way to check timings is to contact the bus company yourself. In Ajaccio you can do this in person at the *terminal routière* (bus station), where each company has its own counter. If these aren't staffed, ask at the information desk, which keeps a folder with the full set of current timetables. Online the most reliable summary of public bus timetables is at 💻 www.corsicabus.com.

The buses vary enormously, ranging from huge luxury coaches (as on the Ajaccio–Bastia route) to small 12-seater minibuses. While some are laid on with visitors in mind, others form essential lifelines to remote villages, carrying post and provisions as well as people.

Tickets are sold in advance at the bus station in the capital but elsewhere you have to pay the driver when you get on the bus. Note, too, that in larger towns where the company may operate through a travel agency (as is the case with the bigger firms) you can sometimes **leave your rucksack** at the agency free of charge until the bus departs.

Taxis

One reason why key tourist destinations such as Calvi Airport and Calenzana (starting point of the GR20) are so poorly served by buses is the influence of the local taxi drivers. Their powerful lobby also keeps fares comparatively high, and once outside the large towns you can expect some hefty meter charges if you catch a cab to or from the trailhead.

Unfortunately, taxis are in many instances the only way (apart from hitching) to reach some villages or *stations de ski*, which is why this guide lists the contact details of registered drivers who serve places on or within reach of the GR20. If you do call out a cab, especially for a long drive, make sure you get a quoted fare over the phone in advance.

Hitching

No self-respecting Corsican would be seen dead hitching, but with a rucksack – and even better, a set of trekking poles – your chances of getting a lift are pretty good. As in most parts of the world, success rates seem to improve as you penetrate the mountains. From late June onwards a steady flow of tourist traffic ensures a dependable supply of potential lifts in all but the remotest areas.

You'll find cars much more likely to stop if you pick your spot well: stand on straight stretches of road with plenty of space to pull over on the hard shoulder (roadsides just past roundabouts are usually safe bets). And avoid busy highways and intersections; it's obviously harder for drivers to stop when they're in fast moving, bunched traffic.

Attacks on hitchers are unheard of in Corsica, but getting into a stranger's car inevitably brings with it a degree of risk, and it's always worth checking the driver out first. Never be afraid to refuse a lift if you feel unsure about it for any reason.

EATING AND DRINKING

Time was when everything you ate or drank on the GR (other than spring or stream water) had to be carried in your backpack, and when re-provisioning meant carefully planned food drops or long detours off the trail to villages. These days, however, the gardiens of most refuges offer trekkers a selection of essential supplies: typically charcuterie, local cheese, tinned fish, pâté, pasta, noodles, condensed milk, chocolate and biscuits. Nearly all of them also do a roaring trade in luxuries such as fresh bread, wine, beer and soft drinks, and some cook up hot soup, omelettes or coffee. Keeping these little businesses stocked at peak season means near-daily trips down to road level with a mule or two, which explains the sky-high prices of food in refuges. Rely on the gardiens' supplies and you'll rip through your money very quickly indeed.

You can re-stock more cheaply at Asco, Castel di Verghio, Vizzavona and Bavella, where the trail crosses tarmac. These hamlets, and *stations de ski*, also have small **restaurants**, which we review in the relevant sections.

In addition to the usual selection of packaged food, vegetables and staples, local épiceries stock a good choice of regional specialities that make ideal trekking fodder. Look out for *canastrelli*, thick calorific biscuits traditionally made from chestnut flour and olive oil. They come in a range of flavours – *anis* (aniseed), *noix* (walnut), *raisin* and *miel* (honey) – but our vote goes to *vin blanc* (white wine), which is the most consistently delicious.

Corsica is also deservedly renowned for its cured meats, or **charcuterie**, whose intense flavours derive from the fact that most pigs on the island roam free, feeding on windfall chestnuts and forest roots. As well as familiar, Parma-style smoked ham (*prisuttu*) you'll come across three main kinds of hard *saucisson* (sausage) hanging in Corsican grocery shops: *coppa* (shoulder), *figatellu* (liver) and, the most prized of all, *lonzu* (lean fillet). Quality charcuterie doesn't come cheap – expect to pay anything from 10€ to 15€ for saucisson from a reputed source – but its strong taste means you have to slice it thinly, which makes it last a long time. Above all, charcuterie provides an excellent, easily portable source of protein.

The same is true of Corsica's notoriously strong **cheese**, the most pungent and expensive of which is make from full-fat ewe's milk collected at altitude. A range of different strength *fromages corses* is offered at village épiceries and supermarkets, but for the real McCoy you'll have to shop at bergeries up in the hills, where shepherds sell direct from their cool stone cellars.

Restaurants

Once away from the few points where the route dips down to road level, bubbling lasagnas and chestnut-flour flans steeped in maquis-scented honey become the stuff of dreams on the GR20. Don't be surprised, then, if you're tempted to splurge on a proper meal when you touch civilization again.

In common with mainland France, *la restauration* is regarded as a true *métier* – a vocation – and it's rare to be served duff food in Corsica, especially in the hills where most restaurants are well-established, family-run places with an exi-

Corsican cuisine

It's commonplace on the island to say that while French food celebrates the genius of the chef, Corsican food celebrates the genius of God. Based on simple, natural ingredients, *la cuisine corse* relies substantially on freshness and quality for its flavours rather than fussy sauces and convoluted cooking techniques.

A prime example is the Corsican-style omelette, which is made with little more than mint (ideally picked at altitude) and that other quintessential component of Corsican cooking, **brocciu**. Produced in bergeries high up in the mountains of the interior, this mild, soft ewe's cheese is regarded as far superior to its continental cousin, *brousse*, and is used to add flavour and creamy texture to a variety of dishes, including desserts. **Soups** are another popular starter, whether based on beans or a peppery fish stock, the latter served with chunky croutons smothered in mustard-enriched mayonnaise.

Before the arrival of the main dish it's customary to serve side plates of *fritella* (griddle-fried fritters) or *beignets* (savoury donuts) made with chestnut flour and knobs of melted brocciu. But the traditional focal point of any major Corsican meal is a meat dish of some kind. During the winter hunting season, freshly shot **wild boar** will frequently dominate the table of Sunday lunches in the villages, served as fillets with roast potatoes, in a rich lasagna or in stews (*tianu di cingale*), flavoured with fresh maquis herbs such as rosemary, tarragon, sage, fennel and wild thyme. Roasted suckling kid (*cabrettu*) and lamb (*agnellu*) are other popular bases for stews, while veal (*veau*) is more classically prepared with olives. All manner of meat and game – including tripe, blackbird and even hedgehog – might end up rolled together and baked as *stifatu*, which is served with a sprinkling of strong, hard ewe's cheese.

To round things off on an appropriately heavy note, *the* most Corsican of desserts is *fiadone*, a flan made from chestnut flour, brocciu, eggs and maquis honey. You'll sometimes be served it flambéed in aromatic *eau de vie* liqueur.

gent local clientele as well as passing tourist trade to cater for. All but the very poshest restaurants generally offer a range of *menus fixes*. With these, you select one dish from the limited choice listed for each course, among which is invariably a *plat du jour* (chef's special or dish of the day). There's usually a cheap and cheerful budget menu for around 16€ and a *menu corse* offering a spread of local specialities for upwards of 20€. The most expensive menus will probably include especially good charcuterie and cheese, fresh fish such as river trout, game or wild boar delicacies, and a home-made dessert.

It generally works out more expensive to eat à la carte (where you select individual dishes from a full-length menu) but in principle you get what you pay for, with access to the full range of house specialities. Note that the French word for menu is 'carte'; ask for 'le menu' and you'll be shown or told about the *menu fixe*.

Pizzas are enormously popular in Corsica and generally the most affordable way to eat out. Baked in wood-fired ovens (look for a sign outside the pizzeria saying 'Au Feu de Bois'), a pizza typically costs between 8€ and 12€, depending on the toppings, which allows you to order a side salad or maybe a dessert and coffee, with a small *pichet* of wine, for less than 15€. A lighter budget option would be to order from the long list of salads offered by most places, which cost around the same as pizzas and are usually large enough to make a meal in themselves. However, they tend to be unexciting: fresh vegetables on the island are mostly imported and tasteless, bulked out in salads with tinned sweetcorn or tuna, and smothered in mass-produced mayonnaise. Only in quality restaurants and at family places in the mountains are you likely to be served fresh, organically grown leaves and vegetables from kitchen gardens.

Drink

Nothing will sap your trekking legs quite so thoroughly as alcohol but it's all too easy to ignore the consequences at the end of a day's walking when pichets of wine and cold bottles of chestnut beer start to flow from the refuge stores.

Down at sea level drinking is a major pastime. Alcoholic drinks are routinely consumed in Corsica before eating (as *apéritifs*), to accompany the different courses and to finish off meals (as *digestifs*). They're also served without food at cafés, where a significant proportion of the island's middle-aged male population pass their lives sipping *pastis* (also known by its various brand names such as Pernod and Ricard) – a dry, clear spirit heavily flavoured with aniseed that turns milky yellow when mixed with water or ice. The other classic Corsican appetizer is a fortified wine called **Cap Corse** (its brand name), whose distinctive bitter-sweet taste derives from a blend of sugar-rich muscatelle grapes and quinine. Now produced in a range of flavours, it was originally drunk as an anti-malaria prophylactic – the Corsican equivalent of British-India's gin and tonic. Ask for '*un Cap*' and you'll be well in with the locals.

More palatable to the uninitiated are the lager-style beers sold even in remote refuges up on the GR20. Arguably the most distinguished of them is Corsica's own brew, Pietra, made from chestnut flour. Although a notch pricier than 1664 and Stella Artois, it's darker, crisper and stronger than the competition. The same company has also brought out a delicious (and even more expensive) *weissbier* called Colomba, sold in bottles in most village bars.

The reputation of **Corsican wine**, which you'll see on sale everywhere, took a knock in the 1970s after it was revealed that some of the large-scale *pieds-noirs* producers on the east coast were illegally adulterating their cheap *vins de pays* to bump up alcohol content (a scandal that eventually provoked an armed siege, see pp51-2). Over the past decade or so, however, the industry has recovered and now turns out some outstandingly good reds (*rouges*), whites (*blancs*) and rosés. The chalky-soil region of Patrimonio, in the north near Bastia, and the sea-facing slopes below Sartène in the far south-west, harbour the most celebrated *domaines*, but vineyards around Ajaccio, Calvi and Porto-Vecchio also enjoy Appellation d'Origine Contrôlée (AOC) status. In addition, Cap Corse, the 40km-long finger-thin promontory extending northwards from Bastia, is famous for its pale-amber **muscat**, a sweet dessert wine with a delicate floral aroma which Corsicans serve as an apéritif or with strong ewe's cheese.

Resembling quality Tuscan chiantis, the best Corsican reds are robust and dark. With the exception of muscat, the whites are far more delicate, with hints of apple and hazelnut that make the perfect accompaniment for the oysters gathered on the lagoons of the east coast (which Napoleon famously had shipped to him while in exile on nearby Elba). Names to look out for in the supermarket or on wine lists include: Domaine Torraccia, Domaine Antoine Arena, Domaine Venturi-Pierreti and Clos Columbu.

In restaurants you'll be offered a selection of bottled AOC wine from around the island, as well as less pricey house wines. These usually come in small jugs, or pichets – ask for 'un quart' (a quarter litre) or 'un demi' (a half litre) – and tend to be undistinguished vins de pays. In reputable auberges and some gîtes d'étape, however, the *patron* or *patronne* may pride themselves on their own local supply of AOC-standard wine which they'll serve at house rates.

No full-scale Corsican meal is considered complete without a small glass of spirit to round things off. The one you're most likely to be offered on the house is ***eau de vie***, a clear rocket-fuel liquid distilled from grape skins. For obvious reasons it's served in tiny quantities, and also used to flambé desserts, to which it imparts a delicate liquorice flavour. Liqueurs are also very popular on the island, especially ***vin de myrte***, whose taste comes from aromatic myrtle berries gathered from the maquis. The best of it seems to be made at home by people's grandmothers, but you can buy inferior stuff in fancy bottles at souvenir shops.

BILLS AND TIPPING

Bills will all include sales tax (IVA) but not necessarily service charges unless you see '*service compris*' (or just '*s.c.*') printed at the bottom. '*Service non compris*' means you're expected to add the discretionary 15% yourself.

ELECTRICITY

Electricity is 220V out of double, round-pin wall sockets. European appliances should work with just a plug-in adaptor; North American ones will need this plus a step-down transformer.

HOLIDAYS AND FESTIVALS

Traditional festivals, pegged to the religious calendar, are still celebrated with enthusiasm and, in some cases, great solemnity in Corsica. The island also boasts a string of more frivolous modern cultural events, introduced to inject a bit of life into quiet times of year or as focal points of the summer tourist season. Neither these nor the conventional French public holidays has much impact on life in the interior villages, where shops, bars and restaurants keep to their normal opening hours.

On the GR20 it can be difficult to remember what day it is, let alone the date, so the festivals and holidays listed below will probably appear as distant irrelevancies if you're up on the haute route. The list includes only Corsica's main events; for a fuller rundown with precise dates, contact a tourist office on the island or browse one of the information websites listed in the box on p81.

● **Good Friday – U Catenacciu** Sartène, in southern Corsica, hosts this famous nocturnal procession, when rows of Ku-Klux-Klan-lookalike hooded penitents imitate Christ's walk to Golgotha. There's a 12-year waiting list to be the Grand Pénitent, who gets to carry a heavy wooden cross through the candle-lit streets with chains wrapped around his ankles. Similar rituals are performed by religious brotherhoods on Easter weekend across the island.

● **June 2 – La Fête de Saint Erasme** The island's fishermen celebrate their patron saint's day with a special mass and firework displays at ports and harbours throughout Corsica.

● **Third week of June – Calvi Jazz** A world-class line-up of musicians perform on a stage set below Calvi's picturesque citadel, and then jam the night through at the quayside bars.

● **First and second week of July – Festivoce, Calvi** A festival dedicated to *a cappella* singing from around the world, with Corsican polyphonic groups contributing to the international line-up.

● **September 8-10 – Santa di u Niolu, Casamoccioli** Corsica's oldest established singing event revolves around an arcane choral joust between singers who trade improvised insults across a crowded bar up in the Niolu Valley. For more on this, see box p133.

● **September 14-18 – Rencontres de Chants Polyphoniques, Calvi** The island's premier polyphonic festival showcases the finest exponents of a singing tradition unique to the island (see box p133).

● **Last week of October – Festiventu, Calvi** The end of the tourist season and return of the autumnal winds is celebrated with a colourful kite festival on one of Corsica's most spectacular beaches.

OPENING HOURS

For most businesses standard opening hours are 8am-noon and 2-6pm, Monday to Friday. Village épiceries tend to stay closed for most of the afternoon but open 4.30-7.30pm (or later in summer); bakeries open at the crack of dawn and keep working through the lunch hour until around 2.30pm, but generally close soon after that. Nearly everywhere closes on Sunday and most shops open for only half a day on Saturday.

MONEY

France's currency is the Euro: **coins** come in eight denominations – 2€, 1€, 50c, 20c, 10c, 5c, 2c, 1c – and there are a total of seven **notes**, all in different colours and sizes, denominated in 500€, 200€, 100€, 50€, 20€, 10€ and 5€.

❏ **Rates of exchange**

	Euro
Aus$1	€0.61
Can$1	€0.68
NZ$1	€0.54
UK£1	€1.34
US$1	€0.68

For up-to-the-minute rates of exchange check the Internet: **www.xe.com**

POST, TELEPHONE AND EMAIL

Post

Distinguished by their yellow-and-blue livery, Corsica's **post offices** are smart and reliable, despite being the repeated target of nationalist bomb and machine-gun attacks. **Stamps** (*timbres*) can be bought at all branches, as well as over the counter at tobacconists (look for the red '*tabac*' signs on most high streets) and at postcard shops. Letters up to 20g cost 55 cents for countries within the EU, or 90 cents for North America and Australasia. Parcels of up to 1.5kg cost 11€, depending on the rate, or 18.10€ for countries out of the EU.

Telephones

Just about everywhere that sells stamps also sells cards (*télécartes*) for **public telephone** booths (*cabines*). These come in two sizes, costing around 7.50/15€ for 50/120 units respectively. To make a call using one, insert it chip-end first into the phone and wait a few seconds until the LCD display registers the number of unused units remaining. You can then dial. For telephone numbers in Corsica or anywhere in mainland France the ringing tones are long beeps. If the line's engaged you'll hear short beeps instead. Should your card run out midway through a call you can replace it by pressing the green button on the console. When the message '*retirez votre carte*' comes up, pull out the used card and wait until you see the words '*nouvelle télécarte*' before inserting the new one.

Coin-operated phone boxes are these days few and far between, although you do occasionally come across them in bars. It's therefore a good idea to buy as many *télécartes* as you think you'll need at the start of your trek as they can be hard to get hold of in more remote villages.

Public phone boxes should all receive **incoming calls**. Look for the cabine's number printed at the head of the instruction panel on the wall in front of you. Tell the person who is to ring you back all ten digits (or only nine, minus the first zero from +04, if they're abroad) and remind them to add the international code plus the code for France (+33).

Mobile phones (*portables*) are of limited use in the mountains, where coverage is very patchy, but function reliably enough in the towns and most villages.

Email

Email and **Internet** access is hard to come by. The few real Internet cafés we unearthed on the island are listed in the relevant accounts. If you're desperate to get online, you could always ask the manager of any hotel you happen to be staying in to help you out.

THINGS TO BUY

Food and drink are the obvious things to take home from Corsica as presents. In the main towns you'll find little boutiques selling artisanally made charcuterie, cheese, honey, maquis herbs and biscuits (*canastrelli*). They also stock a range of quality wines – including muscat, which makes a great souvenir as it's unique to the island – and will package anything you buy in fancy paper and ribbons if you explain it's '*un cadeau*' (a present). The same applies to bakeries, which all prepare their own Corsican speciality cakes and tarts.

(Opposite) Top: Bergeries de Pozzi (1746m, see p170), a forgotten paradise accessible via the Monte Renoso high-level variant route. **Bottom**: The Plateau de Gialgone (see p168) at 1600m, en route to Bocca di Verdi. (Photos © David Abram).

> **Corsica-related websites**
> In spite of the overall sluggish way with which Corsicans have responded to the Internet revolution, the Web these days supports a mass of information about the island. Anyone intending to attempt the GR might also wish to surf some of the many homepages containing illustrated accounts of recent GR20 treks; (stick 'GR20' in your search engine and see what it comes back with).
>
> ● **www.corsica-isula.com** A general site with a wealth of info on every conceivable subject, including mountain trekking
> ● **www.parc-naturel-corse.com** A full rundown of PNRC's projects and background on the park itself (French only)
> ● **www.corsematin.com** Articles from the island's top selling daily (French only)
> ● **www.napoleon.org** Richly illustrated site devoted to Ajaccio's most illustrious son
> ● **www.muvrini.com** Corsica's foremost musical export, who combine traditional polyphony with a modern rock sound
> ● **www.corsicabus.com** Bang up-to-date public transport timetables for all buses and trains on the island – a more reliable info bank than the tourist offices
> ● **perso.wanadoo.fr/tempifaipaesi** A mind-boggling collection of old postcards from around the island, and some great portraits of local characters
> ● **www.visit-corsica.com** Official website of the Corsican tourist board
> ● **www.traincorse.net** Site devoted to Corsica's narrow-gauge train, the Micheline

Supermarkets may feel like less authentic places to shop but the larger ones have substantial Corsican produce sections and much lower prices than the 'Produits Corses' boutiques. Most also have racks of Corsican polyphony CDs, which can make good presents (see the box on p133 for some suggestions).

SECURITY

Corsica may suffer one of the worst rates of violent crime in Europe but the island remains an extremely safe place for tourists. Nationalist attacks are always tightly targeted and never affect visitors; aside from the ubiquitous political graffiti and occasional bombed-out building you'll be completely unaware that 'le problème corse' even exists.

Theft is very rare indeed. Up in the closely knit communities of the interior it's virtually non-existent. Trekkers routinely leave their packs outside bars, shops and gîtes without so much as a second thought. If anyone did steal from a visitor they'd probably soon find themselves staring down the barrel of a hunting rifle. Muggings and sexually motivated violence against tourists are also unheard of, even in the two main towns, although you should take the same precautions you would anywhere when walking around late at night.

The one way you might be drawn into a violent encounter with a local person is if you insult someone. Corsicans are quick to react when they perceive they, their family or their political opinions have been slighted. For advice on conduct and possible gaffes see pp67-9.

Opposite: Approaching the forepeak of Monte Cinto – see p121. (Photo © David Abram).

PART 3: GATEWAY TOWNS

Ajaccio
(Aiacciu)

Ajaccio, capital of Corse-du-Sud and seat of the regional government, is the island's largest town and its principal transport hub. Set against a grandiose backdrop of hills and distant snow peaks, its old port and eighteenth-century core of red-tiled tenements, where Napoleon Bonaparte was born and raised, are hemmed in by ugly suburbs of tower blocks that sprawl around the northern shore of a spectacular bay. Palm-lined promenades, rows of swish terrace cafés, and the notoriously glitzy dressing of its inhabitants lend to the town a strongly French-Riviera feel, a world away from the mountains visible across the gulf.

Napoleon and Ajaccio

Ajaccio's most illustrious son, Napoleon Bonaparte, may be regarded as the archetypal Frenchman but he started life as a staunchly nationalistic Corsican. The son of rebel leader Pascal Paoli's right-hand man, he was born only three months after the crushing defeat of Ponte Nuovo in 1769 when Paoli's army was routed by the French. Thereafter, the Bonapartes were quick to reconcile their political differences with the new overlords and prospered, with young Napoleon gaining a scholarship at a military academy on the continent.

By the time Paoli had rallied sufficiently to mount a second, British-backed attempt to overthrow the French 25 years later, Napoleon's family had become part of the gallicized Revolutionary élite in Ajaccio, making them a prime target for patriot ire. When rebel forces stormed through the town, the Bonapartes' Ajaccio home was among the first to be looted and the family was forced into exile. It is said that the young Napoleon never forgave his countrymen the insult. Apart from a brief visit in 1799 when his fleet was forced into Ajaccio by inclement weather on its victorious return from Egypt, he never came back.

As emperor, Napoleon became vehemently anti-Corsican, suspending the island's Constitution and ruthlessly suppressing any signs of nascent nationalism. He even gallicized his name (from the more Italian-sounding Napoleone). Ajacciens responded by disowning him. When the emperor announced his abdication in 1814 they celebrated by cheering in the streets and pitching a statue of him into the gulf.

These days it's a very different story. France's great leader and his memory have been enthusiastically rehabilitated by the town. Statues of him (wearing Roman togas and laurel leaves) now preside over the three main squares. The town's principal thoroughfare is called cours Napoléon, and there are a couple of small museums dedicated to the Boney cult. But the old animosity, however, still resurfaces from time to time: a few years back, the equestrian statue of Napoleon in place de la République was painted bright yellow.

Ajaccio, 1870 (from *Journal of a Landscape Painter*, Edward Lear)

In short, Ajaccio is somewhere guaranteed to make you feel frumpy in hiking boots but, as the location of Corsica's busiest airport and railhead, it's hard to avoid. It also suffers from a chronic shortage of hotel beds so plan your visit to avoid spending the night here, or far enough ahead to be sure of a room.

WHAT TO SEE

Conventional sights are thin on the ground in Ajaccio. Most people kill time with a leisurely amble around the fishing harbour and the grid of narrow streets packed behind the citadel where, sooner or later, you'll come across Napoleon's birthplace, on place Letizia. **Maison Bonaparte** today houses a small museum (☎ 04.95.21.43.89, 🖥 www.musee-maisonbonaparte.fr (French only); Apr-Sep Tue-Fri 9am-noon and 2-6pm; Oct-Mar Tue-Sat 10am-noon and 2-4.45pm; admission 5€) containing less Napoleonic memorabilia than you might expect, most of the family's possessions having been pillaged by rampaging Paolists.

A more engaging selection of Boney trophies and relics is displayed at the **Salon Napoléonien** (🖥 www.napoleon.org; June 15-Sep 15 Mon-Sat 9-11.45am and 2-5.45pm; Sep 16-June 14 Mon-Fri 9-11am and 2-4.45pm; admission 2.80€), in a grand hall above the entrance of the Hôtel de Ville on place Foch. The prize exhibits here are a replica of the emperor's death mask and a fragment of his coffin.

Napoleon's armies systematically looted the art collections of the European capitals they passed through and many of the period's finest treasures ended up in Ajaccio, where they were acquired by the emperor's uncle, Cardinal Fesch.

Those not sold off by later generations are preserved in the excellent **Musée Fesch** (☎ 04.95.21.48.17, 🖥 www.musee-fesch.com; July-Aug Mon 2-6pm, Tue-Thur 9.30am-6pm, Fri 2-9.30pm, Sat & Sun 10.30am-6pm; April-June and Sep Tue-Sun 9.30am-12noon and 2-6pm; Oct-Mar same hours, but closed Mon and Sat; 5.35€), rue Cardinal Fesch, in the centre of town. Among the superb array of mainly sixteenth- and seventeenth-century masterpieces is an early Botticelli, *Virgin and Child*, and Titian's famous *Man with a Glove*.

Across the museum's courtyard stands the **Chapelle Impériale**, where members of the Bonaparte family, including Napoleon's mother and uncle, are buried (same hours; admission 1.50€). If you're short of time skip this and head for the wonderful town library, the **Bibliothèque Municipale** (Mon-Fri 8am-noon; admission free), in the museum's north wing. The huge collection of leather-bound antique books stacked to its ceiling were mostly confiscated from fleeing aristos during the French Revolution. You can't touch them, but this is also an atmospheric place to browse the local newspapers and magazines.

Of the two **beaches** within easy walking distance of the town centre, plage St François, below the citadel, is the least clean and appealing. You're better off plodding 20 minutes south-west down the promenade to the other beach (Plage Trottel) backed by a row of shops, where the water is much clearer and the sand more salubrious.

ORIENTATION AND SERVICES

Ajaccio's Campo del Oro **Airport** (☎ 04.95.23.56.56) lies 8km south-west of the centre, around the bay. In the arrivals hall you'll find the usual gamut of car rental counters and an ATM. Taxis (20-25€) wait at the rank outside, or you could jump on one of the half-hourly buses that shuttle into town (5€).

The airport bus route passes the train station, just east of the centre, before dropping you at the imposing *terminal routière* (**bus station**), which doubles as a *gare maritime* (**ferry port**). Both the train and bus stations have *consignes* (**left-luggage offices**), but their opening hours vary according to final arrival and departure times, so check when you deposit your gear.

Across the road from the terminal routière is place du Marché (Market Square) where you'll find Ajaccio's **tourist office** (☎ 04.95.51.53.03, 🖥 www .ajaccio-tourisme.com; Sep-June Mon-Fri 8am-6pm, Sat 8am-noon; July and Aug Mon-Sat 8am-8.30pm, Sun 9am-1pm and 4-7pm). The rest of the town's useful services and businesses are dotted along or around the main street, cours Napoléon, which runs the length of the centre. This is where you'll find the **post office**, **banks** (with ATMs) and **pharmacies**, as well as Ajaccio's only **outdoor equipment** shop, Luciani Sports.

For the latest information on Corsica's long-distance trekking routes, visit **Parc Naturel's information office** (☎ 04.95.51.79.10, 🖥 www.parc-naturel-corse.com), 2 rue Sergent Casalonga, just off cours Napoléon. They should have both Topoguides for the island and a range of IGN maps. If not, try Maison de la Presse, five minutes' walk south-east on place Foch.

Ajaccio

Campo del Oro Airport (8km),
Camping Les Mimosas (4km)

Train Station

AVE BÉVÉRINI-VICO

Hôtel du Palais

★TRAILBLAZER

0   100M
APPROXIMATE SCALE

Hôtel le Dauphin

BLVD SAMPIERO

Hôtel Kallisté

Luciani Sports

COURS NAPOLÉON

RUE CARDINAL FESCH

Musée Fesch,
Bibliothèque Municipale,
Chapelle Impériale

Hôtel Napoléon

RUE L VERO

QUAI L'HERMINIER

Post Office

R. SERGENT CASALONGA

Port de Commerce

Parc Naturel
Info Office

RUE MAR D'ORNANO

Hôtel Fesch

Place du Marché

Terminal Routière /
Gare Maritime

Les Halles,
L'Aquarium,
Don Quichotte

Tourist office

Launderette

Maison de la Presse

Hôtel de Ville &
Salon Napoléonien

Place Foch

Marina
Tino Rossi

Jetée de la
Citadelle

Plage Trottel
Hôtel Marengo (750m),
Camping de
Barbicaja (5km)

Place
de Gaulle

Restaurant 20123

RUE DU ROIS-DE-ROME

QUAI NAPOLÉON

QUAI DE LA CITADELLE

Fishing
Harbour

Capitainerie

Maison
Bonaparte

Casino

Launderette
& shower block

Plage
St François

CITADEL

There are two self-service **launderettes** in the centre: one on rue du Maréchal Ornano just off place de Gaulle (place Diamant); the other, on the jetée de la Citadelle, on the south side of the Marina Tino *capitainerie* (Harbour

Master's Office). The latter also houses a useful shower and toilet block where you can scrub up for 3.50€.

WHERE TO STAY

It's hard to overstate just how difficult it can be to find a hotel room in Ajaccio, especially at weekends. Pressure for beds is especially intense at the bottom end of the market, following what seems to have been a conspiracy in recent years to close down the town's cheaper hotels. A good solution is to get together with fellow trekkers and hunt for a triple or four-person room in one of the more upscale places, which can often be less expensive than a double or single in a budget hotel. The following are open year-round unless stated otherwise.

Hôtel Le Dauphin (☎ 04.95.21.12.94, 🖳 www.ledauphinhotel.com), on blvd Sampiero, is a convenient choice. Prices start at around 60€ for a sparsely furnished en suite double, rising to 70€ in July/August. They also have a handful of cheaper rooms (50€; with shared showers and toilets) in an adjacent building, but you'll have to ask specifically for one of these as they try to fill the others first. The tariffs include breakfast, served on the pavement terrace of the slightly seedy bar.

As a fallback, try *Hôtel du Palais* (☎ 04.95.22.73.68, 🖳 www.hoteldu palaisajaccio.com), 5 ave Bévérini-Vico, where rooms cost 70-80€ en suite. Regularly refurbished, this place is clean and good value, and well placed for the train station.

In a similar bracket, though a 20-minute trudge south-west from the centre, is *Hôtel Marengo* (☎ 04.95.21.43.66, 🖳 www.hotel-marengo.com), at 2 rue Marengo. Rates here range from 59€ to 79€ en suite. Although somewhat hemmed in at the end of a cul de sac it's near the seafront and more peaceful than the competition.

If you want to be more in the thick of things on cours Napoléon, much the best option – in fact altogether the nicest mid-range hotel in Ajaccio – is *Hôtel Kallisté* (☎ 04.95.51.34.45, 🖳 www.hotel-kalliste-ajaccio.com). The rooms in this renovated eighteenth-century building are on the small side but well appointed, with en suite bathrooms, comfy beds and cable TV. Prices go from 64€ to 76€.

Moving upmarket, one of the few central three-star hotels that usually has vacancies is *Hôtel Napoléon* (☎ 04.95.51.54.00, 🖳 www.hotelnapoleonajac cio.fr), on rue Lorenzo Vero. Rooms start at 75€ for a double, rising to 100€ in peak season, and they install extra beds for a very reasonable 17€. Breakfast (8€ extra) is a sumptuous buffet.

The other established three-star in this area is *Hôtel Fesch* (☎ 04.95 .51.62.62, 🖳 www.hotel-fesch.com), rue Cardinal Fesch, which became briefly famous in 1980 when the hotel was occupied by a gang of armed nationalists. Fitted out with chestnut-wood furniture and sheepskin rugs, the en suite rooms are all air-conditioned and have satellite TV. Tariffs range from 59€ to 86€ for a double, depending on the time of year and grade of room.

Ajaccio has two **campsites**, neither of them convenient for anyone without a car. Just under 5km west of town, on route des Iles Sanguinaires, *Camping de Barbicaja* (☎ 04.95.52.01.17; open mid-April to September) is the easiest to reach by public transport, but cramped and grotty by Corsican standards. Jump on bus No 5 from place de Gaulle. *Camping Les Mimosas* (☎ 04.95.20.99.85; open April-mid-Oct) gets marginally less crowded and is cleaner, but lies well off the beaten track on the northern outskirts of town. Catch a No 4 bus from place de Gaulle or cours Napoléon to the 'Brasilia' stop and walk north to the big roundabout at the bottom of the hill. After crossing the intersection, head up the lane on its far side and turn left at the signpost, passing a tennis club soon after on your right. The site is another 1km uphill from there. Better still, take a cab for around 12€.

WHERE TO EAT

Ajaccio may suffer a dearth of hotels but it isn't short of places to eat. Purely in terms of location, the row of identikit tourist restaurants lining quai de la Citadelle are hard to beat. The seafood tends to be mediocre but the views of the fishing boats and the gulf are compensation enough. Stick to pizza and a pichet of house red and you'll not go far wrong.

For anything more adventurous, take your pick from one of the open-air restaurants crammed into rue des Halles, the alley behind the covered market just off place du Marché. *Restaurant Les Halles* is a pre-war stalwart that does an excellent-value 14€ set menu of traditional Corsican canelloni with brocciu. *L'Aquarium*, two doors down, is strong on fish from the gulf with menus from 18€ to 25€. At the opposite end of the street, the *Don Quichotte* specializes in T-bone steaks, washed down with better than average local AOC wines. *Menus fixes* range from 18€ to 33€.

If you're splashing out, *Restaurant 20123* (☎ 04.95.21.50.05), 2 rue du Roi-des-Rome, is a safe choice. Decked out with traditional farming implements (and an old Vespa for some reason), it serves top-notch Corsican cuisine: Bastelica charcuterie, pungent ewes' cheese from the Niolu Valley, chestnut-flour desserts from Castagniccia and wine from Partimonio, Ajaccio and Sartène. The menu fixe is 28€.

GETTING TO THE TRAILHEAD FROM AJACCIO

Calvi, jumping off place for Calenzana and the start of the GR20, is a 4½ to 5-hour train ride north across the island. Two services per day leave Ajaccio station to link up with a through service at Ponte Leccia junction. En route the Micheline (see box p160) passes via Vizzavona (see p159), near the foot of Monte d'Oro, from where you can pick up the GR20 at its midway point.

If you're planning to head north from Vizzavona, jump on the first possible train from Ajaccio station and resist the temptation of a leisurely lunch as you'll be hard pushed to cover the monstrous climb and descent to reach Onda refuge before nightfall.

Bastia

Bastia, capital of Haute-Corse, is smaller than Ajaccio but an altogether more authentically Corsican town. Looking east across the Tyrrhenian Sea to the coast of Tuscany, it feels closer to Italy in every way, and decidedly un-French. The industrial estates sprawling south to Poretta airport and the gritty suburbs stacked up the surrounding hillsides remind you that this is primarily a working town. Despite recent efforts to spruce up the citadel and make the centre more visitor friendly, tourism remains peripheral. That said, Bastia is arguably the island's most atmospheric urban point of arrival or departure. If you're passing through try to make time for at least a stroll around the old harbour district and citadel.

WHAT TO SEE

Enfolded by a horseshoe of crumbling Genoan tenements, Bastia's **Vieux Port** is easily the town's most picturesque quarter. Its defining landmark is the spectacular Baroque facade of the **Church of Saint Jean-Baptiste**, whose giant belfries loom above an extraordinary jumble of schist tile rooftops – a scene little changed since Nelson attempted to blow it to pieces in 1794.

Down at water level, cafés and restaurants hug the harbour, overlooking a forest of yacht and fishing boat masts. This is a particularly enjoyable place to come for breakfast, when the sun rising over the Tyrrhenian Sea casts a rich light over the quayside terraces, and for sunset, when the sky is filled with flocks of screeching swifts.

The tranquillity of the Vieux Port, however, masks the fact that the quartier has long been a hotbed of nationalist politics. In 1998 it witnessed one of Corsica's most vicious terrorist attacks, when a car bomb exploded in broad daylight, killing one prominent militant and severely injuring another. As a result, your view of the marina will be obscured at regular intervals by armoured CRS patrols.

The police presence is less noticeable up the hill in the Citadel district, or Terra Nova, a warren of alleys and squares enclosed by its original honey-coloured Genoan ramparts. The main building of interest here is the **Palais des Gouverneurs**, which served as a prison before it was bombarded by Nelson during the British siege. It took another pounding in 1943 when the Americans mistakenly blitzed Bastia the day after it had been liberated, but was beautifully restored to its original state in the 1990s. Nowadays the palace accommodates the town's **Musée Ethnographique**. Charting the history of Corsica from prehistoric times to the post-war period, the exhibition is less impressive than the building itself, tours of which invariably end up in the dungeons, last used to imprison Resistance fighters in WWII.

GATEWAY TOWNS

Bastia, 1870 (from *Journal of a Landscape Painter*, Edward Lear)

ORIENTATION AND SERVICES

Bastia is fairly compact and you shouldn't have to take a taxi anywhere, even from **Poretta Airport**, 16km south. A **shuttle bus** (8€) connects with most flights, approaching the centre via the old quarter of Terra Nova or through the tunnel beneath the citadel. Either way you end up at the train station after a brief stop on place St Nicholas, the town's heart and most obvious reference point. The ferry dock, or Nouveau Port, lies just off its north-east corner, while the train station stands 10 minutes' walk west down ave Pietri and ave Sébastiani. Bastia's main shopping streets, blvd Paoli and rue César Campinchi, are just west of place St Nicholas.

At the north end of place St Nicholas is the **tourist office** (☎ 04.95 54.20.40, 🖳 www.bastia-tourisme.com; June-15 Sep daily 8am-8pm; 16 Sep-May Mon-Sat 8am-6pm, Sun and holidays 8am-12noon) useful primarily for information about bus departures which, in the absence of a proper bus station, can be a tricky business (see Getting to the trailhead from Bastia, on p92). The **post office**, which has an ATM, is three minutes' walk along ave Pietri.

Most other useful services – including the **launderette**, five minutes' walk north of place St Nicholas, near the entrance to the North Ferry Terminal – are at this end of town. **Left-luggage facilities** are available at the train station.

En route south from place St Nicholas to the old quarter of Bastia – the Vieux Port and citadel district, Terra Nova – you'll pass a string of **bookshops** that all stock FFRP Topoguides and IGN maps. Best of the bunch is L'Ile aux Livres on rue César Campinchi, which also has a good range of flora and fauna field guides.

WHERE TO STAY

Camping is not easy without your own transport. The closest sites to town, the *Casanova* (☎ 04.95.33.91.42) and *Les Orangers* (☎ 04.95.33.24.09), both lie next to each other, 5km north in the seaside suburb of Miomo; buses run there twice an hour Mon to Sat, or hourly on Sundays, until 7.30pm, from the top of place St-Nicolas (opposite the tourist office).

Hotels are a notch pricier here than elsewhere on the island and, once again, there's a shortage of rooms at the bottom end of the scale. Unless otherwise stated, the following are open year-round.

In the centre of town one budget place stands out: *Hôtel Central* (☎ 04.95 31.71.12, 🖳 www.centralhotel.fr), at 3 rue Miot, is a cozy, well-run little hotel close to the shops and main square. En suite doubles cost 50-80€, depending on the season. Breakfast (optional) is served in a small dining room.

Central Bastia's other economy option is very popular and hard to get into without advance reservation. Close to the Nouveau Port, *Hôtel Riviera* (☎ 04 95.31.07.16, 🖳 www.corsehotelriviera.com), which has 20 or so well-aired en suite rooms for 50-75€ depending on the time of year.

In a similar bracket, the venerable *Hôtel Posta Vecchia* (☎ 04.95.32.32.38, 🖳 www.hotel-postavecchia.com), on quai des Martyrs, offers a range of rooms from 40€ to 63€ in low season and 48€ to 78€ in July/August. Its location is marginally more inspiring than that of *Hôtel Napoléon* (☎ 04.95.31.60.30, 🖹 04 95.31.77.83), 43-45 blvd Paoli, whose rooms cost 60-100€. Most have a mini-bar and cable TV to justify the somewhat ambitious tariffs. *Hôtel les Voyageurs* (☎ 04.95.34.90.80, 🖳 www.hotel-lesvoyageurs.com), 9 ave Maréchal-Sébastiani, is brighter, more modern, and close to the Nouveau Port and train station. The majority of its rooms go for around 70-90€, though a few are discounted in low season.

If all these are full, you might have to try one of the pricier two- or three-star hotels at the bottom of blvd Paoli. Rates at *Hôtel Impérial* (☎ 04.95 31.06.94, 🖹 04.95.34.13.76), 2 blvd Paoli, and *Hôtel Forum* (☎ 04.95.31.02.53, 🖹 04.95.31.06.60), at 20 blvd Paoli, start at around 75€ for an en suite double.

WHERE TO EAT

Eating out in Bastia is a real pleasure. Kick off with a chilled muscat or Cap Corse at one of the relaxing cafés lining the west side of place St Nicholas, and from there make your way over to the Vieux Port or Citadel, which are packed with snug little restaurants and pizzerias.

For a slightly off-the-wall experience of local cuisine, try *La Braise* (☎ 04 95.31.36.97), 7 blvd Hyacinte-de-Montreal/blvd Général de Gaulle. This is a local institution, renowned as much for the repartee of its garrulous patron (who claims to be a half-Russian-half-Chuwawa-Indian retired boxer from the Côte d'Azur) as for its wholesome cooking. Most of the ingredients, notably the charcuterie and chestnut flour, come straight from Mme La Braise's village in nearby Castagniccia. Prices are low for the district (around 25€ for the works).

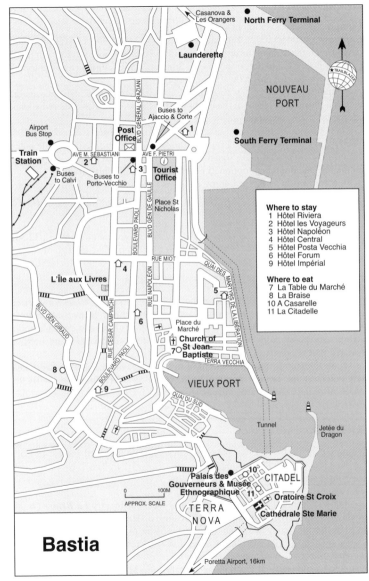

Where to stay
1 Hôtel Riviera
2 Hôtel les Voyageurs
3 Hôtel Napoléon
4 Hôtel Central
5 Hôtel Posta Vecchia
6 Hôtel Forum
9 Hôtel Impérial

Where to eat
7 La Table du Marché
8 La Braise
10 A Casarelle
11 La Citadelle

Casanova & Les Orangers

North Ferry Terminal

Launderette

NOUVEAU PORT

South Ferry Terminal

Airport Bus Stop

Train Station

Buses to Calvi

Buses to Porto-Vecchio

Buses to Ajaccio & Corte

Post Office

AVE M. SEBASTIANI

AVE F. PIETRI

BLVD GENERAL GRAZIANI

Tourist Office

Place St Nicholas

BLVD GEN DE GAULLE

BOULEVARD PAOLI

RUE MIOT

RUE NAPOLÉON

QUAI DES MARTYRS DE LA LIBÉRATION

L'Île aux Livres

BLVD GEN GIRAUD

RUE CESAR CAMPINCHI

BOULEVARD PAOLI

Place du Marché

Church of St Jean-Baptiste

TERRA VECCHIA

VIEUX PORT

QUAI DU SUD

Tunnel

Jetée du Dragon

Palais des Gouverneurs & Musée Ethnographique

CITADEL

Oratoire St Croix

Cathédrale Ste Marie

TERRA NOVA

0   100M
APPROX. SCALE

Bastia

Poretta Airport, 16km

GATEWAY TOWNS

A more serious atmosphere prevails at *A Casarelle* (☎ 04.95.32.02.32), at 6 rue Ste Croix in the citadel, whose chef has made it his mission to revive the old-fashioned cooking style of his home region, Balagne (the area around Calenzana at the start of the GR20). His signature dish, *storzzapretti*, is a mixture of soft ewes' cheese (brocciu), spinach and fresh maquis herbs baked in a rich tomato pesto. The set menus cost 24€ at lunch time and 35€ for dinner.

Just up the alley from A Casarelle on rue du Dragon is Bastia's swishest restaurant, *La Citadelle* (☎ 04.95.31.44.70; Mon-Sat). You won't get much change out of 33€ per head but the food, an innovative blend of Corsican and French haute cuisine, served in a beautifully restored vaulted dining room, is superlative.

More down-to-earth local food, such as traditional Corsican charcuterie, cheeses, pastries, herbs and wine, are the stock in trade of the daily **market**, held on place du Marché behind the Vieux Port. Bustling with shoppers from the surrounding quartiers, this is a lively spot to people-watch over a coffee. The south-west side of the square also has an excellent little restaurant, *La Table du Marché* (☎ 04.95.31.64.25; Mon-Sat) that's particularly popular at lunch. Seafood is the thing to go for here: try their succulent moules marinières (11€), or check out the *plats du jour* board for the best-value fish dish of the day, washed down with a bottle of cold AOC Patrimonio white.

GETTING TO THE TRAILHEAD FROM BASTIA

You can reach **Calvi**, springboard for the GR20 at Calenzana, by train or by bus. Both follow more or less the same route but the bus is cheaper and quicker. Operated by Les Beaux Voyages (☎ 04.95.65.11.35), it leaves from outside the train station twice daily. Departure times are best checked at the tourist office (see p89), or online at 💻 www.corsicabus.com.

Calvi is also served by two trains per day, via Ponte-Leccia junction. The latter is where you have to change trains to reach Corte and Vizzavona (halfway point of the GR20). Current timetables are displayed in the station and at the tourist office.

For **Ajaccio**, you also have a choice of train or bus. Even though it's a lot slower, most people choose the former – the line through the mountains, crossing the watershed below Monte d'Oro, is among the most spectacular in Europe. Two to four services cover the route each day, taking 3 hours 40 minutes. The Ajaccio bus, run by Eurocorse Voyages (☎ 04.95.21.06.30), leaves from a small square opposite the tourist office and only takes three hours.

If you're doing the GR20 from south to north, you'll have to pick up a bus (Rapides Bleues; ☎ 04.95.31.03.79) **towards Porto-Vecchio** and ask the driver to let you off at Sainte-Lucie-de-Porto-Vecchio, from where you can hitch the remaining way to Conca, or else phone for the gîte minibus to collect you (see p199). Timetables for these services are at 💻 www.corsicabus.com.

Calvi

There can be few towns in the world as inherently beautiful as Calvi that are so thoroughly eclipsed by their setting. Its squat citadel and yacht-filled harbour, where the Côte d'Azur jet-set drop anchor in August, are poised at the head of a magnificent turquoise bay and encircled by a gigantic backdrop of snow-streaked mountains. In good weather the grey escarpments seem magnified and it can be a surreal experience to sit on the quayside with a pastis in your hand staring up at the névés splashed across the north face of Monte Cinto, knowing that you'll be crossing them in a couple of days.

For those heading off on the big GR the town's sophisticated pleasures only serve to sharpen anticipation of the trail ahead. Most hikers can't resist the call of the hills for long, heading inland as soon as they've stocked up with cash and other essentials not available in Calenzana. If you've already been trekking, Calvi is a place to ease aching feet with a well-earned break on the beach.

WHAT TO SEE

Packed onto a high bluff above the harbour, Calvi's ochre-walled **citadel**, erected in the fifteenth century by the Genoans, is the best place to get your bearings.

Calvi, 1870 (from *Journal of a Landscape Painter*, Edward Lear)

Its entrance is just above place Christophe Colomb at the top of blvd Wilson, from where a cobbled alley winds up to an enclosed square, dominated by the **Cathedral of Saint Jean Baptiste** and the former Governors' Palace, now a military barracks.

Heading uphill along rue Colomb you'll eventually emerge at a ruined house which local legend asserts was the birthplace of **Christopher Columbus** (Le Maison Columbus). Shreds of tenuous evidence have been unearthed to support the connection but scholars remain unconvinced. Calvi, meanwhile, is milking the supposed link for all it's worth, renaming streets and squares, sticking up plaques and featuring an image of the discoverer of the New World in its tourist brochures.

With such inspiring views from the nearby ramparts it's hard to see why the hype is necessary. Calvi's natural attributes have exerted a powerful-enough pull on visitors for years, as demonstrated by the citadel's most famous café-restaurant, **Chez Tao**. Opened in the 1930s by a couple of Russian émigrés, one of whom was in the group who murdered Rasputin, it quickly established a reputation among the international glitterati. Three generations on it's owned by the same family and continues to attract film and rock stars, whose signed photos hang on the walls.

Chez Tao's view over the marina is legendary but for panoramas of the town and bay head for the **Chapelle de Notre Dame de la Serra**, perched on a ridge high above Calvi. You can walk there; pick up the signs pointing inland from ave de la République to the four-star Hôtel La Villa, and from there follow the lane steeply uphill until you see a path forking to the left into the maquis. Set amid a pile of pink granite boulders that have sheltered a shrine since at least the 1400s, the present chapel dates from the nineteenth century.

From the south side of the marina Calvi's spectacular white-sand **beach** curves for more than 4km around the bay. The further from town you walk, the quieter and cleaner it becomes, though during the high season, crowds of campers from the sites hidden in the huge pine forest behind the beach can fill its entire length.

An alternative to lazing on the sand is to take one of the **boat trips f**rom the marina. At 42-50€ they're not cheap but offer a great way to see the magnificent coast to the south, including the famous red cliffs of the Scandola Nature Reserve (see box p96). Before heading home most boats pull in for an hour at Girolata, a remote former fishing village that's accessible by road. Tickets and timetables are available from the booths dotted along Quai Landry.

ORIENTATION AND SERVICES

Calvi basically comprises one main street, blvd Wilson, which runs from the **train station** (☎ 04.95.65.00.61) to the foot of the citadel. Below its sloping walls, a tangle of narrow stepped lanes, little squares and winding alleys tumble down to quai Landry and the marina, where swish cafés and restaurants open onto a mass of gleaming white luxury pleasure boats. Ferries and hydrofoils from the continent dock at the far northern end of the harbour.

La Maison
Columbus

CITADEL

Cathédrale
St Jean Baptiste

Chez Tao

Place
Christophe
Colomb

Port

Garage d'Angeli

QUAI LANDRY

Voyages Mariani
(bus to
Calenzana)

RUE VILLA-ANTOINE

Halle de la
Presse

BOULEVARD WILSON

RUE CLEMENCEAU

Church of
Ste Marie Majeure

Supermarket

2

3

4

6

5

QUAI LANDRY

7

Boat Trips

Les Beaux Voyages Buses

La Porteuse d'Eau

RUE JOFFRE

Train Station

Marina

Chapelle de Notre Dame
de la Serra (4km)

8

TRAILBLAZER

0   100M
APPROXIMATE SCALE

ROUTE SANTORE

AVENUE DE LA REPUBLIQUE

Where to stay
1 Hôtel le Belvédère
3 Hôtel du Centre
6 Grand Hôtel
8 Hôtel Casa Vecchia

Where to eat
2 Chez Annie
4 Pizzeria Capuccino
5 U San Carlu
7 Abri Côtier

Launderette

Super U

Beach

Calvi

M Cyrnea,
Ste Catherine
Airport (8km)

'U Carabellu' (1km)

GATEWAY TOWNS

Scandola Nature Reserve (Réserve Naturelle de Scandola)

Forming the northern limits of the Golfe de Porto, the distinctive red peninsula of Scandola (named after the island's traditional terracotta rooftiles, *scandule*), comprises one of the Mediterranean's richest biospheres. In 1975, after the disappearance of the monk seal, 7800 hectares of its wind-lashed tip and 4200 hectares of water were accorded special protection; today, as a UNESCO World Heritage site, the area supports a wealth of wildlife, both above and below sea level.

The promontory is believed to have been formed by a volcanic eruption 200-250 million years ago when lava from the crater of Monte Cinto flowed into the sea. Since then, wind, waves and wet weather have been hard at work sculpting its cliffs, which rise to 900m in places, into an astonishingly convoluted mass of fissures, pinnacles, creeks, arches and caves.

As Scandola is strictly off-limits to casual visitors, you'll have to be content with a boat trip from Calvi (see p94) or Porto (see box p104). Birders shouldn't pass up the chance to see some of the 24 pairs of ospreys who nest here (most of them on rocky columns rising out of the sea), as well as andouin gulls, bearded vultures, peregrine falcons and the large flocks of Mediterranean shearwaters.

The clear seas around Scandola harbour a correspondingly rich sub-aquatic ecosystem, underpinned by deep fields of **poseidonion** (*Posidonia oceanica*), a grass that is able, because of the water's exceptional clarity, to photosynthesize at 35m – and thus supply life-giving oxygen to the many creatures who live at that depth (you may come across banks of the stuff on Girolata beach and Cala di Tuara).

Grazing the reefs of exquisite red coral beneath the cliffs, chubby-lipped **grouper**, two-metre barracuda, scorpion fish, moray and conger eels and carnivorous dentex all flourish here, as do three species of lobster, seahorses and a vivid red plant called gorgonian that glows blue when illuminated by diving lights.

Divers are not allowed inside Scandola's exclusion zone but the **sub-aqua schools** in Porto marina lead groups to a string of superb sites nearby. Rates for exploratory dives range from 27€ to 42€; the schools also offer instruction for beginners, leading to PADI accreditation. For more information, check out 🖳 www.plonge eporto.com or www.generation-bleue.com, or call at the dive schools on the quayside.

Buses (Les Beaux Voyages) from Bastia pull into the small square near the train station, known locally as **La Porteuse d'Eau** because of the statue of a woman carrying water at its centre.

Ste Catherine **Airport** (☎ 04.95.65.88.88), 8km south-west of the centre, is a far less convenient and welcoming point of arrival. The cab drivers' mafia has ensured that there's no bus service into town; you'll have to catch a **taxi** for a stiff 15-20€ depending on the time of day.

As the airport is effectively on the way to Calenzana, many trekkers bypass Calvi completely. Taxis charge 25-30€ for the trip so it pays to group together with other hikers. You could try to hitch but you may have to walk a fair way and wait around (see Getting to Calenza from Calvi, p98).

The **tourist office** (☎ 04.95.65.16.67, 🖳 www.tourisme.fr/calvi; June 15-Sep daily 9am-7pm, Oct-June 14 Mon-Fri 9am-noon and 2-5.30pm, Sat 9am-noon) is just above quai Landry. Bus times can be checked there, or better still at the travel agent on La Porteuse d'Eau.

Most of Calvi's other essential services are on blvd Wilson. The **post office** has an **ATM**, as do the big **banks** further up the road. You'll also find a bureau de change on La Porteuse d'Eau. FFRP Topoguides and IGN maps are available at several **bookshops**, including Halle de la Presse, at the top of blvd Wilson.

There's a small **supermarket** on rue Clémenceau but it's far pricier and offers a more limited choice than the huge Super U (June-Sep Mon-Sat 8am-8pm, Sun 8am-1pm; Oct-May Mon-Sat 8.30am-12.30pm and 3-7.30pm), 10 minutes' walk down ave de la République from La Porteuse d'Eau.

Cars may be rented from the usual range of companies at the airport, or from the Hertz office (☎ 04.95.65.06.64) on La Porteuse d'Eau. Europcar (☎ 04 95.65.10.35) has a counter on the west side of ave de la République, near the train station, while Avis (☎ 04.95.65.06.74) works from a cabin in the car park next to the marina. For **mountain bikes** (15-17€ per day) try Garage d'Angeli (☎ 04.95.65.02.13) on rue Villa-Antoine. Deposits are charged by credit card.

Calvi's only **launderette** stands at the top of the car park next to Super U.

WHERE TO STAY

By far the best budget option is *Hôtel du Centre* (☎ 04.95.65.02.01; open June-Sep), tucked away at 12 rue Alsace-Lorraine, near the Church of Sainte-Marie-Majeure. Most rooms in this converted gendarmerie share showers and toilets but the facilities are well maintained. Prices start at 34€ in June and September, rising to only 48€ in July and August – unbeatable value.

Occupying a prime position on one of the hills overlooking the town, the grandly named *Relais International de la Jeunesse 'U Carabellu'* (☎ 04.95 65.14.16, 🖳 04.95.80.65.33; open May-Oct) would be a great fallback were it not more than 2km (one of them uphill) from the centre. Go down ave de la République for 1km, where a signboard indicates the way to the right. Beds cost 24€ per head (30€ half board); the views over the gulf from the terrace are superb.

A little way from the town centre, on route Santore, the relaxing mid-range *Hôtel Casa Vecchia* (☎ 04.95.65.09.33, 🖳 www.hotel-casa.vecchia.com) comprises 10 pleasant bungalows set in a pretty garden. The hotel is handy for the beach and well secluded. Rates range from 40€ for the most basic double rooms (with exterior toilets) in low season to 60€ in high season. Half-board (112€ for two people) is obligatory in July and August.

In a similar bracket, but much better value, is the *Cyrnea* (☎ 04.95.65 03.35, 🖳 www.hotelcyrnea.com), on route de Bastia. The rooms are large for the price and there's a pool. The only catch is that it's a 20-minute walk from the centre. To find it keep going down Ave de la République and along the main Bastia road for around 20 minutes (on foot); the hotel is on your right, facing the road.

If you're splashing out, try the *Grand Hôtel* (☎ 04.95.65.05.74, 🖳 www .grand-hotel-calvi.com; open April-Oct), at the bottom of blvd Wilson. Dating from Calvi's heyday at the turn of the 20th century, it has lots of period charm, with huge rooms and old fashioned fittings. Don't be put off by the slightly dowdy reception area. Rates start at around 76€ for a double, rising to 115€ for the larger rooms in peak season: good value for money.

WHERE TO EAT

Calvi is crammed with restaurants. The wealth of competition ensures fair prices except along quai Landry where you pay for the location. One exception is *Pizzeria Capuccino* (☎ 04.95.65.11.19), a refreshingly unpretentious place serving delicious home-made pasta, salads and pizzas for 10-15€.

Overlooking the quayside from the corner of rue Joffre, *Abri Côtier* (☎ 04 95.65.12.76) offers the best value among the larger seafood joints in this strip. Grilled fish from the gulf is the thing to go for here (consult the plats du jour board for the chef's recommendation) but they also offer fresh salads livened up with delicious local brocciu and herbs, as well as inexpensive pizzas. Their set menus cost 20€ to 35€.

Deeper into the old quarter, *U San Carlu* (☎ 04.95.65.92.20), just off rue Clémenceau, is another of the town's old favourites, with no less than five set menus (18-27€) and a vast choice of à la carte dishes. The terrace, in a courtyard overhung with trees and flowering shrubs, is especially pleasant in the evening.

For relatively inexpensive Corsican specialities to take away, try *Chez Annie* at No 5 on the same road. All kinds of pastries, ewes' cheese, charcuterie and chestnut-flour flans and biscuits are sold here, as well as a good selection of quality local AOC wines.

GETTING TO CALENZANA FROM CALVI

The village of Calenzana, 15km south of Calvi, marks the start of the GR20. Unfortunately, despite the huge numbers of hikers passing through between May and mid-September, getting there cheaply can be difficult – a fact attributable to the pressure brought to bear on the council by local taxi drivers.

The village is served by a regular **bus** but timetables tend to be erratic. From mid-September until the end of June the service is essentially a school run, pegged to holiday dates; check times with the tourist office or at the travel agent on La Porteuse d'Eau. During the summer months, however, Les Beaux Voyages (☎ 04.95.65.15.02) operates a twice-daily service, with regular departures at around 2pm and 7pm. Voyages Mariani (☎ 04.95.65.00.47) also operates a bus on this route, leaving at 6.30pm (Mon-Sat) from the car park below the citadel. The fare in both cases in 6€ one way. Timetables can be consulted at 🖳 www.corsicabus.com.

If you miss the bus your only options are to take a **taxi** (☎ 04.95.65.30.36, 15-20€ from La Porteuse d'Eau or the airport), walk, or hitch. That said, it is notoriously difficult to catch a lift, though your chances will improve considerably once you're off the main N197 onto the Calenzana road. From there it's a 10km plod across the plains and up the hill to the village, a grim prospect if you're weighed down with provisions and intending to make a dawn start the following day.

Thanks to its regular year-round train service, Calvi is well connected to Bastia, Corte and all points south along the line to Ajaccio, including Vizzavona where you can join (or leave) the GR20 at its midway point.

Corte

As the seat of the island's independent government in the eighteenth century and now the home of its only university, Corte occupies a unique position in the Corsican psyche. Ajaccio and Bastia may be the main economic centres but this is the undisputed spiritual capital.

When the FLNC decided to stage a mass show of strength prior to its cease-fire of 1996 it's no coincidence that the site they chose lay on the opposite side of the valley from the town. Rising above its Tibetan-monastery-like tumble of tiled rooftops, Corte's citadel, where Faustina Gaffory and her rebels held out against a Genoan siege in 1750, is dwarfed by an appropriately epic mountain backdrop – a vision that for many Corsicans symbolizes the island's defiant essence.

Despite an abundance of political graffiti, Corte strikes a more peaceful profile than its nationalist significance would suggest. Bombings and machine-gun attacks on civic buildings are actually much rarer here than in Ajaccio, Bastia and Calvi, and the presence of so many students gives the town a lived-in atmosphere missing from much of the interior.

If you've been on the trail for some days this is the perfect place to see a bit of island life, especially during term time when Corte's main drag, café-lined cours Paoli, is the liveliest spot for miles. Cours Paoli is also the home of Corsica's best-stocked outdoor equipment shop, Omnisports, see p102.

WHAT TO SEE

The logical place to begin a walk around Corte's historic *haute ville* is **place Paoli**, dominated by the statue of the man affectionately dubbed 'Babu di a Patria, or 'Father of the Nation' by Corsicans.

Although originally from the Castagniccia region in the north-west of the island, Pascal Paoli is most closely associated with Corte, the town from where he launched the rebellion of 1754 and where he revived the island's National Assembly the following year (see p46).

Heading up the stepped ramp on the south side of the square brings you to the smaller **place Gaffori**, where the seeds of Paoli's success were sown. The house flanking its north side belonged to the first leader of independent Corsica, General Gian' Pietri Gaffori, whose wife Faustina famously defended it against a Genoan attack long enough for her husband to arrive with reinforcements (she allegedly threatened to ignite a keg of gunpowder and blow both herself and her troops up if they failed to fight to the last). You can still see the old Genoan bullet marks on its facade.

The seat of Paoli's first government, **U Palazzu Naziunale**, stands just above place Gaffori, to the left of the entrance to the citadel. After serving as a parliament building it was handed over to the Franciscan Order to become Corsica's first university and today houses the Corsican Studies department.

Beyond the ornamental gateway the Genoan **citadel**, dating from the early fifteenth century, was recently given a massive makeover to accommodate the state-of-the-art **Museu di a Corsica** (summer daily 10am-8pm, winter Tue-Sat 10am-6pm; 5.30€). The complex, designed by Italian architect Andréa Bruno, forms an incongruously modern counterpoint to the collection inside it, dominated by farm implements and peasant costumes collected by the ethnographer Révérend Père Louis Doazan. The admission price includes entrance into the citadel proper, from where the views over Corte's hinterland and its convoluted roofscape are spectacular.

ORIENTATION AND SERVICES

The trail from A Sega refuge and the Tavignano Gorge approaches Corte from the west, arriving in town on the north side of the citadel. Follow the lane downhill and you'll eventually hit cours Paoli, running from place Duc de Padoue in the north to place Paoli in the south; this is Corte's principal thoroughfare. On its south-west side, the old quarter, a mildewing mass of Genoese-era tenements stacked up the hillside below the university and citadel, holds most of the town's picturesque buildings and atmosphere.

Buses from Ajaccio and Bastia, operated by Eurocorse Voyages (☎ 04 95.21.06.30) stop at the top of ave Xavier Luciani, just off the south side of cours Paoli.

The **train** station (☎ 04.95.46.00.97), on the eastern edge of town, has four services daily from Ajaccio and Bastia (via Vizzavona and Vivario). It's within easy walking distance of the town centre; the quickest route on foot is to turn left out of the main exit and follow allée du 9 Septembre past the sports stadium, shortly after which a lane cuts on your right down to a footbridge across the confluence of the Tavignano and Restonica rivers. The steps on the opposite side bring you out on ave Président Pierucci, five minutes from the bottom of cours Paoli.

Taxis (☎ Michel Silvani 04.95.46.04.88 or mobile ☎ 06.03.49.15.24; or Thérèse Feracci ☎ 04.95.61.01.17 or mobile ☎ 06.12.10.60.60) queue at the rank outside the train station. If it's not closed as a security precaution, you can **leave luggage** at the *consigne* in the ticket office, or better still lug it up the hill to the Café du Cours, on cours Paoli, which keeps rucksacks in its locked store room while you wander around town. The service is free but it's a good idea to return the favour by ordering a drink at the bar if you've time. In another of this café's backrooms you'll find Corte's only **Internet access**, where you can send and receive email for nominal rates.

Information on current bus and train timings is the main reason you might want to visit the town's main **tourist office** (☎ 04.95.46.26.70, 🖳 www.corte-tourisme.com; Mon-Sat 9am-1pm and 3-6pm, Sun 3-6pm from mid-June to Sep); it's inside the citadel, to the right of the museum's main entrance.

GATEWAY TOWNS

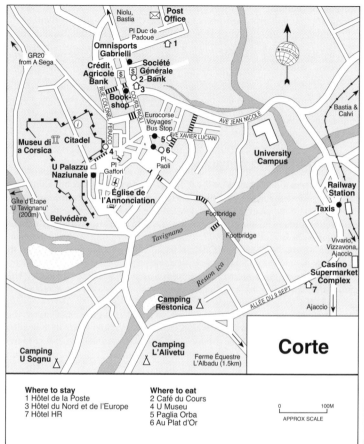

Where to stay
1 Hôtel de la Poste
3 Hôtel du Nord et de l'Europe
7 Hôtel HR

Where to eat
2 Café du Cours
4 U Museu
5 Paglia Orba
6 Au Plat d'Or

0   100M
APPROX SCALE

Corte

FFRP **Topoguides** and IGN **maps** of the island are also sold at all the newsagents and bookstores dotted along cours Paoli. In the same street you'll find a string of **ATMs** and **banks** (normal hours Mon-Fri 8.15am-noon and 2-4.30pm) where you can change money. The **post office** (Mon-Fri 8am-noon and 2-5pm, Sat 8am-noon), on a road leading north off place Duc de Padoue, also has an ATM.

The best and cheapest place for provisions is the **supermarket** on the southern edge of town near the train station. **Omnisports Gabrielli**, at the top of cours Paoli, is the place to go for trekking and camping gear.

WHERE TO STAY

On the whole, accommodation is cheaper here than on the coast and there's plenty of it. Unless specified places listed are open all year.

For those happy to walk a little way, the pleasant **Ferme Équestre L'Albadu** (☎ 04.95.46.24.55), a horse-riding centre and working sheep farm, offers inexpensive bed and breakfast accommodation for 33€ per double room (shared shower and toilets), or 40€ per person half-board.

Located on the hillside above the town, the farm enjoys fine views over the hills from its olive orchards, where you can pitch tents or bivouac for 8€; this includes unlimited hot showers and use of the clean toilet block. Don't miss the wonderful evening meals here (see opposite). To reach it, follow the old Ajaccio road uphill for 15 minutes.

After Ferme Équestre L'Albadu the best of the many **campsites** dotted around the town is **U Sognu** (☎ 04.95.46.09.07; May-Sep), 15 minutes' walk from the centre and at the bottom of the road leading up the Restonica Valley. It has views of the citadel, a seasonal wood-fired pizzeria (for campers) and is altogether cleaner and more congenial than the nearby **Restonica** and **L'Alivetu** sites across the bridge.

Gîte d'étape 'U Tavignanu' (☎ 04.95.46.16.85; Easter-Oct), secluded in the woods behind the citadel, is the most convenient budget option for trekkers. Peaceful, close to the centre yet inaccessible by road, it has a scruffy garden terrace overlooking the valley and a ping-pong table. Dorm beds cost 18€ (breakfast included) or 33€ per person half-board.

Other accommodation in Corte is serviceable but largely uninspiring. For rock-bottom rates try **Hôtel HR** (☎ 04.95.45.11.11, 🖹 04.95.61.02.85), on allée du 9 Septembre. Basic double rooms in this vast, institutional block (a converted gendarmerie) go for as little as 29€, or 33€ en suite.

Up in the centre of town, the little **Hôtel de la Poste**, on place Duc de Padoue (☎ 04.95. 46.01.37, 🖹 04.95.46.13.08) has a lot more character. On the ground floor of an old building, its rooms range from simple doubles with WC on the corridor (40€) to larger en suites (53€). They also have a few triple-bedded rooms (again, with washbasins but no toilets) for 58€. Unlike many places its rates do not fluctuate according to the season.

Moving up the scale, **Hôtel du Nord et de L'Europe** (☎ 04.95 46.00.68, 🖳 www.hoteldunord-corte.com), on cours Paoli, holds more of a period feel than most, with original stone steps and wood floors. Rooms start at 75€. This is a smart, friendly, efficient place within easy reach of the train station and bus stops.

WHERE TO EAT

When looking for somewhere to eat in Corte, the golden rule is to avoid anywhere with photos outside it. These places, most of which are dotted around the squares, cater solely for tourists and are not in the same league as the town's four bona fide restaurants, which offer fine dining for no more expense. The

THANK YOU
HONEY -
I NEEDED THAT
TALK ! -

XO

SOMEDAY WOULD
LIKE TO HAVE BRIAN,
COATES & BOOKER IN
ONE ROOM !
LOVE YOU

I love you

xxo

best situated is **U Museu**, up in the haute ville on rampe Ribanelle (open daily in summer, Mon-Sat during the winter). It does a roaring trade so get there early in the evening to secure a table outside with views of the valley. The cost of their set menus (15-23€) varies according to the number of courses you choose, not the dishes on offer. Most of the mains are local specialities, such as wild boar and myrtle stew, stuffed trout in red pepper sauce, and sweetmeats in red wine. Among their copious selection of salads, the *chèvre chaud* (hot goat's cheese) stands out; served on a bed of croutons and cubes of bacon, it's filling enough to be a complete meal.

Just off cours Paoli on ave Xavier Luciani, **Paglia Orba** (☎ 04.95.61.07.89) is a safe choice for a cheap and cheerful pizza (6-8€), or pricier à la carte splurge. For once, vegetarians are well catered for, with dishes such as aubergine baked with chestnuts and stuffed onions, and a generous choice of salads.

Around the corner, on place Paoli, **Au Plat D'Or** (☎ 04.95.46.27.16) is the classiest restaurant in Corte. Wild river trout, and brochette of local beef with mushrooms are their two specialities (18€ à la carte); they also offer a tempting selection of desserts. Menus range from 20€ to 28€.

Well worth the 20-minute walk out of town, **Ferme Équestre L'Albadu** (☎ 04.95.46.24.55) is the most sociable option. Evening meals (fantastic value at only 19€ for a fixed three-course menu) are served on a long table in a communal dining hall. The accent is firmly on traditional Corsican cuisine, with superb local cheese and charcuterie, as much wine as you can drink, and warm hospitality from the host, Jean Pulicani. Book in advance as numbers are limited and the food is prepared to order each afternoon.

Porto-Vecchio
(Porto Veghju)

Porto-Vecchio has been south-west Corsica's principal town since it was found-ed by the Genoans in the sixteenth century. Controlled from the confines of its crumbling citadel, which still overlooks the gulf from its hilltop vantage point, a flourishing trade in cork and wine originally ensured the town's prosperity, which endured well into the 20th century despite the perennial threats of malar-ia and pirate raids.

Today, with a permanent population of around 10,600, Porto-Vecchio remains a well-heeled town, only nowadays tourism forms the backbone of its economy. Shiploads of visitors, the majority of them wealthy Italians, pour through each summer en route to the famous white-sand-and-turquoise-water beaches to the south. This, however, is where they come to shop and strut their stuff in the evenings. Consequently the narrow lanes of the old town are crammed with designer boutiques and chic souvenir chops – Corsica at its most bijou.

Lumbering out of the hills with a backpack, you'll probably feel under-dressed and out of place here. After a laze in the square and an amble around the back lanes of the citadel, most hikers make a beeline for the bus office and

---

Beaches around Porto-Vecchio

Postcard racks across the island gleam with images of the translucent water and inviting white sands that lie south down the coast from Porto-Vecchio, but for most of the year the best of these beaches are hard to reach without some form of transport. In July and August, however, a shuttle bus (*navette*) runs out to the most developed of them, Palombaggia and Santa Giulia, starting at Camping Matonara (see map p107) and stopping at various points along the road behind the marina. For details ask at the tourist office or campsite reception.

Backed by ranks of distinctive umbrella pines, **Palombaggia** is a long, perfect-ly white curve dotted with clumps of pink granite. Get there early in the morning to enjoy it before the rush starts. If the crowds become too much walk south to the qui-eter **Plage d'Asciaghju**, where there's an excellent campsite, the *Asciaghju* (☎ 04 95.70.37.87) just 300m behind the beach. **Santa Giulia**, further down the coast, is perhaps the most spectacular, with brilliant turquoise water, but is spoilt by a huge holiday villa complex behind it.

An alternative way to see some of the beautiful coast south of Porto-Vecchio is to take one of the **boat trips**, costing around 62€, offered at the marina. The excur-sions last a full day, taking you down as far as Bonifacio and the Îles Lvezzi marine reserve, with a stop for lunch and a swim at one of the more remote coves along the way. Look for the 'Le Ruscana' sign opposite the capitainerie.

Finally, if you've just finished the GR20 and are considering a spell on the beach, check the box on p199 for suggestions for places closer to Conca.

Figari-Sud-Corse Airport
Southern Corsica's airport, Figari-Sud-Corse (☎ 04.95.71.10.10), lies 20km south-west of Porto-Vecchio. Shuttle buses, run by Transports Rossi (☎ 04.95.71.00.11), operate from mid-June until early September, connecting with flight arrivals and departures. Leaving town you can pick them up from the marina opposite the capitainerie. Tickets cost 10€.

Taxis charge 42-50€ depending on the time of day. The only other option, apart from hitching, is to catch Eurocorse Voyage's Ajaccio bus from Porto-Vecchio and get off at Figari village, which straddles the main road, and walk or hitch the remaining 5km to the airport.

---

head off in search of somewhere more low-key. With hotel rates among the island's highest and the fabled beaches difficult to reach without your own transport for much of the year, this is not the ideal place to rest up.

ORIENTATION AND SERVICES

Although surrounded by an unprepossessing belt of supermarkets and roundabouts, Porto-Vecchio's heart comprises a quaint, compact grid of late-medieval streets encircled by fragments of Genoan walls and gateways. Its focus, place de la République, is a sunny square which for nine months of the year metamorphoses into one large café-terrace, overlooked by the stately Church of Saint-Jean-Baptiste.

Across the square you'll find the helpful **tourist office** (☎ 04 95.70.09.58, 🖥 www.accueil-portovecchio.com; July & Aug Mon-Sat 9am-8pm, Sun 9am-1pm; June & Sep Mon-Sat 9am-1pm & 3-6pm; Oct-May Mon-Fri 9am-noon & 2-6pm, Sat 9am-noon). Most of the town's hotels and restaurants lie within five minutes' walk of here. The **post office**, however, stands just outside the citadel, past the mairie on rue Général-Leclerc. It has an ATM as does the Société Générale **bank** nearby.

Porto-Vecchio's **marina** is not the most picturesque on the island but it's as good a place as any to kill an hour or two, especially in the midday heat. To reach it, walk under Porte Génoise, the grand old gateway at the south-east corner of the citadel, and follow the road downhill. The main **port de commerce**, the arrival and departure point for the ferry boats, lies further east.

Buses drop and pick up passengers at several locations, depending on the route. **Eurocorse Voyage**'s service to and from Ajaccio via Propriano uses the small car park opposite the Trinitours travel agency (☎ 04.95.70.13.83) on rue Pasteur, two minutes' walk north of the citadel. For destinations up the east coast (including Sainte-Lucie-de-Porto-Vecchio, the turn-off for Conca and the GR20 trailhead, and Bastia), **Rapides Bleues**' bus (☎ 04.95.70.10.36) uses the Corsica Tours office at 7 rue Jean-Jaurès. Always check bus times at the relevant office (the timetable is usually displayed in the window), not at the tourist office, which is notoriously unreliable. Fares are usually paid to the driver when you get on. Note, too, that the travel agents will usually look after your luggage if you're leaving town on the next bus; Porto-Vecchio has no official left-luggage facility. The bus to **Figari-Sud-Corse Airport** (see box p105) leaves from opposite the capitainerie.

For serious **shopping**, both provisions and and outdoor bits and bobs, you won't do better than the huge Hyper U supermarket next to rondpoint Quatre Chemins, 20 minutes' walk north of the citadel. A bakery and a pharmacy are in the same complex. The bookshop here stocks a good range of IGN maps but you're more likely to get hold of the latest FFRP Topoguides at **Maison de la Presse** on rue Pasteur, which also sells a modest range of foreign newspapers.

The only **launderette** in Porto-Vecchio is in the marina, next to the capitainerie. **Internet access** is available at Cyberlink, rue Jean-Jaurès, which has fast ADSL connections (5€/hr or 1.50€/15min).

WHERE TO STAY

Much the most convenient **campsite**, although a correspondingly busy one, is *Camping Matonara* (☎ 04.95.70.37.05; May-Oct), near rondpoint Quatre Chemins, whose terraces are shaded by old cork trees.

In spring and autumn Porto-Vecchio is a prime destination for bus parties of French pensioners, so pressure on rooms is intense even outside peak season; during peak season every hotel seems to be block booked by Italians. Whenever you come, therefore, reserve well in advance and brace yourself for higher-than-average room rates.

A safe mid-price bet is *Hôtel Panorama* (☎ 04.95.70.07.96, 📄 04.95 70.46.78; open June-Sep), at 12 rue Jean Nicoli, where en suite doubles cost 50-60€ depending on the season. It's a modest place that's frayed around the edges, but clean enough for a night. Otherwise try the elegant three-star *Hôtel Goéland* (☎ 04.95.70.14.15, 🖥 www.hotelgoeland.com; open Apr-Oct), on ave Georges-Pompidou, down on the water's edge; tariffs (which include breakfast) range from 70€ to 100€ depending on the level of comfort. Alternatively check out the more run-of-the-mill *Hôtel Holzer* (☎ 04.95.70.05.93, 🖥 www.corse-eter nelle.com; open March to mid-Nov), at 12 rue Jean-Jaurès, where a double room will set you back 75€ in June and September, or twice that in July and August. *Hôtel Le Mistral* (☎ 04.95.70.08.53, 📄 04.95.70.51.60; open Mar-Nov), at 5 rue Toussaint-Culioli, is a comfortable, well-maintained two-star, with a selection of double rooms costing 49-80€/110-150€ low/high season. It's down the hill, past the post office on the left (south) side of the road.

WHERE TO EAT

Cheap eats in the citadel are in short supply, to say the least. For a quick snack, try the *boulangerie* on place de la République, which does the usual savoury bakes – hot pizza or brocciu-and-spinach *bastelles* (pasties), or *Sur la Pouce*, down the lane leading to Porte Génoise, where you can order from a vast range of filling, inexpensive paninis (hot baguettes) from around 4€. Nearby on rue Joseph Pietri, facing the church, *Le Shirley* is an efficient, inexpensive little fast

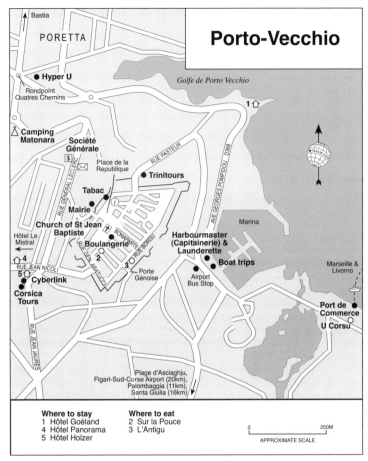

Golfe de Porto Vecchio

Marina

Marseille & Livorno

Where to stay
1 Hôtel Goéland
4 Hôtel Panorama
5 Hôtel Holzer

Where to eat
2 Sur la Pouce
3 L'Antigu

0   250M

APPROXIMATE SCALE

food joint serving the cheapest sitdown meals in town, including salads, quiches and crêpes.

If you're celebrating and fancy a more serious meal, much the most dependable option in the citadel is ***L'Antigu*** (☎ 04.95.70.39.33; closed Sun lunchtime), on rue Borgu, which serves Corsican specialities on a romantic terrace overlooking the gulf. Menus range from 16.50€ at lunch to 21-35€ in the evenings. Alternatively, head down to the ferry dock (port de commerce), where *U Corsu* (☎ 04.95.70.13.91) is indisputably the best pizzeria in town. Everything is fresh and tasty, and there's a fine rear terrace literally overhanging the water. Pizzas cost 11-15€ .

PART 4: ROUTE GUIDE AND MAPS

The route

CALENZANA

Calenzana, the village marking the start of the GR20, has been a major centre of olive production since the time of the Romans. Set against the awesome backdrop of Monte Grossu's massive cliffs, its nucleus of old granite houses, grouped around the Baroque belfry and façade of the Church of Saint Blaise, preside over a swathe of gnarled trees that tumble downhill to meet the coastal maquis behind the Golfe de Calvi. It's an archetypal Mediterranean hill village, with twisting lanes that open onto a square where you can join the old boys in their blue overalls sipping strong coffee in the shade of plane trees.

But beneath Calenzana's sleepy feel, broken only by the steady stream of trekkers that plod through to begin the **GR20** (and the Tra Mare e Monti winding down the west coast) trail, lurks a decidedly dubious underbelly. Among Corsicans the village is infamous as a taproot for organized crime on the Côte d'Azur, the so-called *Milieu*. It is often asserted that its prosperity, which has endured generations of emigration and economic decline,

---

The Battle of Calenzana

A small plaque on the south-west wall of Calenzana's church bell tower reminds customers in the Café Le Royal that beneath their feet around 500 Austrian mercenaries are buried, casualties of a bloody battle that took place here on February 2, 1732.

The foreigners formed part of a force of 8000 dispatched by Emperor Charles VI to bail out his Genoan allies, who had been struggling to quell an uprising on the island since the previous year. But the Corsicans, marshalled by the legendary Général Ceccaldi, were far better prepared and more highly motivated than the opposition. Rather than laying siege to Calenzana, where the rebels had dug in, the 600 attackers streamed headlong through the village, only to be met with fierce resistance from the locals. Boiling oil was poured over them from the upper storeys of narrow alleyways, and beehives and flaming branches were thrown from rooftops. As the mercenaries fled, bulls whose hides had been set on fire were released, allowing the defenders, aided by women and young boys armed with farm implements, to pick them off at will.

Led by General Camille Doria, the attempt to flush out the rebels had been a total debacle: only 100 of the mercenaries survived. Doria, shocked at the ferocity of the Corsicans' close-quarter combat, never repeated the mistake. After licking his wounds, he marched with heavy artillery on the bastions of nearby Algajola and Saint-Florent and successfully routed the rebels' defences using old-fashioned cannonades. Some concessions were made by the Genoans in the ensuing treaty, but the islanders would have to wait another two decades before tasting true independence from Italian rule.

derives from gangsterism in Marseille, a short ferry hop across the water.

This might merely be jealous slander but few would deny that Calenzana remains discernibly better off than its neighbours. Come here in August and you'll notice a disproportionate number of luxury German cars sporting '13' (Marseille) number plates.

After a nose around the **church**, whose ornate, gloomy interior is dominated by an early eighteenth-century altar and very gory tabernacle, there's not much to do other than fortify yourself for the trial ahead.

Orientation and services
Advice on how to get to Calenzana by **public transport from Calvi** appears on p98. A taxi here will set you back around 20-30€ one-way. Heading in the other direction, from Calenzana, call Taxis Biancardini on ☎ 04.95.62.77.80 or ☎ 06.08.16.53.65.

Anyone who didn't stock up with supplies before leaving the coast can do so at the large Spar **supermarket** on the main Calvi road. Fresh bread and pastries are sold there and at the small **bakery**, five minutes' walk east of the square.

Where to stay
In peak season, Calenzana struggles to cope with the influx of trekkers, in spite of the large, well-equipped *Gîte d'étape Municipal* (☎ 04.95.62.77.13; open May-Sep). Situated just below the village proper, a stone's throw off the main road, this is where most people heading off on the GR20 hole up. Its four-berth dorms, ranged around a gravel-chipping courtyard, have en suite bathrooms and cost 14€ per head.

Bivouackers are charged 5.50€ for a pitch under the trees in the garden, plus 4.50€ per tent, for which you also get the use of an impressive power shower and toilet block. Self-catering facilities are limited to a tiny kitchen equipped with a single electric hob and some pans; a move obviously designed to encourage you to eat in

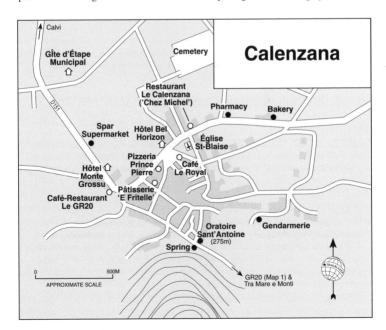

Calenzana

Calvi

Cemetery

Gîte d'Étape
Municipal

D151

Restaurant
Le Calenzana
('Chez Michel')

Pharmacy

Bakery

Spar
Supermarket

Hôtel Bel
Horizon

Église
St-Blaise

Pizzeria
Prince
Pierre

Café
Le Royal

Hôtel
Monte
Grossu

Pâtisserie
'E Fritelle'

Café-Restaurant
Le GR20

Oratoire
Sant'Antoine
(275m)

Gendarmerie

Spring

0   500M
APPROXIMATE SCALE

GR20 (Map 1) &
Tra Mare e Monti

TRAIL BLAZER

one of the restaurants up in the village. For the same reason, breakfast is not available here but see Café le Royal in the column opposite.

Two hotels up in the village centre offer more comfortable alternatives. Neither is particularly swish but their rates are low compared with Calvi. *Hôtel Monte Grossu* (☎ 04.95.62.70.15, 📠 04.95.62 83.21; open May-Sep) stands to the left of the main street and has 10 simple, clean double rooms (all with en suite showers but toilets *à l'étage*). Rates range from 44€ to 48€ depending on the month. Opposite the square, *Hôtel Bel Horizon* (☎/📠 04.95.62.71.72; open May-Sep) is in much the same mould, with rates from 40€ to 50€.

Where to eat

There's only one restaurant worthy of note: situated opposite the main façade of the church, *Le Calenzana 'Chez Michel'* (open daily Mar-Dec, Tue-Sun in Jan/Feb) offers staunchly traditional, delicious Corsican mountain cuisine and wood-baked pizzas.

If you're not expecting to be within range of a decent meal for a while, splash out on one of the set menus (15€ and 20€). These kick off with a rustic *soupe corse* (complete with the bones) or *terrine de*

figatellu (fragrant liver-sausage pâté), followed by wild-boar spaghetti, pan-fried veal with broad beans, or the restaurant's signature dish, tender suckling lamb and wheat-rolled roast potatoes.

Although marginally cheaper, neither of its competitors down the road, *Pizzeria Prince Pierre* and *Café-Restaurant Le GR20*, offers comparable value for money, nor the same degree of hospitality. You may, however, be tempted by the set breakfasts at *Café le Royal*, served on a terrace behind the church. Since the gîte was forced by the municipality to stop serving breakfasts (in order to *faire travailler les cafés*), something of a price war has broken out in the village. A string of places now open at 6am to catch the dawn trekking exodus; the Royal is the friendliest and best situated.

On your way up the hill towards the trailhead, another place to carb up is the stark *Pâtisserie E Fritelle*, on a lane called U Chiasu, which runs to the right off the main street just after the bend. Open from 6am, it's renowned for its hot Corsican doughnuts (*beignets*) and Calenzana's own speciality biscuits, *cuggielli*, made with appropriately calorific chestnut flour. Ask for a bag hot out of the oven.

STAGE ONE: CALENZANA→ REFUGE D'ORTU DI U PIOBBU
[MAP 1, opposite]
Overview

Leading you from the coastal belt around Calenzana to the windy heights of the watershed, the first day of the GR20 is an unremittingly tough slog involving a net altitude gain of 1245m (think of Ben Nevis and then some). Weighed down with two or three days' provisions and three litres of water (there's no dependable source along the route once out of sight of Calenzana), most trekkers find it a gruelling introduction to the joys of Corsican trekking. You'll certainly make life a lot easier for yourself by getting an early start, which will enable you to cover the first major climb in cool shadow.

The stage's highlights are a succession of extraordinary panoramas revealed from the passes. Encompassing a large chunk of the Balagne coast, these grow steadily more impressive as you climb, culminating in your first glimpse of the Cinto massif and Paglia Orba, which flag the onward route.

Because of the length and overall difficulty of the next (second) étape, this is not a leg of the GR20 to double up unless you are already fit and comfortable

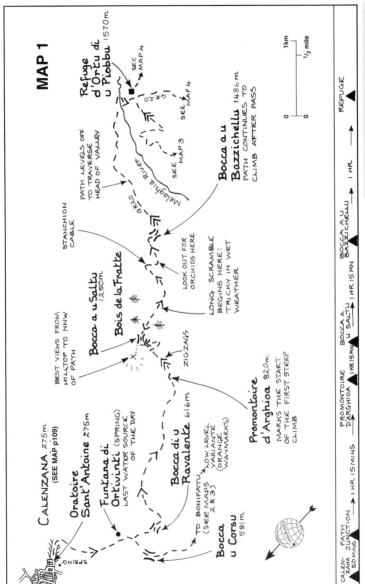

MAP 1

Refuge d'Ortu di u Piobbu 1570m

SEE MAP 4

SEE MAP 4

Bocca a u Bazzichellu 1486m
PATH CONTINUES TO CLIMB AFTER PASS

SEE MAP 3

Melaghia River

B120

B120

PATH LEVELS OFF TO TRAVERSE HEAD OF VALLEY

STANCHION CABLE

LOOK OUT FOR ORCHIDS HERE

Bocca a u Saltu 1250m

Bois de la Tratte

LONG SCRAMBLE BEGINS HERE: TRICKY IN WET WEATHER

BEST VIEWS FROM HILLTOP TO NNW OF PATH

X

ZIGZAGS

Promontoire d'Arghioa 820m:
MARKS THE START OF THE FIRST STEEP CLIMB

CALENZANA 275m
(SEE MAP p109)

Oratoire Sant'Antoine 275m

Funtana di Ortiventi (SPRING)
LAST WATER SOURCE OF THE DAY

Bocca di u Ravalente 616m

LOW LEVEL VARIANTE (ORANGE WAYMARKS)

TO BONIFATU (SEE MAPS 2 & 3)

Bocca u Corsu 581m

SPRING

1km

½ mile

0

0

REFUGE

CALEN-ZANA JUNCTION ▲ 50 MINS — PATH → 1 HR 15 MINS ▲ PROMONTOIRE D'ARGHIOA 1 HR 15 MN ▲ BOCCA A U SALTU 1 HR 15 MN ▲ BOCCA A U BAZZICHELLU 1 HR. ▲ REFUGE →

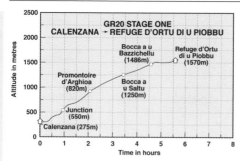

with the altitude. Anyone arriving early in the afternoon at the Refuge d'Ortu di u Piobbu would do better to consider the ascent of Monte Corona (see p116) as an extension.

A *Variante* route to the refuge runs along the Tra Mare e Monti trail to Bonifatu and thence up the Melaghia Valley (see p114). Keeping to easy gradients for most of the way it has little to recommend it other than as a safe bad-weather approach to the main trail. Basically, if the first étape seems too much for you in favourable conditions you should probably think twice about attempting the GR20 at all.

Route guide

PNRC signboards dotted along the road from the Gîte d'Étape Municipal and around Calenzana's square point the way to the GR20/Tra Mare e Monti **trail-head** at the top of the village.

The official start is marked by a tiny chapel, the **Oratoire Sant'Antoine** (275m), opposite a gushing **spring** of the same name where you can fill up your water bottle. Beyond it a paved mule track squeezes between old retaining walls to start a steady climb through a mix of Laricio pines, ferns and maquis dotted with lightning-charred chestnut trees.

A stately old pine, roughly 45 minutes up the trail, heralds your arrival at a second spring, the **Funtana di Ortivinti**, which stands to the left of the trail a short way before it splits; this is the last dependable source of drinking water before Ortu di u Piobbu. At the **junction** (550m), the orange waymarks of the Tra Mare e Monti/GR20 *Variante* run west (to the right).

The main GR20, meanwhile, presses south (left) uphill through spiny maquis to cross a shoulder pass, the **Bocca di u Ravalente** (616m), from where you can see up the whole Figarella Valley to the Cirque de Bonifatu.

Once over the spur a steady traverse sweeps around the eastern flank of the valley to a distinctive rock outcrop, the **promontoire d'Arghioa** (820m). Take a break here to steel yourself for the hard, zigzagging ascent of more than 400 metres through scruffy heather and pines to **Bocca a u Saltu** (1250m). Affording grandiose views across the wild Frintogna Valley to the summit of Monte Grossu, this pass forms the GR's gateway to the high mountains and is a great spot from which to admire the panorama of the Balagne coast (clearest from atop the outcrop immediately north-north-west of the pass itself).

(Opposite) Top: The Cinqui Frati ('Five Monks') rock pillars, crenellating the southern flank of the Cinto Massif. **Bottom**: Calenzana, starting point of the GR20, and the start of a long first day's climb. (Photos © David Abram).

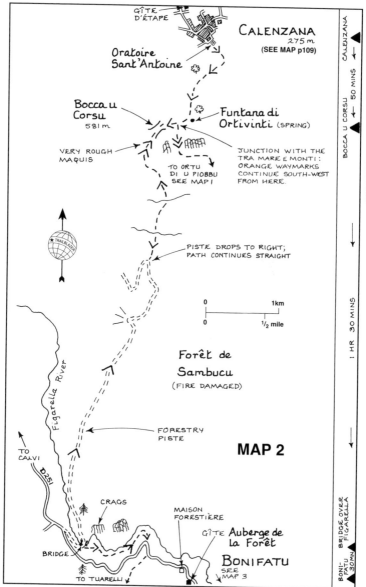

CALENZANA
275 m
(SEE MAP p109)

GÎTE
D'ÉTAPE

Oratoire
Sant'Antoine

Bocca u
Corsu
581m

Funtana di
Ortivinti (SPRING)

VERY ROUGH
MAQUIS

JUNCTION WITH THE
TRA MARE E MONTI:
ORANGE WAYMARKS
CONTINUE SOUTH-WEST
FROM HERE.

TO ORTU
DI U PIOBBU
SEE MAP I

★ TRAILBLAZER

PISTE DROPS TO RIGHT;
PATH CONTINUES STRAIGHT

0   1km
0   ½ mile

Forêt de
Sambucu
(FIRE DAMAGED)

Figarella River

FORESTRY
PISTE

MAP 2

TO
CALVI

D251

CRAGS

MAISON
FORESTIÈRE

GÎTE Auberge de
la Forêt

BONIFATU
SEE
MAP 3

BRIDGE

TO TUARELLI

CALENZANA
50 MINS
BOCCA U CORSU

1 HR 30 MINS

BRIDGE OVER
FIGARELLA
BONIFATU
30MN

(Opposite) Corte (see p99). (Photo © David Abram).

The Bocca a u Saltu also heralds a marked transition in the trail. After a short, easy descent through a beautiful Laricio pine forest (**Le Bois de la Fratte**) the waymarks thread steeply uphill though a messy mass of exposed granite that should be approached with caution, especially in wet weather. A **stanchion cable** (broken when we last passed through!) has been attached to one of the trickier pitches. Although a welcome help in slippery conditions it can prove a bottleneck in peak season.

Above it, more enjoyable scrambling across rocks dotted with spotted orchids and hellebore brings you eventually to the second major pass of the étape, **Bocca a u Bazzichellu** (1486m). The col is more rounded and wooded than the previous one but has less imposing views; you'll probably want to get straight on with the climb through the pine forest above it. Once clear of the trees a wonderful panorama opens up to the south across the Melaghia Valley to Monte Cinto and Paglia Orba on the horizon.

With the last significant ascent of the day behind you, the traverse that follows, contouring around the headwaters of the Melaghia River, is a real joy. After crossing a stream the path rounds a boulder-strewn spur and ascends for one last push to the plateau on which Refuge d'Ortu di u Piobbu is situated.

Refuge d'Ortu di u Piobbu
Nestled below the summit of Monte Corona, the Refuge d'Ortu di u Piobbu (1570m) is one of the most attractively sited on the GR20. A perfect spot for sunset, the refuge sits on the site of an old bergerie at the head of the Melaghia Valley, looking west over ranks of receding ridges towards the coast. Arriving here from sea level in fine weather you'll be struck by the clarity of the light and shimmering silver birch wood that spills down the stream gully nearby. The high-mountain ambience is accentuated by prayer flags fluttering from a cairn behind the hut; the flags were erected by the gardiens and some Nepali friends they met on an expedition to climb Mansulu in 2000.

The refuge itself accommodates 30 people (9€ per person), with a spacious dining area and adjoining stove room. Dry-stone bivouac and camping shelters are dotted around the building. If you're sleeping in the open without a tent, expect to be hassled by cattle during the night. Note, too, that this mountainside can get especially chilly in the small hours as the warm westerly from the sea dies off and cooler air currents drift down from Monte Corona; so bed down in one of the round, tall-walled shelters rather than semi-circular windbreaks if you can.

Hot drinks and cooked food, such as soupe corse and omelettes, are available here, in addition to the usual range of basic supplies when the refuge is staffed (from June until mid-September).

Low-level *Variante*: Calenzana → Bonifatu → Ortu di u Piobbu
[Map 2, p113; Map 3, opposite]
This low-level *Variante* section, which follows the Tra Mare e Monti trail south to Bonifatu and then cuts back in a north-easterly direction to scale the Melaghia Valley, is only worth taking in especially poor weather, if driving rain or snow render the principal route impassable. Although less strenuous it's a comparatively dull option, keeping for much of the time to monotonous

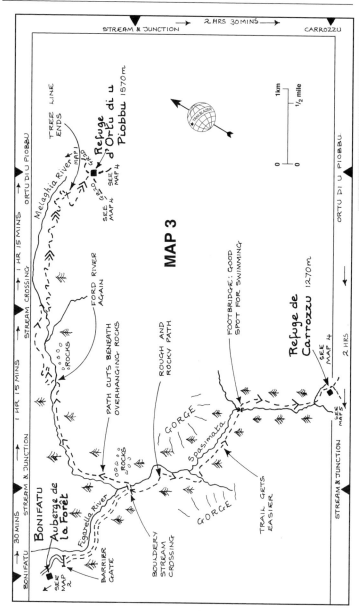

MAP 3

forestry tracks. During the summer this *Variante* also exposes you to a greater risk of heat stroke as its first half is almost devoid of tree cover.

From the **path junction** above Calenzana the *Variante*, indicated with orange waymarks, peels right (west) and after crossing **Bocca u Corsu** (581m) descends sharply through dense, scratchy maquis to the Sambuccu stream Here it levels off, following the contours of the hillside, and then climbs slightly to reach a clearly defined **forestry track** which runs gently downhill for roughly 3km to meet the **Figarella River**.

Under a large outcrop of weirdly eroded orange granite, the path crosses the river via a motorable bridge, veers east along the true left bank for one kilometre and then cuts steeply uphill in a series of tight zigzags to join the road (D251). A left turn here will take you past the Maison Forestière to **Bonifatu** where the excellent *Auberge de la Forêt* (☎ 04.95.65.09.98) offers restaurant meals and gîte d'étape accommodation.

The piste resumes beyond the auberge at the far side of the coach park and barrier, winding for 1.5km alongside the river before coming to an abrupt end after around 30 minutes. At the junction where a signboard marks the meeting point with the GR20's *Variante* from Carrozzu bear left to cross the river and follow the **yellow waymarks** along a rough piste as it cuts beneath a series of cliffs and then climbs steadily through maritime pine and oak forest to ford the stream a second time. After another sequence of broad zigzags the track comes to a third and final crossing of the Melaghia, beyond which it turns into a steeper line that cuts straight up the valley via a succession of tight switchbacks. Having emerged from the trees you veer sharply to the right (southwest) and follow the path up an open ridge to the refuge, visible above.

Low-level *Variante*: Ortu di u Piobbu → Carrozzu   [Map 3, p115]

It's possible to bypass the GR20's second étape by dropping down the thickly forested Melaghia Valley from Ortu di u Piobbu to the river bridge just east of Bonifatu, and from there heading up the Spasimata Valley to rejoin the main path at Carrozzu.

Taking around five hours, this low-level *Variante* is a much easier option than the conventional route, but misses out on some of the GR's most impressive landscapes. Trekkers tend to use it only when **bad weather** shrouds the high path, pressing on to Carrozzu rather than waiting at Ortu di u Piobbu for the clouds to lift.

The first section of the route, which is outlined in reverse above, is waymarked in yellow and easy to follow throughout. Allow two hours to reach the path junction near Bonifatu and 2½ hours for the zigzagging ascent to the Carrozzu refuge through some of the island's loveliest Laricio pine and holm oak forest.

Ascent of Monte Corona   [Map 4, p119]

Anyone not totally wiped out by the climb from Calenzana should consider this superb extension from Ortu di u Piobbu. Reachable in a round-trip of 2½ hours, the summit of Monte Corona (2144m) ranks among Corsica's most spectacular viewpoints, giving uninterrupted vistas of the north face of the Cinto massif as well as the rest of the interior watershed and north-west coast – well worth the labour to reach it.

The route, indicated with yellow waymarks, begins behind the refuge, skirting the side of the birch wood. Rough, loose and dusty at the outset, it zig-zags steeply through the trees towards the windswept **Bocca Tartagine** (1852m). This impressive pass formed a major transhumant gateway in past centuries. Shepherds used to drive their animals across it en route between the Melaghia Valley and the Giunssani region to the east. These days the only animals you're likely to come across are shy mouflons (*muvra*) scouring the scree above the col (for more on this reclusive and very rare animal, see box p128).

From the pass, turn right and follow the line of the ridge steeply uphill through a dense carpet of scratchy, malodorous alder. **Cairns** sketch a rough zigzagging route through the rocks but you can also pick up the odd stretch of path across the bank of vegetation (being careful not to stray to the right into the alder scrub). This section can be frustratingly hard going in places, but after 45 minutes you emerge on the scree which covers most of the summit. A clearly discernible path leads to the top, marked by a large cairn and stone hollow, from where a truly extraordinary view extends all the way from Cap Corse in the north-east to Paglia Orba in the south-west. From the south flank of the summit you overlook the snow-flecked bulk of Monte Cinto, rising from the arid Asco Valley.

The descent by the same route is rapid (scree down the first bit and rock-hop much of the more difficult lower slope to the Bocca Tartagine).

STAGE TWO: ORTU DI U PIOBBU → CARROZZU [MAP 4, p119]

Overview

After an easy initial climb and short descent through forest, stage two of the GR20 gets stuck into to a hefty ascent, followed by a long ridge traverse and, to wrap things up, a very sharp drop. Taking you above 2000m for the first time it also features one of the most memorable sections of the walk, the traverse of Capu Ladroncellu's deso-

late south face. In the course of the day you'll be exposed to some testing terrain as the GR winds up slippery rock slabs, through tight corridors, past wind-eroded breaches overlooking dizzying drops, and down stretches of precipitous, loose shale.

GR20 STAGE TWO
ORTU DI U PIOBBU → REFUGE DE CARROZZU

Once again, **water** is in short supply and, given the length and steepness of some gradients on this étape, you'll need to carry plenty of it – at least three litres in warm weather. There are two springs along the route but they're too near the beginning to be of real use. Don't be tempted to scrimp on liquid to save weight. The toughest portions of the étape towards the end of the day are south-facing and thus subject to the full force of the afternoon sun. To avoid this consider taking the low-level variante, see p116.

Route guide

From Ortu di u Piobbu the path winds south past a **spring** and into birch woods to begin a short, sharp climb that soon levels off. Following the contours of the hillside it crests a spur at 1627m and descends steeply down the drier, southern side of the ridge, where Laricio pines now predominate. Shortly before fording a perennial stream you pass the picturesque **Bergeries de la Mandriaccia**, where there's a **spring.**

A low, bouldery pass after a second stream crossing heralds the day's hardest climb, which strikes south up a tributary valley of the Melaghia. Interspersed by patches of alder and arbutus bushes, huge, smooth-backed rocks carry the route steeply uphill, with impressive pinnacles and crags towering above. Around mid-way through the ascent, arrows show the way off the main path to a small **spring**. The steepest stretch, however, is still to come. There's precious little let-up in the gradient until you near the pass, a clearly defined niche in the ridge between Punta Pisciaghia (to the right) and Capu Ladroncellu (to the left).

By the time you reach **Bocca Piccaia** (1950m) you're well and truly initiated into both the travails and payoffs of the GR. The long slog up the stream valley is rewarded with a view that comes as a spectacular surprise (if you didn't make it up Monte Corona). Plunging near vertically below you, the bare south wall of the Ladroncellu valley faces a vast sweep of eroded granite mountains, riddled with pinnacles, rock towers and vast cliffs. On the horizon, the serrated summits of Monte Cinto, Paglia Orba and Capu Tafonatu complete an unforgettable vista.

The views intensify as you press on from the pass, following the line of the ridge left (east) to an altitude of 2020m where the route levels off to begin the famous traverse of Capu Ladroncellu. For the next half-hour or so you keep to a more or less even gradient of around 150m below the summit, crossing scree and clumps of blue-grey rock. Make the most of the views here as in a short while you'll need to concentrate on a protracted, and at times tricky, descent over loose shale, which begins beyond a prominent overhang.

Bending southwards along the curve of the cirque, the path, after an initially sheer drop, negotiates a succession of steep, and in places awkward, scrambles on its gradual descent to **Bocca d'Avartoli** (1898m), a rugged, knife-edge ridge separating Capu Ladroncellu from Punta Ghialla to the south. The next 45 minutes or so involve more short ups and downs, with the waymarks winding from one side of the ridge to the other via a sequence of impressive gaps. It's important to keep your eye on the paint blobs throughout this stretch as several (unmarked) minor paths peel off the GR20; lose your concentration and you could find yourself heading steeply down the wrong valley.

At the final gap, known as the **Bocca Carrozzu** (Bocca Inuminata; 1865m), the path suddenly plunges due south down a rugged, steep couloir that gets baking hot on summer afternoons. Dusty and loose underfoot, the descent, which takes around 80 minutes, is unrelentingly tough on the knees. With the refuge visible far below, it takes you through more alder bushes and, further down, silver birch woods before crossing the stream twice and easing off on its approach to Refuge de Carrozzu.

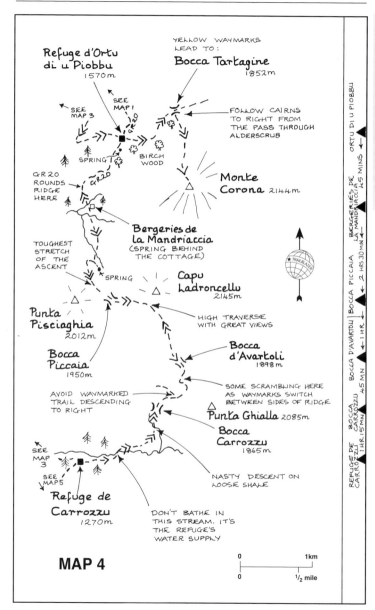

Refuge d'Ortu
di u Piobbu
1570m

YELLOW WAYMARKS
LEAD TO:
Bocca Tartagine
1852m

FOLLOW CAIRNS
TO RIGHT FROM
THE PASS THROUGH
ALDERSCRUB

SEE
MAP 3

SEE
MAP 1

SPRING

BIRCH
WOOD

Monte
Corona 2144m

GR20
ROUNDS
RIDGE
HERE

GR20

Bergeries de
la Mandriaccia
(SPRING BEHIND
THE COTTAGE)

TOUGHEST
STRETCH
OF THE
ASCENT

SPRING

Capu
Ladroncellu
2145m

HIGH TRAVERSE
WITH GREAT VIEWS

Punta
Pisciaghia
2012m

Bocca
Piccaia
1950m

Bocca
d'Avartoli
1898m

AVOID WAYMARKED
TRAIL DESCENDING
TO RIGHT

SOME SCRAMBLING HERE
AS WAYMARKS SWITCH
BETWEEN SIDES OF RIDGE

Punta Ghialla 2085m

SEE
MAP 3

SEE
MAP 5

Bocca
Carrozzu
1865m

Refuge de
Carrozzu
1270m

NASTY DESCENT ON
LOOSE SHALE

DON'T BATHE IN
THIS STREAM. IT'S
THE REFUGE'S
WATER SUPPLY

MAP 4

0   1km

0   1/2 mile

ORTU DI U PIOBBU

BERGERIES DE
LA MANDRIACCIA ← 45 MINS →

BOCCA PICCAIA ← 2 HRS 30 MIN →

BOCCA D'AVARTOLI ← 1 HR. →

BOCCA
CARROZZU ← 45 MN →

REFUGE DE
CARROZZU ← 1 HR.15 MN →

Refuge de Carrozzu

Flanked by a Herculean pair of orange granite crags that peak at nearly 2000 metres, Refuge de Carrozzu occupies an idyllic spot in the heart of the Cirque de Bonifatu. The hut's wooden deck, looking west over the treetops to the distant sea, is a great place to enjoy the sunset and socialize over a beer.

Sadly, Carrozzu has become a victim of its own success over the past decade. Its enviable location, proximity to the roadhead at Bonifatu, and strategic position between two of the route's toughest étapes ensure it's invariably swamped at the height of the summer. The toilet facilities, in particular, strain to cope with the onslaught, making this a less than pleasant place to be towards the end of the year.

Sanitation aside, the refuge is well set up, with gushing cold showers, shaded camping-bivouac space, external gas hobs, and interior accommodation for 30 trekkers, as well as a fully equipped kitchen. The gardien and his team provide a good selection of cooked food, including delicious soup served with chestnut-flour bread, and drink. Prices, it has to be said, are top whack but the location may well tempt you to splash out.

The one real gripe with Carrozzu has to be that, in order to maximize profits from the menu, its gardiens do not stock supplies; you'll have to wait until Asco Stagnu to reprovision.

STAGE THREE: CARROZZU → ASCO STAGNU (HAUT' ASCO)
[MAP 5, p123]

Overview

More superb scenery lies in store on day three. The crux of the étape is the long ascent of the Spasimata Valley to Bocca di a Muvrella, from where you get a magnificent close-up view of the Cinto Massif's north face. Far below, the ski station of Asco Stagnu (Haut' Asco), dwarfed by the surrounding mountains, sweetens the steep descent with the prospect of a cold beer and a hot meal.

Committed trekkers with supplies in hand may opt to forgo the hedonistic pleasures of the station to follow the rugged Muvrella ridge up the Tighjettu Valley, Michel Fabrikant's original GR20 route, which will put them in prime position for an early start on the infamous Cirque de la Solitude the following day.

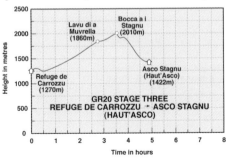

Although a relatively short stage, this is one that's hard to extend without bivouacking illegally (unless you've got the stamina and provisions to press on to the Refuge de Tighjettu on the far side of the cirque). Once beyond the lower reaches of the Spasimata Valley, it's also devoid of drinking water.

Finally, bear in mind that the ski station is the most convenient springboard for the ascent of Monte Cinto (see below). Spend an additional night at road level and you'll be able to scale the island's highest peak for a vivid taste of high mountain terrain. For the route guide see p122.

Ascent of Monte Cinto [Map 5, p123]

Overview The ascent of Monte Cinto is the icing on the GR20 cake. Peaking at 2706m, Corsica's highest summit provides an unrivalled viewpoint over the route and its environs. The experience of standing on the peak with the entire central range spread below you will shift your perspective of the island's mountains; it also takes you through scenery quite unlike anything you'll encounter elsewhere.

The standard route from Asco Stagnu, although approaching the massif via its colder, harsher and more rugged north face, presents no technical obstacles. It's essentially a long, hard slog requiring a small pack and plenty of stamina. That said, the ascent shouldn't be taken lightly. In the course of the seven-hour round trip you notch up more than 2500 metres of altitude change, most of it over very steep rock, boulders and precipitous, loose scree. This is certainly one trek where you'll be glad of a pair of walking poles. The only thing to really worry about is the weather, which is notoriously fickle above 2000m. Clouds carrying sleet and snow can sweep in at any time of year and with very little warning, transforming your hike into a full-on battle with the elements. Just how dangerous Cinto's micro-climate can be was brought home in 1996 when, after being overtaken by a freak blizzard in early July, seven people died on the mountain in a single day. Check the forecast (see p38) the night before and remain vigilant throughout. If the weather looks like turning nasty it's always better to get off the mountain as quickly as you can rather than press on in the hope that conditions will improve.

Route guide The trail starts on the opposite side of the car park from **Hôtel Le Chalet** (look for the 'Monte Cinto' sign daubed on a boulder). Marked with red-paint blobs (the orange waymarks at the beginning lead to Punta Minuta, one of Cinto's sister summits), it follows a descending traverse past the old Austrian Alpine Club hut where Félix Von Cube (see box p129) used to hole up and through old-growth Laricio pine forest to the Stranciaccone stream. Once across the stepping stones here, you follow the true left bank of the Tighjettu uphill to a small **footbridge**, with the magnificent Cirque de Trimbolacciu and its crown of 2500m peaks rising to the south. Beyond the footbridge the ascent proper gets underway as the route, dotted with red way-marks and small cairns, zigzags steeply up slabby rock and then bends south and eastwards to enter a spectacular side ravine. From a small shoulder at roughly 2100m you can look across to the Tour Penchée ('Leaning Tower'), the most distinctive among many amazing rock formations on the opposite flank of the ravine, standing out against gigantic red-brown cliffs.

Gradually the route progresses towards a large scree field which you traverse to reach the lip of an open depression beneath a saddle pass called **Bocca Borba** (2207m). A hollow under a big boulder here has been encircled by stones to create a shelter that makes a good place to pause. Once past this point, the way ahead over the Borba cwm is less clearly defined, splintering into a web of cairned routes that fans out across the enormous scree slopes below the summit. Keep heading south-east along any of them and you'll eventually hit **Lac d'Argentu**, a beautiful little lake that remains frozen well into the summer. Around it huge névés spread up the mountain; this is the snow visible on the far horizon from Calvi. Look out too for the weird, day-glo yellow lichen coating some of the shadier buttresses below Cinto's forepeak.

From the lake, you press on steeply uphill in a south-south-westerly direction across a couple of large névés and an increasingly sheer scree slope towards the **ridge**. This is the crux of the ascent, although the ridge itself, a flat saddle from which you can get your first sight of the Niolu Valley and mountains to the south, is something of a false summit. You've still a good 45 minutes ahead as the waymarks lead you first along the line of the crest towards the forepeak and then south off the ridge to start the last strenuous scramble to the top, up steep terraced slabs and grooves.

If you've been lucky with the weather the view from the top should be astounding. On very clear, windy days it's even possible to see the Alps and the French Riviera.

Allow 4^1/$_2$ hours for the ascent and 2^1/$_2$ hours for the descent (not including rest time).

Route guide

A short but sharp 10-minute descent from Refuge de Carrozzu gets the third day underway. It brings you to what must be the most photographed feature of the GR: a 35m **suspension bridge**, la passarelle suspendue de Spasimata, which spans the stream against an impressive backdrop of escarpments.

The climb starts as soon as you're across it, as the waymarks guide you through a narrow river gorge via a succession of huge, water-worn **slabs**. Presenting no difficulty in dry conditions, these can be treacherous in wet weather, hence the stanchion cables to help you up the steepest. The first sight of the Spasimata slabs tends to be the point at which anyone who found the first two days of the route too much turns around and heads for Bonifatu.

With the pass still high above the valley it can feel like a test of resolve, but within an hour or so you're clear of the shadowy gorge and (weather permitting) contouring in bright sunlight across the open mountainside through patches of alder scrub. A steep squeeze through a couloir followed by another climb to the top of a huge round-topped outcrop, 2^3/$_4$ hours into the walk, brings your first glimpse of the beautiful **Lavu di a Muvrella** (1860m), a tiny lake at the bottom of a suspended glacial shelf. Frozen throughout the winter, it doesn't support any aquatic life; nor is it safe to drink. Moreover, bivouacking and camping are strictly forbidden at this exquisite spot which, warmed by morning sunshine and with fine views all the way down to Calvi, makes a good place to break before the final haul to the pass.

From the lake you also get a good view of one of the GR20's most distinctive rock formations, a huge eminence overhanging the pass that looks uncannily like a sculpted head of a Native American Indian, complete with feather headdress. The path threading through the boulder-choked gully below it holds patches of snow and ice well into the summer, which adds a bit of interest to the steep approach to the **Bocca di a Muvrella**.

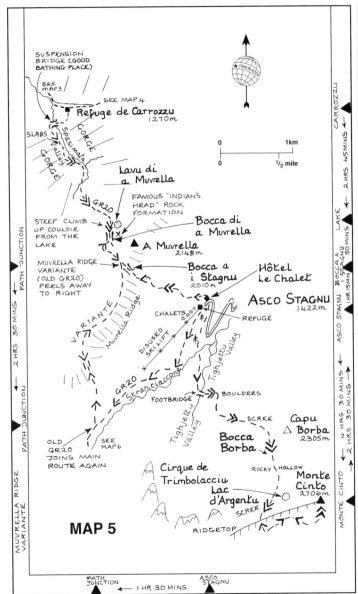

SUSPENSION
BRIDGE (GOOD
BATHING PLACE)

SEE
MAP 3

SEE MAP 4

Refuge de Carrozzu
1270m

SLABS

Spasimata Valley

GORGE

GORGE

GORGE

Lavu di
a Muvrella

GR20

FAMOUS "INDIAN'S
HEAD" ROCK
FORMATION

STEEP CLIMB
UP COULOIR
FROM THE
LAKE

Bocca di
a Muvrella

▲ A Muvrella
2148m

MUVRELLA RIDGE
VARIANTE
(OLD GR20)
PEELS AWAY
TO RIGHT

Bocca a
i Stagnu
2010m

Hôtel
Le Chalet

ASCO STAGNU
1422m

VARIANTE

Muvrella Ridge

CHALETS

REFUGE

DISUSED
SKI LIFT

GR20
Stranciaccone

Tighjettu Valley

FOOTBRIDGE

BOULDERS

SCREE

Capu
△ Borba
2305m

Tighjettu Valley

Bocca
Borba

OLD
GR20
JOINS MAIN
ROUTE AGAIN

SEE
MAP 6

Cirque de
Trimbolacciu

Lac
d'Argentu

ROCKY \ HOLLOW

Monte
Cinto
2706m

SCREE

RIDGETOP

MAP 5

0   1km

0   ½ mile

TRAILBLAZER

PATH JUNCTION ← 2 HRS 30 MINS

MUVRELLA RIDGE VARIANTE

PATH JUNCTION

CARROZZU

2 HRS 45 MINS ←

BOCCA A I STAGNU LAKE

1 HR 50 MINS ←

ASCO STAGNU

1 HR 15 MINS ←

4 HRS 30 MINS →

2 HRS 30 MINS →

MONTE CINTO

Standing at the border of the island's Balagne and Filosorma regions, the pass reveals another stupendous view that takes in the entire central chain and red-granite cliffs of the west coast. Once over it the red-and-white waymarks plunge steeply to the right through a mass of broken rock before switching direction to begin a steadily ascending traverse to the second pass of the day, **Bocca a i Stagnu** (2010m).

With an early-enough start from Carrozzu you should be able to get here before clouds obscure the top of Monte Cinto; this is the most impressive view of Corsica's highest peak you'll get from the GR20 and few trekkers are in a hurry to put it behind them. Hopping down a precipitous jigsaw of creviced boulders, the 500-metre descent to Asco, whose rooftops, car park and helipad you can make out way below, is none too enticing. Allow at least $1^1/4$ hours and stop regularly if your knees start feeling the strain. You'll need them to be in top shape for the next stage, which includes the GR20's steepest ascent and descent.

Variante: Muvrella ridge to the Ancien Refuge d'Altore
[Map 5, p123; Map 6, p127]
The GR20 forks shortly before reaching the Bocca a i Stagnu, with the *Variante* path peeling south along the Muvrella Ridge towards the Ancien Refuge d'Altore. Until the mid-1980s, when the refuge was mysteriously destroyed by fire, this formed the main GR20 route as envisaged by Michel Fabrikant. However, pressure from the failing ski station, which desperately needed summer business, combined with the destruction of the refuge and the obvious logistical problems of a route that otherwise didn't touch a roadhead between Calenzana and Col de Verghio, eventually forced the PNRC into re-routing the GR to the valley floor.

The old waymarks have faded but the original route is still easy to follow. Apart from the dramatic views it affords over the Filosorma Valley, the main incentive to choose the old path is that it bypasses Asco Stagnu (no bad thing if you're reluctant to return to 'civilization'), bringing you out at the head of the valley below **Bocca Tumasginesca**, gateway to the Cirque de la Solitude. It is thus the preferred route for anyone aiming to double up étapes between Carrozzu and the Refuge de Tighjettu.

To deter people from bivouacking at the old refuge the PNRC has concreted over the old spring so you'd have to be well stocked with **water** to overnight there and then press on over the cirque the following day. Unless you melt snow off the névé leading to the pass or make a detour to fill your bottles from the river, the next dependable source of water would be the Refuge de Tighjettu. This is a very long way from the previous one (Carrozzu/Spasimata) if you've walked along the Muvrella ridge.

Bank on between two and two-and-a-half hours for the *Variante* between Bocca a i Stagnu and the junction with the main GR route.

ASCO STAGNU (HAUT' ASCO)
The former winter sports station at Asco Stagnu, or Haut' Asco as it's otherwise known, presents a bleak spectacle, its incongruous chalets and rusty ski lifts surrounded by scarred, deforested slopes. But for GR20 trekkers, the hotel, gîte d'étape

and refuge here – not to mention the restaurant and bar – provide a welcome excuse to pause and recover from the exertions of the previous days. The complex also boasts a tempting terrace which, if you can ignore the dusty car park next to it, affords an inspiring view of the Cinto massif. After a hot shower and a couple of beers, the lure of the snow fields seduces many people into loosening their itineraries and slotting in the ascent the following day.

Orientation and services

Arriving from the Muvrella Ridge, bear left at the bottom of the pine forest for Hôtel Le Chalet or right, on the route indicated by the waymarks for the PNRC refuge. Below the latter you'll find a small Portacabin that houses Asco's **shop** (open all day and most of the evening; if it's closed ask the gardienne of the refuge to unlock it), which stocks the best range of trekking supplies (including fresh bread and fruit) between Calenzana and Vizzavona. Prices are lower than at the refuges.

There's no ATM here but the manager of Le Chalet will advance **cash** against a Visa or MasterCard if you've patronized the bar or restaurant (100€ maximum, plus 3€ charge).

The complex has two public **telephones**: one (which takes only coins) in the corner of the bar and a France Telecom booth (cards only) below the refuge. Anyone wishing to leave the GR20 here will have to phone for a **taxi** from Corte (see p100) and should expect to pay around 80-90€ for the luxury as there's no public transport to Asco. Hitching, however, is fairly reliable if you wait until afternoon when the daytrippers start to head home. Alternatively, ask at the hotel if any of the staff are driving into town that day.

For those who arrive in Asco Stagnu wishing they hadn't packed quite so much gear, the larger-than-life gardienne of the refuge, Martine Franceschetti, offers a handy **luggage-transfer** service. For the princely sum of 15€ she'll arrange to have your excess stuff sent home in a parcel, or else delivered to the SNCF train stations at Bastia or Ajaccio for you to collect at a later date. If you go for the latter option, bear in mind you'll have to pick up your package during office hours on weekdays (ie, don't leave it until the Saturday or Sunday of your flight home).

Where to stay and eat

Asco Stagnu's institutional *refuge* overlooks the complex from the edge of the tree line. Rates are standard and the facilities spartan but adequate. The one compensation for its grim aspect are the blissfully hot showers. You can also cook in a fully equipped kitchen. Sheltered bivouac and camping sites are dotted among the fir trees next to the building, although many have been spoiled by people shitting in the bushes beside them.

By comparison the dorm beds in *Gîte d'étape GR20*, part of *Hôtel Le Chalet* (☎/🖷 04.95.47.81.08; open May-Sep) are luxurious. Rates here (7€ per bed or 28€ for half-board) are rock-bottom (lower, in fact, than at the PNRC's refuge). In the hotel proper, double rooms with shower and a small balcony cost 38€, or 50€ with an en suite toilet.

Le Chalet's *restaurant*, off the left of the foyer as you enter the hotel, does a roaring trade. Most people eat here as part of a half-board deal but you'll do a lot better by spending a little more to eat à la carte (the half-board portions are on the small side). This will allow you to order their steak-frites, which (somewhat undeservingly it has to be said) enjoys near legendary status on the GR20. Count on around 22€ for a three-course meal, or 15€ for the *menu fixe*.

In the new building directly opposite *Le Chalet*, there's also a pleasant café, *Snack L'Altore*, whose bar stays open late serving good value 12€ menus, and offers breakfast from very early in the morning for 6€.

ROUTE GUIDE AND MAPS

STAGE FOUR: ASCO STAGNU (HAUT' ASCO) → REFUGE DE
TIGHJETTU → BERGERIES DE VALLONE   [MAP 6, opposite]

Overview
If one stage could be said to define the GR20 it would have to be this one. The passes on the fourth étape may not be the highest but the terrain they enclose – namely the infamous Cirque de la Solitude – tends to linger in the memory more vividly than any other on the route. The main reason is a series of sheer stepped pitches, negotiated by means of fixed chains and a metal ladder, which take you across the head of a steeply concave valley.

Although undeniably strenuous, the scrambling is no more difficult than that experienced on some sections of the previous three days. In fact, with the fissured profile of Paglia Orba looming above you, this has to be one of the most intensely enjoyable legs of the whole GR20. Yet for some reason the cirque's reputation endures, a fact that probably accounts more than the actual terrain for the people-jams that form here. At the height of the summer trekkers who are normally comfortable and quick on steep, exposed rock will find themselves held up unless they get to the cirque early in the day before the queues form. Those of more nervous disposition should take solace in the fact that very few people fail to complete this section (not least because to avoid it you'd have to make a huge detour by road to Corte and another to Col de Verghio). If you do get the jitters in the cirque you'll be that much more proud of yourself once it's behind you.

By comparison, the rest of the étape – comprising one long, gradual ascent (the last bit of it across a névé) and a somewhat steeper descent through a huge boulder field – is easy going. Starting out from Asco Stagnu, it's not unusual for trekkers to press on to the Refuge de Ciottulu a i Mori after a leisurely lunch at the Bergeries de Vallone, one of the nicest pit-stops on the GR.

Route guide
The red-and-white waymarks lead out of Asco Stagnu along the line of the ski lift initially, bearing left towards the pine woods above. As you progress up the valley the imposing profile of the Cirque de Trimbolacciu's peaks rise to the

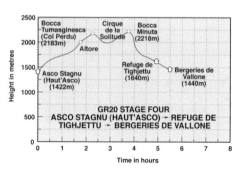

south through gaps in the trees. The path emerges from under the pines to open, grazed ground carpeted in juniper, with clumps of crocuses and the odd orchid dotting the grassier patches during the early summer. The route then makes a sweeping ascent of the valley's north side, nearing the stream towards the top.

ROUTE GUIDE AND MAPS

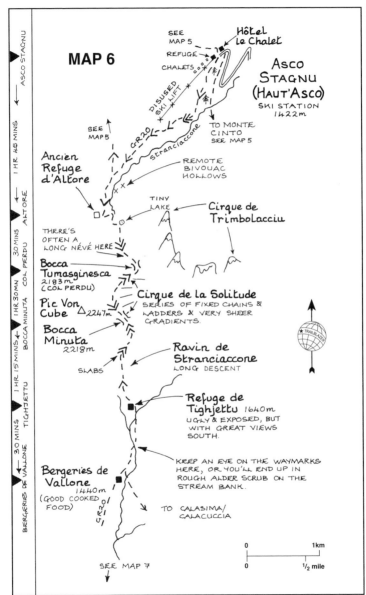

MAP 6

SEE MAP 5

Hôtel le Chalet

REFUGE

CHALETS

DISUSED SKI LIFT

GR20

Stranciaccone

Asco Stagnu (Haut'Asco)

SKI STATION 1422m

TO MONTE CINTO SEE MAP 5

ASCO STAGNU ← 1 HR. 45 MINS → ALTORE ← 30 MINS → COL PERDU ← 1 HR 30MN → BOCCA MINUTA ← 1 HR 15 MINS → TIGHJETTU ← 30 MINS → BERGERIES DE VALLONE

SEE MAP 5

Ancien Refuge d'Altore

REMOTE BIVOUAC HOLLOWS

XX

THERE'S OFTEN A LONG NÉVÉ HERE

TINY LAKE

Cirque de Trimbolacciu

Bocca Tumasginesca 2183m (COL PERDU)

Pic Von Cube △2247m

Cirque de la Solitude
SERIES OF FIXED CHAINS & LADDERS & VERY SHEER GRADIENTS.

Bocca Minuta 2218m

SLABS

Ravin de Stranciaccone
LONG DESCENT

★ TRAILBLAZER

Refuge de Tighjettu 1640m
UGLY & EXPOSED, BUT WITH GREAT VIEWS SOUTH.

KEEP AN EYE ON THE WAYMARKS HERE, OR YOU'LL END UP IN ROUGH ALDER SCRUB ON THE STREAM BANK.

Bergeries de Vallone 1440m
(GOOD COOKED FOOD)

GR20

TO CALASIMA/ CALACUCCIA

0		1km
0		½ mile

SEE MAP 7

Muvra

Hear rocks clattering from the cliffs above you and chances are if it's not a GR20 trekker it'll be a muvra. Corsica's elusive, short-fleeced sheep – mouflon in French – may be the symbol of the island's mountains but it's a far less sure-footed creature than the chamois and its other goat cousins on the continent. This is because it was originally a grassland animal, descended from domestic sheep thought to have been imported from the Middle East by early Neolithic peoples and forced by centuries of hunting, fires and competition from other animals to seek refuge in the mountains.

Males, distinguished by their long coiled horns and white facial markings, weigh up to 50kg. Females typically weigh 30kg and have stumpier, straighter horns. Only a vestigial population of around 600 survives, mostly in the higher reaches of Filosorma, Fango, Asco and Bavella.

During the winter – five months after the summer rut – the muvrini flee the snow to secluded, south-facing valleys that hold warmth throughout the year, where females give birth to their lambs. As the snow line recedes, they creep back up the mountainsides, spending the hottest months at the highest altitudes feeding on *arbutus* (strawberry trees) and alder.

On the GR20 you're most likely to catch a glimpse of a muvra on: Monte Corona (at the end of stage one); on the Muvrella ridge (*muvrella* means baby muvra) above Asco; at the head of the Asco valley and in the Cirque de la Solitude; around Paglia Orba; on the upper slopes of Monte Alcudina in the south; and on the Alpine section through the Bavella needles. First light and dusk, when the animals are most active, are the best times for muvra spotting.

A short, steeper section up a gravelly path brings you to the site of the **Ancien Refuge d'Altore**, which burned down in 1982. Its remains are scattered on a balcony below the first of the day's challenges, the 30-minute climb to **Bocca Tumasginesca** (also called Col Perdu; 2183m). This sheltered, north-facing slope often holds snow until well into the season. Towards the top of it you may be lucky enough to catch a glimpse of the Alps on the far horizon.

Most minds, however, tend to be on what's ahead. From the lip of the pass the ground falls away almost vertically into the upper Filosorma Valley, bounded by the imposing profile of Paglia Orba and its surrounding mantle of rock towers.

To cross the **Cirque de la Solitude** to reach the Bocca Minuta, the niche visible on the opposite side, you have to descend 200 metres and clamber all

---

(Opposite) Top: Cirque de la Solitude – something of a misnomer in mid-season. (Photo © Peter Gorecki). Bottom: Lac de Nino (see p137) – the Corsican mountains at their most bucolic, and one of the only level stretches on the GR. (Photo © David Abram).

the way back up again. In dry conditions proficient rock climbers will have little need of the chains whose clanking reverberates around the ravine, but these are essential aids when the granite is wet and slippery. Keep a close eye on the waymarks throughout and avoid dislodging loose rock onto people climbing below you.

With a clear run you can be across the cirque in 90 minutes or less. Once at the **Bocca Minuta** (2218m) a radically different landscape is revealed to the south. Visible on the horizon for the first time are the mountains of the central Corsican watershed, which you'll be crossing in the days ahead. The descent from the pass to the rocky **Ravin de Stranciaccone**, across a mixture of broken boulders and giant lichen-covered slabs, is straightforward though hot work in the afternoon; it's south-facing and almost entirely shadeless.

Refuge de Tighjettu and Bergeries de Vallone

Surrounded by a vast mass of green-tinged rock, **Refuge de Tighjettu** is perched atop a spur between the Stranciaccone and Stagni ravines, looking south across the Vallée de Vallone and the ridgetops of Niolu to Monte Rotondo in the distance. Built of wood, it's an angular modern construction with beds for 45 trekkers. The bivouac area is directly below the main building. A huge range of supplies is also available from the gardien.

The size, popularity and overall ugliness of Tighjettu encourage many trekkers to continue down the valley for another half-hour to the more congenial **Bergeries de Vallone**, where a shepherd and his family have set up a small

Félix Von Cube

The relative accessibility of Corsica's mountains compared with the Alps or the Pyrenées means that few climbing reputations have been forged here over the years. One name, however, is closely associated with early exploration of the island's major peaks. Félix Von Cube, an Austrian doctor, first travelled to Corsica in 1899 and opened up a series of new routes around the Cinto massif. Three years later he returned with a group of friends to map and explore Monte Cinto more thoroughly and it was then that his team fixed the route that subsequently became the standard approach from the Asco side (described on p121). Von Cube's final visit was in 1904 when he became the first man to scale Capu Tafonatu, the famous pierced peak next to Paglia Orba.

His achievements (honoured by the re-naming after him of a peak overlooking the Cirque de la Solitude (see map 6) are all the more impressive when you consider the kind of clothing and rudimentary equipment mountaineers had to contend with at the beginning of the 20th century. A couple of delightful old photos displayed in the bar of Hôtel Le Chalet at Asco Stagnu perfectly capture the mood of the times, when beards, pipes and suits were still de rigueur. One wonders what Von Cube and his cronies would have made of the ski station, which has so radically disfigured the area they used as a base for their groundbreaking forays onto Monte Cinto in 1902.

(Opposite) Top: The mighty red shark's fin of Paglia Orba (2525m), despite appearances, a straightforward non-technical ascent. **Bottom**: Lac de Capitellu (see p147) in mid spring thaw. The GR20 wriggles over the ridgeline in the background. (Photos © David Abram).

café offering hot meals, snacks, drinks and basic accommodation. A couple of old canvas tents provide sheltered beds (5€); you can also bivouac or camp here for 3.50€ (including the use of a flush toilet). The food, served on their lovely wooden deck or rear terrace, is authentic and delicious (particularly the home-made charcuterie and Niolin ewe's cheese); the prices are reasonable too considering how far supplies have to be brought. If your budget can stretch to it go for the full 18€ four-course menu, which might include wild-boar stew or an omelette made with fresh mint and *brocciu*, rounded off with melt-in-the-mouth *fiadone*.

STAGE FIVE: BERGERIES DE VALLONE → CIOTTULU A I MORI
[MAP 7, opposite]

Overview
Sweeping around the base of Paglia Orba and over Bocca Foggiale into the Golo Valley, this relatively short, undemanding stage is easily doubled up. By doing so, however, you miss out on the chance of climbing Paglia Orba, Corsica's third-highest peak.

Route guide
Beyond the Bergeries de Vallone, the path rises gently to begin with and then follows a fairly level gradient south through pine forest. Having dropped down-hill to cross the **Ravin de Paglia Orba** it then winds around another two wood-ed shoulders before swinging definitively south-west up the Foggiale Valley.

The route forks as it approaches the **Foggiale** stream; one (unmarked) branch heads left towards a cluster of bivouac circles on the bank. The other, the GR20, strikes uphill towards the col, steepening considerably as it leaves the forest and takes to the bare rock. As you ascend, with the waymarks cutting across a succession of seasonal streams, the Niolu Valley, dominated by the Calacuccia barrage, unfolds behind you.

The **Bocca di Foggiale** (1962m) is a bleak, windswept saddle covered in deep-red scree on whose upper slopes you might catch sight of grazing mouflons. To reach the refuge, the waymarks cut uphill to the right and then descend through a channel flanked by juniper and broom scrub. If you're planning to bypass Ciottulu a i Mori and press on to Castel di Verghio, follow the unmarked trail west from the pass which drops straight down the line of the Golo basin to river level; this cuts out an unnecessarily long, sweeping traverse, saving you a good hour or so.

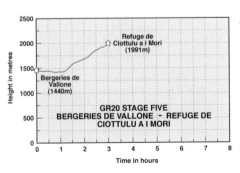

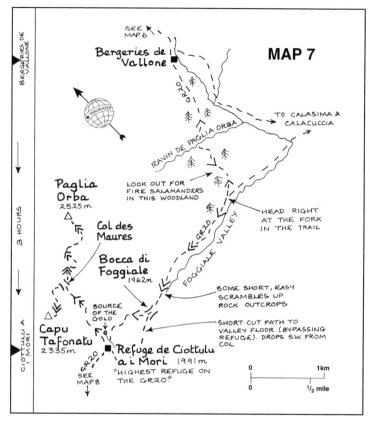

Refuge de Ciottulu a i Mori

Along with Petra Piana and Usciolu, Ciottulu a i Mori (literally 'Hole of the Moors') ranks among the hot contenders for the title of 'most spectacularly sited refuge' on the GR20. Clinging to the south flank of the mighty Paglia Orba at an altitude of 1991m, it's certainly the highest mountain hut on the island. From its terrace you get a matchless view over the Golo basin, flanked by red-granite ridges that taper away to a jagged horizon dominated by the pyramidal Punta Artica.

The refuge is small, with beds for 26 people, and offers scant shelter for bivouackers; you'll be grateful for a snug sleeping bag or a tent if you're overnighting outside. There's a good range of supplies on offer, in addition to hot meals and wine sold by the glass.

Paglia Orba and Capu Tafonatu   **[Map 7, p131]**
Of the big three peaks over 2500m passed by the GR20, Paglia Orba (2525m),
Corsica's distinctive shark's-tooth-shaped mountain, is the most readily accessible. You can get to the summit and back from the refuge in an easy half-day.
With Monte Cinto only a sheep's cough across the valley and the sea close by,
the views from it are as magnificent as you'd expect. However, the ascent –
while technically straightforward, requiring neither ropes nor rock-climbing
skills – involves some highly exposed, tricky scrambling so you most definitely need a good head for heights. This is even more true for **Capu Tafonatu**
(2335m), the extraordinary 'pierced peak' next to Paglia Orba, to which you
can make a short but compelling detour en route. Think twice about attempting either in wet weather, or if you've found any of the ascents described so
far in this book unnerving.
    The approach to Paglia Orba, indicated by a PNRC signboard, starts from
immediately behind Refuge de Ciottulu a i Mori. It begins with a leisurely
ascent across boulders and scree to a pass called the **Col des Maures**, where
you turn left if you wish to attempt Capu Tafonatu. Cairns mark the route up
the peak whose characteristic arched hole Corsican mythology claims was
made by the Devil in a fury. The stones trace the path south-west along a narrow ledge that snakes around the base of the peak. On arriving at a seam of
white rock you have to make a vertigo-inducing climb around a large projec-
tion. Beyond it the route drops down and picks up another ledge which you follow most of the way to the giant arch. Allow two hours for the round trip to
Capu Tafonatu from Col des Maures.
    The route up **Paglia Orba** turns right from just below the col, at the point
where the Capu Tafonatu path veers left. Threading around a couple of low
cliffs and gullies by means of eroded slabs and boulders, it's simple enough to
begin with but grows steeper and more challenging when you penetrate a
couloir crammed with fallen chunks of rock. With the arch of Capu Tafonatu
visible for the first time behind you, the cairns lead to the right of the cleave,
then squeeze through a niche above it, and from there around an exposed ledge
that will have vertigo sufferers rooted to the spot. Jutting into a void, it over-
hangs the vast north face of the mountain above the Fango Valley.
    On reaching a secondary peak on the east side of the massif soon after, the
route drops through a breach to the **Combe des Chèvres** ('Goats' Combe'), a
sheltered dip often lined with névés, from where a well-defined path strikes
uphill to the ridgetop and summit. Count on reaching the top in a little under
two hours, with one hour for the descent.

STAGE SIX: CIOTTULU A I MORI → CASTEL DI VERGHIO
                                                     [MAP 8, p135]
Overview
Stage six of the GR20 is a leisurely half-day's amble down the Golo Valley,
offering plenty of potential for R&R along the way. Many trekkers combine it
with the previous étape from Vallone or continue from Castel di Verghio to
Manganu, but if you take your time you can linger around some of the gorgeous
rock pools that line the river, blissing out to the clank of cowbells and the scent
of pine resin from the giant Laricios.

Corsican polyphony

'It was like hearing a voice from the depths of the earth; a song from the dawn of time; from a beginning that one never dares believe is accessible', wrote historian and traveller Dorothy Carrington in 1948 of her first encounter with Corsican polyphonies.

The island's extraordinary *a cappella* singing tradition encapsulates perhaps better than anything else Corsica's essential otherness. Derived from a mixture of Roman-Christian liturgy, Genoan madrigals, Islamic prayer and pagan chant, its characteristic blend of soaring harmonies overlaid with transient, eerie dissonances seem to bear the imprint of every invading culture since Megalithic times.

The region most closely associated with Corsican singing is the **Niolu Valley**, whose remote churches remained bastions of the art long after it had died out almost everywhere else. Its greatest exponents were always shepherds, which may account for the melancholic tone of much polyphony (as often as not through vendetta or exposure to the elements) and perennial separation from loved ones being integral to transhumant life.

Bleakest of all the island's vocal forms, and the Niolu's speciality, is the **paghjella**, a lament usually performed by three male voices: a bass, or *bassu*; a mid-range singer, *a secunda*; and *a terza* above them, providing heavily ornamented improvisations over the basic chords and cadences. Before the advent of organs in village churches, mass was sung in this style, with the three vocalists leaning together, often with their elbows resting on each other's shoulders and hands shielding their ears – the classic Corsican polyphony pose.

You can be guaranteed to hear live singing at the annual **Santa di u Niolu** fair, held on 8th September at **Casamaccioli**, across the lake from Calacuccia. Its centrepiece is a typically Corsican contest between local bards called **chiami e rispondi**, literally 'call and response'. Contestants improvise a stream of invective, political parody and insult, strictly phrased in 16-syllable lines and designed to outwit their opponent. When one of them fails to respond, the other is declared the winner. In recent years Corsican polyphony has enjoyed a remarkable renaissance. Having become almost extinct after WWII it was revived by the nascent nationalist movement in the early 1970s when its rousing patriotic strains stirred crowds at political rallies.

The power of polyphony was considered so potent by Giscard d'Estaing's government that at one stage several of the most respected young groups, including Cantu u Populu Corsu and Bastia's I Muvrini, were banned. Since then both have become household names in France while a younger generation of singers, notably Les Nouvelles Polyphonies Corses, has experimented with traditional forms to produce platinum-selling World Music albums. More groundbreaking still, an all-women group, Donnisulana, formed in the mid-1990s, shocked traditionalists, who insisted polyphony was an exclusively male art, by recording the CD of the decade, *Per Agata* (on the Silex label and available at good record shops in most towns in Corsica). Other commendable recordings include anything by the island's two professional choirs: A Filetta and Le Choeur d'Hommes de Sartène.

Route guide

The stage starts with a sweeping traverse of the west flank of the Golo Basin. After dropping gently to a ridge that overlooks the Forêt d'Aïtone to the west, the well-worn path plunges down to join the river just south of the disused

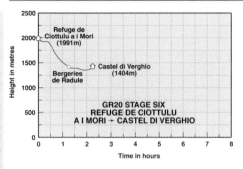

Bergeries de Tula. Note that if you're in a hurry you can cut out this section by following the cattle track due south down the line of the basin from in front of the refuge.

Once at river level the path keeps to an even course; this is one of the few lengths of the GR where you don't have to watch your footing. On reaching a bend in the valley overhung by large outcrop, the path switches to the left bank of the river and zigzags downhill through stands of pines via an old paved transhumant path to a well-known bathing spot that attracts day-trippers off the main road.

Once you've crossed the river a second time at the **Cascades d'E'Radule** – another lovely place to swim – the next landmark is the **Bergeries de Radule**, a picturesque cluster of dry-stone shepherds' huts around 1¹/2 hours from the refuge. This marks the midway point of the étape. From here on you'll be walking more or less continually on springy trails through pine forest. The unfamiliar swoosh of motor traffic on the D84 heralds your arrival at Castel di Verghio, although you still have what can feel like an endless plod through the forest to get there.

CASTEL DI VERGHIO

Originally the GR20 bypassed Castel di Verghio, the ski station below the Col de Verghio. Like the station at Asco Stagnu this one has suffered from the warming of Corsica's climate over the past decade or so. A few years back, however, the owner decided to splash some red-and-white paint around and 'redirect' the GR through the hotel. His detour has since been rubber-stamped by the PNRC, offering a comfortable alternative to Ciottulu a i Mori and Manganu.

Resembling an early 1970s Eastern-bloc ski resort, the hotel, which sits on a spur above the Niolu Valley overlooking Paglia Orba and Monte Cinto, has accommodation to suit everyone: bivouacking and camping space, refuge, gîte d'étape and rooms in the hotel as well as a bar-restaurant. Poorly maintained by Corsican standards, it's an ugly blot on the landscape that gets mixed reviews, but many trekkers welcome the respite it offers from refuge life.

Orientation and services
Verghio lies on a seasonal **bus** route connecting it with Porto in the west and Corte, via Calacuccia and Albertacce, in the other direction. The service, run by Autocars Mordiconi (☎ 04.95.48.00.04), operates daily between mid-July and the end of September. Other than the bus or hitching, the only way to get to or from the ski station is by **taxi**: Michel Salviani (☎ 06.10.60.55.24) from Calacuccia will drop you in Corte, the nearest railhead (see p100) for around 80€.

Where to stay and eat
The cheapest beds at **Castel di Verghio** (☎ 04.95.48.00.01; open May to mid-Oct) are in the **refuge**, a separate block next to the

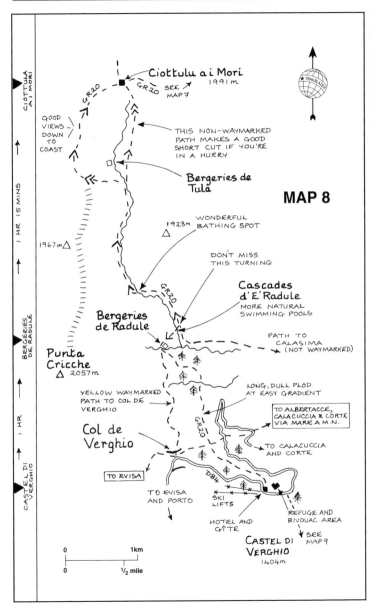

CIOTTULA A I MORI | ← 1 HR 15 MINS → | **BERGERIES DE RADULE** | ← 1 HR. → | **CASTEL DI VERGHIO**

★ TRAILBLAZER

Ciottulu a i Mori 1991m

GR20

GR20

SEE MAP 7

GOOD VIEWS DOWN TO COAST

THIS NON-WAYMARKED PATH MAKES A GOOD SHORT CUT IF YOU'RE IN A HURRY

Bergeries de Tula

MAP 8

1923m △ WONDERFUL BATHING SPOT

1967m △

DON'T MISS THIS TURNING

GR20

Cascades d'E'Radule
MORE NATURAL SWIMMING POOLS

Bergeries de Radule

PATH TO CALASIMA (NOT WAYMARKED)

Punta Cricche △ 2057m

YELLOW WAYMARKED PATH TO COL DE VERGHIO

LONG, DULL PLOD AT EASY GRADIENT

TO ALBERTACCE, CALACUCCIA & CORTE VIA MARE A M.N.

GR20

Col de Verghio

TO CALACUCCIA AND CORTE

TO EVISA

D84

TO EVISA AND PORTO

SKI LIFTS

REFUGE AND BIVOUAC AREA

HOTEL AND GÎTE

SEE MAP 9

CASTEL DI VERGHIO 1404m

0   1km
0   ½ mile

main building with grotty dorms (9.50€ per bed) and dirty bathrooms. In good weather you'd be better off bivouacking or camping in the adjacent field (6€), though if you do be sure to shut the gate firmly or you could find yourself raided by hungry pigs in the night.

The **gîte d'étape**, in the basement of the hotel, is just as shabby as the refuge though it does have steaming hot showers. Beds cost 14€, or 40€ half-board.

To be confident of a comfortable night's sleep indoors you'd have to shell out on a room in the **hotel**. Doubles with attached showers and toilets à l'étage cost 41€, or 41€ per head half-board; they're much better maintained than the dormitories but still a touch overpriced.

Meals are served in the spacious, bright dining hall on the ground floor with fish-bowl windows overlooking Paglia Orba and Monte Cinto – a lovely sunny spot for breakfast (6.30-9am; 7.50€). In the evenings, suppers (menu fixe 18€) are dished up to long tables of hungry trekkers. The food is nothing to write home about but copious enough.

Bone breakers

The lammergeier or bearded vulture (see p62; *gypaète barbu* in French or *altore* in Corsican) is the B52 of the island's skies. Sporting a maximum wingspan of just under 3m, this majestic vulture is known locally as 'le casseur d'os' (bone breaker) after its ingenious feeding habits. When crows and other carrion feeders have cleaned up the carcasses left lying around the mountains, the lammergeier moves in to suck what goodness may be left from the bones. To do this, however, it first has to break them open by dropping them from a height of between 30 and 50 metres onto flat-topped rocks – one of the island's great natural spectacles.

In times past the bone breakers were persecuted almost to the point of extinction by shepherds, who mistakenly believed they preyed on lambs. Another cause for their decline was the disappearance of large sheep flocks from the Corsican mountains, which deprived them of their chief source of carrion. Only around eight couples survive here, despite recent attempts by the PNRC to revive the population with feeding stations, where carcasses are left for the lammergeiers to tuck into.

Sifting through the fragments left on their bone-breaking rocks has revealed that the vultures' territory may extend to 50 kilometres (scientists have even found remains in the mountains of southern Corsica brought across the sea from Sardinia).

Their pinkish-gold breasts, long diamond-shaped tail and colossal size (adults can weigh up to 6kg) make lammergeiers relatively easy to distinguish from golden eagles. Top spots to sight them along the GR20 are around Lac de Nino, where there are three nesting pairs, and the crags above the Refuge de Carrozzu.

STAGE SEVEN: CASTEL DI VERGHIO → REFUGE DE MANGANU
[MAP 9, p139; MAP 10, p141]

Overview

Another gentle but hugely scenic day's trekking awaits as the GR20 climbs out of the Niolu Valley via Bocca San Pedru and follows the ridges above it to Lac de Nino – an exquisite high-altitude lake cradled by 2000m+ peaks. The lush green *pozzines* surrounding it, headwaters of the Tavignano River, are grazed by herds of wild horses. Together with the profile of snow-streaked Monte Rotondo nosing above the southern horizon this unique spot has an air curiously reminiscent of the Central Asian steppes.

From the lake the trail winds steadily downhill along the river, crossing a broad triangular-shaped plain, Pianu di Campotile, on its approach to the refuge. The comparative easiness of the path, together with the temptation to linger on the idyllic shores of Lac de Nino, give this étape the feel of a day-off.

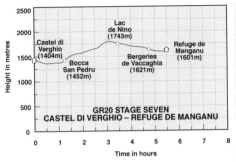

ROUTE GUIDE AND MAPS

Route guide

To pick up the trail from Castel di Verghio, follow the D84 downhill for 20m or so until you see a signboard indicating the route onward through the forest, to the right-hand side of the road. After a steady drop through the forest the path hits a level gradient which it follows for the next hour or more around the contours of the hillside, passing through some wonderful Laricio pine and beech forest.

The first ascent of the day, to **Bocca San Pedru** (1452m), begins just over an hour into the étape, cutting up the dry hillside through a series of zigzags. Laid down with horses and mules in mind, most of this stage's climbs are well paved and set at easy gradients, as you'll soon realize on leaving the small oratory at the col.

From the ridge south-east of Bocca San Pedru the views improve, with Paglia Orba and the Monte Cinto massif dominating the horizon to the north. The sea is also visible for the first time since stage three.

Halfway to the summit of a subsidiary peak called U Tritore the path peels away across the hillside to the left, picking up the ridge again at 1800m. A gentle ascent over open, rocky terrain ensues. Just as the slope begins to steepen markedly on its run up to Capu a u Tozzu (2007m) the trail cuts off the ridgeline again, this time dropping slightly downhill to the right through a niche before striking a steady rising route to **Bocca â Rete** (1883m).

A leisurely descent over rolling stony ground leads you down from the pass to **Lac de Nino**, one of the most photographed landmarks of the GR20. Just under 400m long and 250m wide, it is the source of the Tavignano River, which flows down to Corte (this wonderful waymarked route is described on p142) where it merges with the Restonica River.

Although only 11m deep, the lake supports a thriving population of trout (hence all the local fishermen you'll see here at the weekend). The spongy grass banks and sinuous rivulets linking the pools dotted around it, known in Corsican as *pozzi* (whence their French name pozzines), are home to a thriving population of wild horses and pigs. With the snow peaks reflected in the still water, this can be a dreamy spot. It is, however, rarely deserted. In addition to the flow of trekkers along the GR20, large numbers of day-hikers *(continued on p140)*

Pastori

Thousands of years before the first trekking boot stepped onto the island, Corsica's mountain trails were busy lines of communication between valleys. Modern waymarked routes such as the GR20 are only contemporary versions of ancient pathways along which shepherds (*pastori*) drove their flocks between the winter pastures at sea level (*a piaghja*) and the summer pastures high in the mountains (*a muntagna*).

Replicating the animals' own natural migratory cycle, this annual movement (transhumance) dictated patterns of rural life well into the 20th century. Until WWI cut a swath through the male population, the menfolk would spend half the year with their flocks three or more days' walk from home. For shepherds from high regions such as the Niolu Valley, the long separation from families and friends would take place on the coast during the cold months. The annual migration for shepherds in the arid south-east of the island, on the other hand, would occur in the summer, when the grass growing in the wake of receding snowfields provided an alternative to the sun-scorched grasses of their home patch.

In some parts of Corsica, families decamped en masse for the big migration, setting up home in their **bergeries** – tiny dry-stone cottages where the flocks would be driven to in the evenings and the milking carried out. Except for the introduction of metal implements, matches and rifles, life in the bergeries of the 1950s and 1960s had changed little since Neolithic times. Hunting, story-telling and traditional polyphonic singing (see box p133) filled fireside hours at the end of the day, maintaining traditions that had virtually died out by the modern era.

From its high point in the mid-nineteenth century transhumance fell into a sharp decline as the pan-European economy gathered pace. Emigration also took its toll, along with the severe overgrazing that left whole forests and mountainsides scarred beyond recovery. Now, only 30 to 40 full-time shepherds remain on the island, dependent on EU subsidies and with rigid quotas limiting the ratio between grazing land and flock sizes.

Of the handful of bergeries still worked throughout the summer, **Vaccaghia**, overlooking Pianu di Campotile near Refuge de Manganu, is one of only a few that survive along the line of the watershed (another is the **Bergeries de Gialgo** near Petra Piana). One of the reasons it continues to flourish is the number of trekkers streaming past its door, many of whom leave trailing the pungent aroma of a newly acquired cheese behind them.

The modern shepherd's raison d'être, Corsica's famed **cheese**, is renowned throughout France for its overpowering smell (as you'll already know if you've read *Asterix in Corsica*, in which a cheese is so strong it spontaneously combusts – a play on the adjective 'explosif', which is often applied to describe the taste of *le fromage corse*). Its fresh and milder form, **brocciu**, is made by warming ewe's milk until it starts to coagulate into lumps, which are strained off and set in molds. Used to add flavour and texture to omelettes, flans, doughnuts and tiramisu, it is *the* quintessential ingredient of quality Corsican gastronomy and today enjoys its own prized Appellation Contrôlée status. Just don't, whatever you do, compare it to mozzarella in the presence of a shepherd.

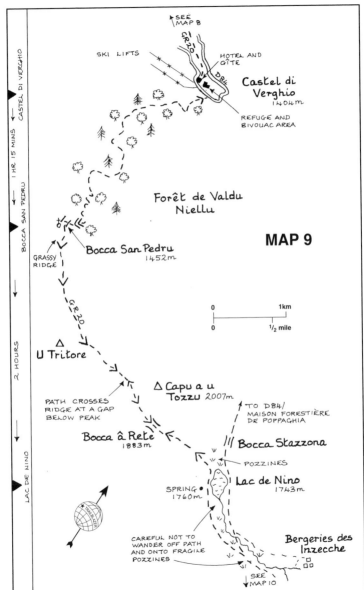

SEE
MAP 8

GR 20

SKI LIFTS

HOTEL AND
GÎTE

D84

Castel di
Verghio
1404m

REFUGE AND
BIVOUAC AREA

Forêt de Valdu
Niellu

MAP 9

Bocca San-Pedru
1452m

GRASSY
RIDGE

GR 20

0   1km
0   1/2 mile

△
U Tritore

△ Capu a u
Tozzu 2007m

PATH CROSSES
RIDGE AT A GAP
BELOW PEAK

→TO D84/
MAISON FORRESTIÈRE
DE POPPAGHIA

Bocca â Rete
1883m

Bocca Stazzona

POZZINES

Lac de Nino
1743m

SPRING ●
1760m

Bergeries des
Inzecche

CAREFUL NOT TO
WANDER OFF PATH
AND ONTO FRAGILE
POZZINES

SEE
MAP 10

CASTEL DI VERGHIO

1 HR. 15 MINS

BOCCA SAN PEDRU

2 HOURS

LAC DE NINO

ROUTE GUIDE AND MAPS

(cont'd from p137) walk up from the Maison Forestière de Poppaghia on the main road. A gardien is posted to the lake during the summer to ensure its fragile ecology is protected; camping, bivouacking and fires are strictly prohibited. You should also avoid leaving the path as the pozzines are easily eroded.

Having reached the lake the GR20 turns right and follows the shoreline past a **spring** and thence east along the valley floor. Ahead of you the serrated, snow-flecked ridges of the Rotondo massif are visible in the distance. Shortly after passing the ruined **Bergeries des Inzecche**, a cluster of stone huts clinging to the hill on the opposite side of the stream, the path bends decisively south-east to follow the wriggling course of the Tavignano across rougher, stonier ground interspersed with alder and beech.

Not long after emerging from a large wood you'll crest a rocky ridge just below which, in a sheltered hollow facing across the valley, stand the **Bergeries de Vaccaghia**, one of the few working shepherds' camps on this route. Three varieties of ewe's cheese (from pungent to eye-wateringly strong) are sold here; express an interest and the berger might show you the cool underground **caves** where they mature on large planks. It's sometimes possible to stay here, though usually only for groups of four people or more on a full-board basis.

From the bergeries you get a great view of the remaining stretch to the Refuge de Manganu across a dead-flat, grassy plain, the **Pianu di Campotile**, where the Tavignano bends north-east.

A **liaison path**, waymarked in yellow, turns left (east) off the GR just below the huts, winding along the northern side of the valley to the Refuge A Sega in around $3^1/_2$ hours. From there you can head down the Tavignano Gorge to Corte, see maps 12 and 13, p142.

At the **Bocca d'Acqua Ciarnente**, at the southern end of the plain, another yellow-waymarked route, indicated by a signboard, turns south-west down the Zoicu valley towards Soccia (see pp144-6), while the GR makes the short final ascent to the refuge.

Refuge de Manganu

Thanks to its proximity to both Lac de Nino and the roadhead at Soccia, Manganu is one of the busiest refuges on the GR20, attracting a mix of trout fishermen, fell runners and trekkers. Its dark but cosy interior accommodates 27 people and a dozen or more tents pitched around the back of the hut soak up the overspill during peak season. The refuge's terrace, which overlooks Bocca d'Acqua Ciarente and Pianu di Campotile, is a great place to hang out, especially when the great pyramidal peak to the north, Punta Artica (2373m), is snow-covered.

The best ground behind the refuge is taken up by the gardien's tents, leaving campers and bivouackers little flat space to pitch on; you might have to hunt beyond the alder bushes for shelter. The toilet and shower block is to the right of the hut as you're facing it from the front terrace. A small selection of expensive **supplies** – from cheese and sausage to fresh bread, soft drinks and beers – are sold by the gardien; do your shopping in the evening as he doesn't open up the following morning. You can also order a hot meal for 9€.

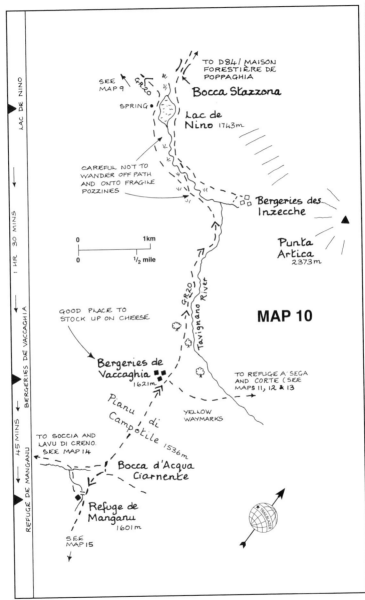

TO D84/ MAISON
FORESTIÈRE DE
POPPAGHIA

Bocca Stazzona

SEE
MAP 9

GR20

SPRING •

Lac de
Nino 1743m

CAREFUL NOT TO
WANDER OFF PATH
AND ONTO FRAGILE
POZZINES

Bergeries des
Inzecche

Punta
Artica
2373m

0   1km

0   ½ mile

GR20

Tavignano River

MAP 10

GOOD PLACE TO
STOCK UP ON CHEESE

Bergeries de
Vaccaghia
1621m

TO REFUGE A SEGA
AND CORTE (SEE
MAPS 11, 12 & 13

Pianu di
Campotile 1536m

YELLOW
WAYMARKS

TO SOCCIA AND
LAVU DI CRENO.
SEE MAP 14

Bocca d'Acqua
Ciarnente

Refuge de
Manganu
1601m

SEE
MAP 15

LAC DE NINO

1 HR. 30 MINS

BERGERIES DE VACCAGHIA

45 MINS

REFUGE DE MANGANU

ROUTE GUIDE AND MAPS

Liaison path: A Sega Refuge to Corte
[Map 11 opposite, Map 12 p144, Map 13 p144]

A Sega Refuge, in the dramatic Tavignano Valley, can be reached in around $3^{1}/_{2}$ hours from the path junction at the Bergeries de Vaccaghia on the GR20. The onward walk to Corte takes another 3hrs 45min, taking you through one of Europe's most spectacular gorges via a paved medieval mule track.

The original refuge at A Sega was blown up by the FLNC in the mid-1990s, but has since been replaced by a state-of-the-art structure that's monstrous from the outside but much airier, more comfortable (and a good deal less crowded) than most other mountain huts.

As it's officially a refuge and not a gîte, the 36 bunk beds (9.50€) are allotted on a first-come-first-served basis, with a dingier, grubbier annexe on the far side of the footbridge taking the overspill. You can also bivouac or camp in the woods outside for 6€, which includes the use of a gas stove. Hot meals are served here by the hospitable gardien, M Marc-Pascal Biancardini (☎ 06.10 71.77.26 or ☎ 04.95.46.07.90). Half-board costs 50€ if you're staying indoors, or 29€ for campers/bivouackers, and you can order a packed lunch with fresh bread and cheese for only 5€.

From the far side of the footbridge, follow the waymarks down the right bank of the river valley. For the next 15km or so to Corte it is virtually impossible to lose your way thanks to the remarkably intact old pack path, the most extraordinary of its kind on the island, that threads down the entire length of the Tavignano. How long the walk takes will depend on how often you pause to admire the landscape, which will probably be more often than you intend so allow plenty of time – $3^{1}/_{2}$-4 hours if you hike non stop – to complete this stretch.

Paved with timeworn granite slabs, the mule track winds around a succession of steep, densely wooded spurs, climbing high above the river as it does so to avoid some vertigo-inducing crags. Relatively restrained at first, the sides of the gorge, flanked by ridges of 1500-2000m, surge to a height of 800m in the middle of the valley, where the vast cliffs are streaked with pale-green mineral traces.

On some of the higher ledges, lone Laricio pine trees cut striking silhouettes. Sadly, many were lost in the devastating fire that swept through here in the summer of 2000 and you'll probably have to negotiate a succession of fallen trees along the route. Look out as you do so for morelle mushrooms, which thrive in pine cinders during early summer. A rare, fragrant fungus that's highly prized for the magic it works with meat sauces, *morilles* sell for insane sums in the markets of Lyon and Paris. On a good day here, you can literally fill rucksacks with them.

The first major landmark about halfway along the Tavignano is the **cable bridge** (*passarelle suspendue*), beneath which a small beach provides an ideal camping or bivouac spot (though flooding is possible in wet weather). More spectacular scenery awaits beyond the bridge, as the forest gradually gives way to low maquis. By the time you get your first glimpse of Corte at the distant mouth of the valley you'll probably be exposed to the full strength of the sun on this south-facing slope – another good reason you should get an early start and carry plenty of water.

For an account of **Corte**, see pp99-103.

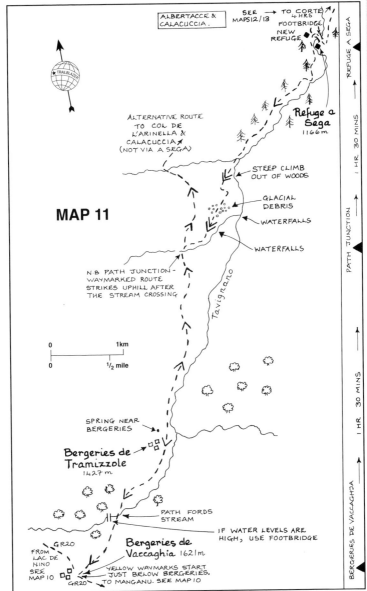

ALBERTACCE & CALACUCCIA.

SEE → TO CORTE
MAPS12/13 4 HRS
FOOTBRIDGE
NEW
REFUGE

REFUGE A SEGA

ROUTE GUIDE AND MAPS

TRAILBLAZER

ALTERNATIVE ROUTE
TO COL DE
L'ARINELLA &
CALACUCCIA
(NOT VIA A SEGA)

Refuge a
Sega
1166 m

1 HR. 30 MINS

MAP 11

STEEP CLIMB
OUT OF WOODS

GLACIAL
DEBRIS

WATERFALLS

WATERFALLS

PATH JUNCTION

N.B PATH JUNCTION-
WAYMARKED ROUTE
STRIKES UPHILL AFTER
THE STREAM CROSSING

Tavignano

0   1km
0   ½ mile

SPRING NEAR
BERGERIES

Bergeries de
Tramizzole
1427 m

1 HR. 30 MINS

PATH FORDS
STREAM

IF WATER LEVELS ARE
HIGH, USE FOOTBRIDGE

BERGERIES DE VACCAGHIA

FROM
LAC DE
NINO
SEE
MAP 10

GR20

Bergeries de
Vaccaghia 1621 m

YELLOW WAYMARKS START
JUST BELOW BERGERIES.
GR20 TO MANGANU. SEE MAP 10

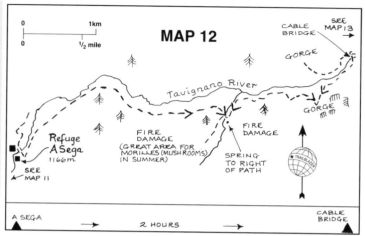

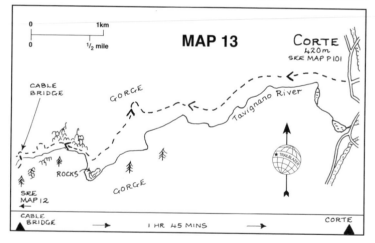

Liaison route to Soccia via Lavu di Crenu and Monte Sant'Eliseo
[Map 14, opposite]

From Manganu it's possible to reach road level at the village of Soccia in a little under 2½ hours. The route, waymarked in yellow, peels west off the GR20 just below the refuge (a signboard shows the way), threading through the rocks above a rushing stream to cross the Rau de Zoicu on the floor of the valley. After winding above the right bank of the river through rough terrain for an hour or so, it switches to the left bank and from there rises gently through old-

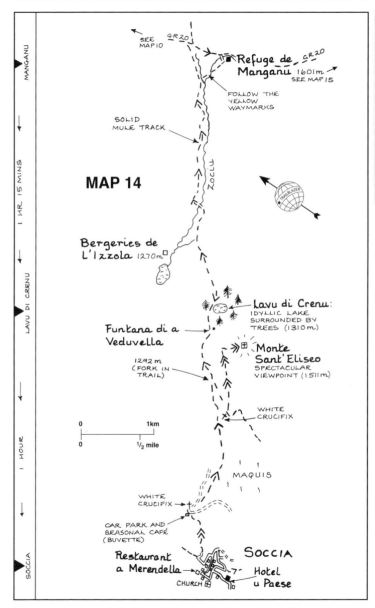

MAP 14

SEE MAP 10

GR 20

Refuge de Manganu 1601m
GR 20
SEE MAP 15

FOLLOW THE YELLOW WAYMARKS

SOLID MULE TRACK

ZOCLU

Bergeries de L'Izzola 1270m

Lavu di Crenu: IDYLLIC LAKE SURROUNDED BY TREES (1310m)

Funtana di a Veduvella

Monte Sant'Eliseo SPECTACULAR VIEWPOINT (1511m)

1292m (FORK IN TRAIL)

WHITE CRUCIFIX

0   1km
0   1/2 mile

MAQUIS

WHITE CRUCIFIX

CAR PARK AND SEASONAL CAFÉ (BUVETTE)

Restaurant a Merendella

SOCCIA

Hotel u Paese

CHURCH

MANGANU

1 HR 15 MINS

LAVU DI CRENU

1 HOUR

SOCCIA

growth pine woods to the **Lavu di Crenu**. The only high-altitude lake in Corsica surrounded by Laricio pines, Crenu is a popular picnic spot in summer, when daytrippers hike up to admire the lotus flowers that bloom on it. A gardienne is on hand to ensure no-one camps, bivouacs or lights fires here.

Beyond the lake, a well-trodden path winds at contour level past a spring, the **Funtana di a Veduvella** which is renowned for the quality of its water, and later (at 1292m) a fork in the trail.

If you're not in a rush consider making the detour to **Monte Sant'Eliseo**, a superb viewpoint a little over 200 metres above you. Bearing left at the fork, the route to it continues downhill for 15 minutes as far as a ridge. At this point you reach another path that cuts back sharply to the left (you'll know you've missed this turning if you arrive at a large white crucifix). Follow this new path in a north-easterly direction as it drifts away from the ridge and then, around 15 minutes later, switches decisively to the south to begin a much steeper, zigzagging approach to the peak. A **chapel** sits on the summit, site of an annual pilgrimage in August when the inhabitants of the surrounding villages, their numbers swollen by relatives holidaying from the continent, follow the priest from Vico up here to celebrate mass. The view is magnificent, stretching from the snows of Monte D'Oro to the Golfe de Sagone, while to the north, Cimatella and Punta Artica flag the line of the watershed.

If you don't make the detour to Monte Sant'Eliseo keep heading straight on and you'll soon emerge from woods to start a long, easy descent through maquis to a **car park** where a *buvette* offers welcome shade and sustenance. From here you can either hitch the remaining few kilometres along the road to Soccia or pick up the path that continues steeply down the hillside.

Soccia, one of the most picturesque villages in the region, has neither a shop nor a bank or restaurant, nor is it served by public transport. To reach the coast you'd have to hitch (ideally from the car park at the Lavu di Crenu trailhead, which sees more through traffic than the village).

STAGE EIGHT: REFUGE DE MANGANU → REFUGE DE PETRA PIANA [MAP 15, p149]

Overview

Stage eight is one of the GR20's classic étapes. Taking you from the restrained environs of the Pianu di Campotile back to the extremes of the high watershed,

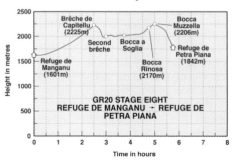

the initial 650m ascent from Manganu strikes a stark contrast with the preceding day or two. But as recompense you'll have what many trekkers regard as the route's most dramatic landscapes to look forward to. In particular, the ridge section between the famous Brèche de Capitellu (at

2225m the GR's highest point) and Bocca Muzzella is a non-stop parade of stupendous scenery. Overlooking the head of the Restonica Valley on one side and the hinterland of the Golfe de Sagone on the other, the views stretch from glacial lakes surrounded by vast, vertical cliffs all the way to the sea, with glimpses of Monte Cinto and Paglia Orba in the distance.

On the downside, awaiting you during the descent from the brêche are a couple of especially steep passages that can be tricky in wet weather, as well as one or two large névés to negotiate early in the season. As you'll be more or less following the island's backbone, water is at a premium: take enough to last you most of the day (2-3 litres depending on the temperature). The étape's altitudes and high degree of exposure can also make this a difficult section in bad weather. If conditions look unstable seek the advice of the gardien at Manganu and be prepared to dig in for a day if storms or persistent rain are forecast. This is definitely one stage whose views you wouldn't want to miss out on.

Route guide
The day kicks off with a long climb that starts gently enough but steepens as you gain height. From the refuge the waymarks cross a **footbridge** and strike immediately uphill to the right along the stream bank. Crossing a succession of slabs and grassy slopes strewn with large boulders, you press on towards a more open area of pozzines at 1783m, the site of a now-drained glacial lake. Beyond this point the route steepens again, levelling off briefly at 1969m where there's a small lake. Above you a moraine splashed with patches of eternal snow stretches up to a cirque of peaks, interrupted by the distinct niche of **Brêche de Capitellu** (also called Bocca a e Porte; 2225m), which you should reach in around $2^1/2$ hours.

An amazing view opens up on the far side of the pass, dominated by **Lac de Capitellu** and **Lac de Melu**, which sit at the bottom of an awesome cirque. From this altitude an optical illusion makes them appear on the same level but Melu, to the right as seen from the brêche, is actually more than 200 metres below Capitellu. Both are popular targets for day trips from Corte. A paved road, recently revamped with a whopping EU grant, funnels traffic up to a car park at the head of the valley, from where a path (complete with fixed chains and a steel ladder) provides access to the lakes. You can also reach the lakes from the GR20 via waymarked paths that drop steeply from the ridgetop (see below) but most trekkers prefer not to yield their hard-won height, instead admiring the water from above.

Leading to the right from Brêche de Capitellu the descent involves several drops down steep crevices and over smooth slabs and boulders. It starts with a memorable névé crossing which, with the peaks of the watershed silhouetted to the south, provides one of the GR's more striking photo opportunities.

After a convoluted traverse, you arrive around 30 minutes later at the ridge. Its first landmark is a second **brêche**, flanked by a pair of pinnacles, from where yellow waymarks plunge steeply down to Lac de Capitellu. The GR20, however, continues south-west, winding repeatedly to the sides of the ridgeline as it approaches **Bocca a Soglia** (2052m). Here another yellow-waymarked route, indicated by a sign, drops to the left; this one leads down to Lac de Melu, offering a quick route off the mountain to Corte via the Restonica Valley.

Bocca a Soglia marks the point at which the GR20 bends decisively northeast to get stuck into another long, rocky traverse. At 1960m, however, it cuts suddenly into the line of the mountain and starts a short but stiff ascent through boulders and patches of alder scrub to **Bocca Rinosa** (2170m). Beyond here a spectacular moraine, crossed at a more gentle gradient, affords great views of the Lac de Rinoso below and back along the range to Monte Cinto and Paglia Orba in the distance.

The best views come at **Bocca Muzzella** (2206m) where an impressive panorama to the south is revealed. Once across the pass you start the hour-long descent to Petra Piana. Beginning with an easy traverse across compacted scree and boulders, the route steepens considerably once the waymarks switch left to cross a southerly spur of Punta Muzzella. From there on you'll have the refuge firmly in your sights as you crisscross downhill through a messy mixture of granite boulders and alder scrub.

Refuge de Petra Piana

The Refuge de Petra Piana occupies a prime spot at the foot of Monte Rotondo, whose rugged south face forms an appropriately impressive backdrop after a memorable day spent clambering around the ridges. The hut, which accommodates up to 27 trekkers, is small but cosy with a rear terrace affording sublime views of Monte d'Oro across the valley and beyond towards the east coast. Close to the nexus of some of the island's key dividing ridges, it lies within comfortable walking distance of valleys that would be hours apart by car. This explains why the refuge becomes a de facto stray dogs' home in the summer: when they're not needed for hunting, the hounds tag along with trekkers for walkabouts that can take them into entirely different regions of the island. Somehow, a disproportionate number end up at Petra Piana.

The one downside of Petra Piana's great location, at least for campers and bivouackers, is that it provides comparatively little **shelter**. If you're sleeping under the stars and arrive too late to get a decent pitch, hunt around on the far side of the stream running to the left of the hut, where some considerate souls have piled stone windbreaks.

A major makeover is planned for Petra Piana in the future, but in the meantime this remains one of the GR20's more old-fashioned refuges, offering a modest supply of **provisions**: beers and staples such as pasta, biscuits, cheese and sausages, plus good hot meals for 8€.

The best way to savour the area's geography is to climb **Monte Rotondo** (see p150). Considering Petra Piana is effectively halfway up surprisingly few GR20 trekkers bother, but a compelling ascent of just under 600m skirting the magnificent Lavu Bellebone, is all that separates you from one of Europe's finest viewpoints.

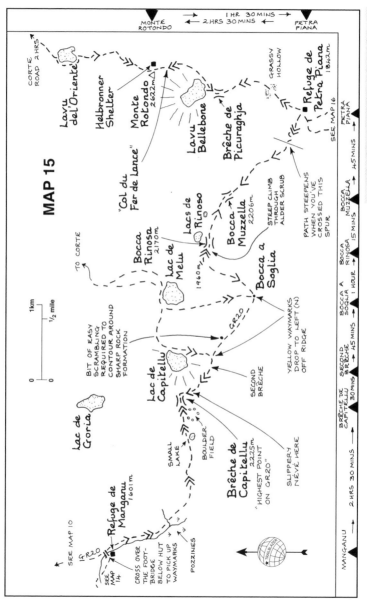

MAP 15

SEE MAP 10
SEE MAP 14
SEE MAP 16

ROUTE GUIDE AND MAPS

MONTE ROTONDO
1 HR 30 MINS →
← 2 HRS 30 MINS ←
PETRA PIANA

CORTE ROAD 2 HRS
Lavu del'Oriente
Halbronner Shelter
Monte Rotondo 2622m△
Lavu Bellebone
Brèche de Picuraghja
"Col du Far de Lance"
Refuge de Petra Piana 1842m
GRASSY HOLLOW
Lacs de Rinoso
Bocca Rinosa 2170m
Bocca Muzzella 2206m.
STEEP CLIMB THROUGH ALDER SCRUB
PATH STEEPENS WHEN YOU'VE CROSSED THIS SPUR

TO CORTE
Lac de Melu
Bocca a Soglia
1960m
GR20
YELLOW WAYMARKS DROP TO LEFT (N) OFF RIDGE

Lac de Goria
Lac de Capitellu
BIT OF EASY SCRAMBLING REQUIRED TO CONTOUR AROUND SHARP ROCK FORMATION
SECOND BRÈCHE

0   1km
0   ½ mile

Refuge de Manganu 1601m.
SMALL LAKE
BOULDER FIELD
Brèche de Capitellu 2225m. "HIGHEST POINT ON GR20"
SLIPPERY NÉVÉ HERE

GR20
CROSS OVER THE FOOT-BRIDGE BELOW HUT TO PICK UP WAYMARKS
POZZINES

TRAIL BLAZER

MANGANU ← 2 HRS 30 MINS → BRÈCHE DE CAPITELLU ← 30 MINS → SECOND BRÈCHE ← 45 MINS → BOCCA A SOGLIA ← 1 HOUR → BOCCA RINOSA ← 15 MINS → BOCCA MUZZELLA ← 45 MINS → PETRA PIANA

Ascending Monte Rotondo [Map 15, p149]

The ascent of Monte Rotondo (2622m), Corsica's second highest mountain, is arguably the most dramatic day trek on the island. Starting out from Refuge de Petra Piana, the route is considerably shorter and easier than the equivalent climb from Asco up its big sister, Monte Cinto (see pp121-2).

With a 6am departure you can be on the summit by 8.30am, well before the convection cloud blisters up and obscures the wonderful views. Well-equipped trekkers might consider making the climb towards the end of the day and bivouacking on top at, the Helbronner shelter, to be there for sunrise.

Don't attempt this route in wet or misty weather. Most of it crosses exposed, rocky terrain that can be treacherous in bad conditions. Note, too, that there are three or four different cairned routes to the top. The one outlined below is the most straightforward. If you decide to go for it, consider leaving your name with the gardiens at Petra Piana as a precaution (in which case don't forget to let them know you've descended safely).

Marked at regular intervals by **cairns** (not paint waymarks), the standard approach follows the stream flowing past Refuge de Petra Piana north-east up a steep and rocky slope. Once past a small grassy hollow you ascend in a series of zigzags along the line of a rounded ridge to a little gap, the **Brêche de Picuraghja**. Beyond this, the south face of Rotondo is fully revealed, along with ice-encrusted **Lavu Bellebone** which often remains partly frozen until well into the summer. Dropping to skirt the south-east shore of the lake, the route then begins a steep traverse of the rugged scree- and boulder-covered cirque below the summit.

It reaches the ridgetop at a prominent rock pinnacle marked on IGN maps as the **Col du Fer de Lance** and from there climbs steeply across large slabs and boulders to the top, which you should reach in around $2^{1}/2$ hours. The final little section, from the **Helbronner shelter** (a rough wood and tin shack left open year-round) to the crow's nest summit, involves a bit of exposed scrambling.

From the top you can see all of Corsica's highest peaks, from Alcudina in the south to Monte Cinto in the north, as well as the Golfe de Ajaccio. Many Corsican mountaineers regard this as the island's ultimate viewpoint.

Allow around $1^{1}/2$ hours for the descent by the same route if you're aiming to pick up the GR again. Alternatively you could climb down the north flank of the mountain into the **Restonica Valley**. This is a considerably longer descent which drops steeply into a gloomy couloir just below the summit and then wriggles over a rough moraine to the exquisite **Lavu del'Oriente**.

From there it more or less follows the course of the main stream northwards before switching to a north-east-running spur, which the path zigzags down to the Bergeries de Timozzo. Beyond this a long descent through pine forest (the latter part along a piste) brings you out on the Corte road. Well cairned as far as the lake, and thereafter waymarked in red and yellow, this northern descent takes around three hours.

STAGE NINE: PETRA PIANA → REFUGE DE L'ONDA [MAP 16, p153]

Overview

At Petra Piana the GR20 splits in two, offering a choice of routes to the next refuge at Onda. The conventional red-and-white waymarked **low-level** one, followed by the majority of trekkers, drops south-east down the Manganello Valley to the passarelle de Tolla. There it crosses the river to follow a broad forestry piste south-west

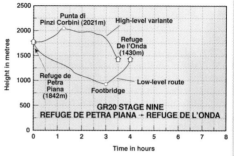

that gradually steepens as it nears the head of the Grottaccia Valley. Essentially a long forest walk passing a string of secluded bathing spots, this is the softer option and the obvious choice in poor weather or if you feel like an easy day.

The **haute route**, on the other hand, is a more challenging proposition following the ridges (*les crêtes*). Although much of it has been badly overgrazed, the landscape lining the path is unremittingly spectacular. With valleys falling steeply away to the sea on both sides, you get a strong sense of being at the sharp edge of the island's watershed – the essence of the GR20. There's quite a lot of scrambling – of much the same kind as on the previous day – but what sticks in the memory from this ridge route are the long, gloriously open sections.

The one thing that should deter you from choosing the latter path is bad weather. In winter this stretch becomes a full-on Alpine-style route requiring ropes and crampons; even in summer, snow patches persist until late in the year and the wind can whip over it at impressive speeds. If in doubt ask the advice of the gardiens at Petra Piana or, better still, trekkers arriving from the other direction.

Petra Piana → Onda: the low-level route

Running west along level ground from Petra Piana to begin with, the red-and-white waymarks drop downhill to the south-east at their bifurcation with the yellow marks of the haute route; the dividing point is indicated by a signboard. A steep descent through alder bushes brings you to the **Bergeries de Gialgo**, where you can buy ewe's cheese and top up your water bottle.

From there the path winds gently east to cross the Gialgo stream, whose true left bank it follows for a while before peeling away to the right at contour level. The descent starts again in earnest once you've forded the **Rau de Monte Rotondo**, which the route follows down to its confluence with the Manganello.

For the next $2^1/2$ hours or so a lovely old mule track winds along the approximate course of the Manganello as it crashes through a thickening forest of

R O U T E   G U I D E   A N D   M A P S

Laricio pine and beech. En route, a succession of tempting pools and waterfalls make perfect places to break the easy descent.

The **Bergeries de Tolla**, reached in just under three hours, sells its own delicious, freshly made goats' cheese in addition to a better range of **provisions** than that found at Petra Piana. Hot stews, snacks and even full three-course meals are also available (though usually only in July/Aug), as well as bottled beers and wine.

About 10 minutes further down the hill you arrive at **la passarelle de Tolla**, the footbridge across the confluence of the Manganello and Grotaccia that marks the lowest point of the étape. A PNRC signboard on the far side indicates the route of the **Mare a Mare Nord** *Variant*, veering left (east) towards Canaglia where a surfaced road winds out to Tattone and Vivario (see p154).

The GR20, however, bends south-west here, following the Grotaccia upstream through more old-growth Laricio pine on a rough forestry piste. Having rounded a sharp bend near a large waterfall it grows considerably steeper and the pines gradually give way to gnarled beech trees. Only when you're clear of the woods, after around 1½ hours, is the refuge visible high above you at the head of the valley.

Petra Piana ↪ Onda: the high-level *Variante*

The early part of this stage's high-level *Variante* can be traced from the Refuge de Petra Piana as the gently curving ridgeway curves south in a succession of smooth-stepped summits. A pale line running along the top of the crest, the path presents a mouth-watering prospect for anyone who loves high, dry hiking, although it is far less of a straightforward yomp than it looks at this distance.

The first of the day's short scrambles begins just after the signboard showing the bifurcation of the main low route ('par la vallée') from the high one ('par les crêtes'). Note that from here on you should follow the yellow waymarks. They lead you through a jumble of granite up to the ridge, which you clamber onto for the first time just before the **Bocca Manganello**. From there an orange-way-marked liaison path drops into the Fiume Grossu Valley and, after three hours, the village of Guagno (see p154).

More scrambling, interspersed with stretches of grassy ridge walking, takes you to just below the **Punta Murace**. From there the *Variante* runs along the aptly named **Serra Bianca** crest to **Punta di Pinzi Corbini** (2021m), a star-shaped peak from where the views back to Petra Piana and Monte Rotondo are magnificent. A short, steep descent brings you to **Bocca a Meta** where the waymarks drift to the east side of the ridge to avoid a sheer outcrop.

The next section involves a steep but enjoyable scramble to regain the crest of the **Serra di Tenda**. Once on the ridge, though, a more clearly defined path takes over as the route drops 500m in a little over 1km.

The most sustained and steepest descent of the étape ends at the **Bocca d'Oreccia** (1427m), a broad, eroded saddle pass. Here the GR20 intersects the Mare a Mare Nord *Variant*, which falls steeply to the right (west) from the pass towards Pastricciola. The yellow marks, however, climb again from the bocca to the top of the rise where they meet the red-and-white waymarks of the main

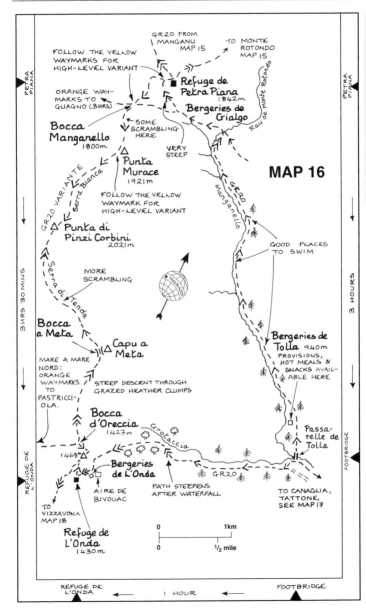

GR20 FROM MANGANU MAP 15

TO MONTE ROTONDO MAP 15

FOLLOW THE YELLOW WAYMARKS FOR HIGH-LEVEL VARIANT

ORANGE WAY-MARKS TO GUAGNO (3HRS)

Refuge de Petra Piana 1842m

Bergeries de Gialgo

PETRA PIANA

PETRA PIANA

Bocca Manganello 1800m

SOME SCRAMBLING HERE

VERY STEEP

Rau de Monte Rotondo

Punta Murace 1921m

MAP 16

Serra Bianca

FOLLOW THE YELLOW WAYMARK FOR HIGH-LEVEL VARIANT

GR20 VARIANTE

Punta di Pinzi Corbini 2021m

GR20 Manganello

GOOD PLACES TO SWIM

Serra di Tenda

MORE SCRAMBLING

TRAILBLAZER

3 HOURS

3 HRS 30 MINS

Bocca a Meta

Capu a Meta

Bergeries de Tolla 940m PROVISIONS, HOT MEALS & SNACKS AVAIL-ABLE HERE

MARE A MARE NORD: ORANGE WAYMARKS TO PASTRICCI-OLA.

STEEP DESCENT THROUGH GRAZED HEATHER CLUMPS

Bocca d'Oreccia 1427m

Grotaccia

Passa-relle de Tolla

FOOTBRIDGE

REFUGE DE L'ONDA

1468m

Bergeries de L'Onda

AIRE DE BIVOUAC

PATH STEEPENS AFTER WATERFALL

GR20

TO CANAGLIA, TATTONE, SEE MAP 17

TO VIZZAVONA MAP 18

Refuge de L'Onda 1430m

0   1km

0   ½ mile

REFUGE DE L'ONDA   ←   1 HOUR   ←   FOOTBRIDGE

GR20. Turn left here for Onda, or carry straight on to begin the long ascent up the north side of Monte d'Oro if you're continuing to Vizzavona.

Refuge de l'Onda

Perched at the head of the Grotaccia Valley, only metres below the line of the watershed, Refuge de l'Onda looks across the richly forested country above Vivario and Venaco to distant Monte Cardo, whose pale-grey humpbacked bulk dominates the north-east horizon. Above it the crags of Monte d'Oro surge sheer from the treeline, splashed with névés until well into the summer. The location is memorable enough, but the hut itself, which only has 14 beds, is decidedly poky. Most trekkers end up camping or bivouacking in the fenced (pig-proof) enclosure below it, where a rushing spring and *bloc sanitaire* (open mid-June to mid-Sep) are the only amenities. Overlooking the *aire de bivouac*, the **Bergeries de l'Onda** sells a good range of **supplies** including cheese, charcuterie, fresh fruit, bread and wine at the usual inflated prices. Even if you are sleeping in the refuge you'll need to walk down to the bergeries to pay; the friendly shepherd family also serve good hot meals for 9.50€.

Onda is not somewhere you'd relish spending much time. However, the next étape to Vizzavona is tougher than it might seem. To double up and leapfrog Onda you should reach here as early in the day as possible and, in hot weather, wait until the heat subsides before beginning the long initial climb to the Crête de Muratello. The refuge has a small kitchen where you can cook up lunch and there are plenty of shady spots around it for a restorative snooze.

Liaison route to Tattone and Vivario   [Map 17, opposite]

From the **passarelle de Tolla** it takes only 1³/₄ hours to trek downstream to Tattone via the hamlet of Canaglia. Waymarked with **orange** paint spots the path, which keeps to the true right bank of the river, follows the rocky route of the Mare a Mare Nord *Variant*.

Tattone lies on the main railway line so you can hop on a train from there to Corte, Bastia or Ajaccio, or leap-frog to Vizzavona. The nearest shop, however, is at Vivario.

Liaison route to Guagno

At **Bocca Manganello** (see Map 16, p153) a liaison path, marked by a signboard and orange paint spots, strikes steeply down the head of the Fiume Grossu Valley to Guagno – an easy 3-hour descent with a final 4km stretch along the D23. This is a much longer exit from the GR than the one via Tolla and Canaglia and ultimately brings you out at a very remote village that is not connected to the rest of the island by public transport. Guagno does, however, have a gîte d'étape.

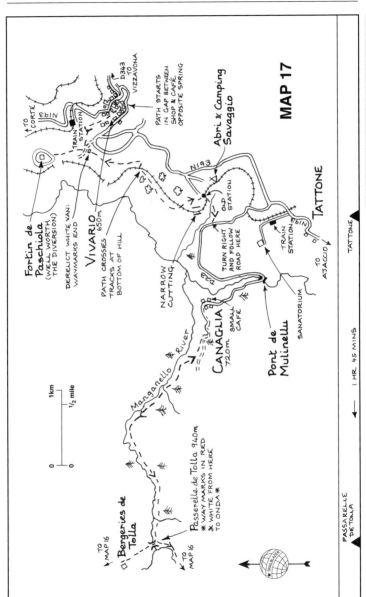

Fortin de Paschiola
(WELL WORTH
THE DIVERSION)

TO CORTE

N193

D343 TO VIZZAVONA

PATH STARTS
IN GAP BETWEEN
SHOP & CAFÉ
OPPOSITE SPRING

TRAIN STATION

DERELICT WHITE VAN:
WAYMARKS END

VIVARIO
650m

PATH CROSSES
TRACKS AT
BOTTOM OF HILL

Abri & Camping
Savaggio

N193

OLD
STATION

MAP 17

TATTONE

NARROW
CUTTING

D343

TURN RIGHT
AND FOLLOW
ROAD HERE

TRAIN
STATION

TO AJACCIO

N193

TO TATTONE

Manganello River

CANAGLIA
720m

SMALL
CAFÉ

SANATORIUM

Pont de
Mulinellu

1km

½ mile

0

0

TO MAP 16

Bergeries de
Tolla

TO MAP 16

Passerelle de Tolla 940m
* WAY MARKS IN RED
& WHITE FROM HERE
TO ONDA *

PASSARELLE
DE TOLLA

1 HR 45 MINS

TATTONE

ROUTE GUIDE AND MAPS

STAGE TEN: REFUGE DE L'ONDA → VIZZAVONA [MAP 18, opposite]

Overview

After the twists and turns of the previous étape, stage ten of the GR20 seems straightforward enough: a stiff ridge climb up to a pass, followed by a long descent down the valley on the other side. A close look at the chart below, however, reveals that the altitude changes involved are considerable. The 670m ascent from Onda to the Crête de Muratello might not be too intimidating by the standards of this route but the descent – at 1100m the longest on the whole GR20 – is a real knee-cruncher, especially if you've doubled up stages from Petra Piana.

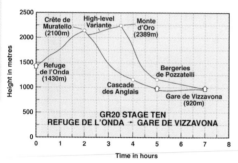

For those with plenty more walking left in them when they reach the ridge, a superb high-level *Variante* (see p158) beckons to the east. Routing you over the summit of Monte d'Oro, Corsica's fifth highest peak, it climbs to nearly 2400m before plunging down the forested flank of the mountain to Vizzavona. To get its most rugged, challenging sections behind you early in the day before the cloud forms, however, you have to start out from Onda rather than Petra Piana.

Whichever way you choose, be sure to take enough **water** as there are no springs along either route.

Route guide

The stage begins with a climb back to ridge level (you need to retrace your steps to begin with, following the path you arrived on), from where the path south towards the Crête de Muratello stretches steeply up the mountain above you.

Although relentlessly steep and rocky in places, the 2¹/₂-hour ascent is an enjoyable one, with superb views of Monte d'Oro, as well as Monte Rotondo and the pale line of the GR20 winding across the ridges to the north.

From the **Crête de Muratello** (2100m), the red-and-white waymarks run down to the left (east), traversing the rocky head of the Vallée de l'Agnone. At the point where the yellow markers of the high-level *Variante* peel off to the left the main route cuts more steeply downhill.

The next couple of hours or so take you across a mixture of steeply inclined slabs, boulders, streams and alder scrub. Later, patches of deciduous woodland create welcome shade as you approach the first real landmark of the descent, the **ruined refuge** of the Club Alpin Français, which stands close to an attractive waterfall. Beyond it the **passarelle de Tortetto**, where the path switches to the right bank of the Agnone, leads down to the **Bergeries de Porletto** and, once

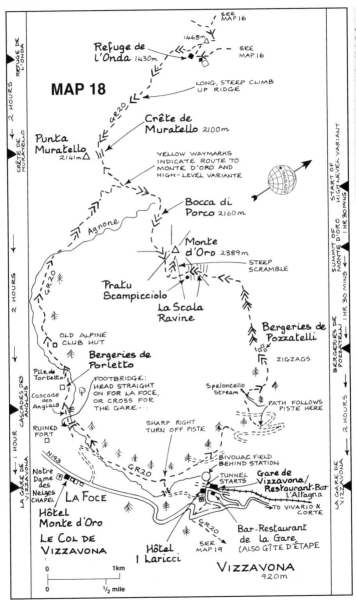

SEE MAP 16

1468m

SEE MAP 16

Refuge de l'Onda 1430m

LONG, STEEP CLIMB UP RIDGE

MAP 18

Crête de Muratello 2100m

Punta Muratello 2141m△

YELLOW WAYMARKS INDICATE ROUTE TO MONTE D'ORO AND HIGH-LEVEL VARIANTE

Bocca di Porco 2160m

TRAILBLAZER

Monte d'Oro 2389m

Agnone

STEEP SCRAMBLE

Pratu Scampicciolo

La Scala Ravine

Bergeries de Pozzatelli

OLD ALPINE CLUB HUT

Bergeries de Porletto

ZIGZAGS

Pile de Torketto

FOOTBRIDGE: HEAD STRAIGHT ON FOR LA FOCE, OR CROSS FOR THE GARE...

Speloncello Stream

PATH FOLLOWS PISTE HERE

Cascade des Anglais

RUINED FORT

SHARP RIGHT TURN OFF PISTE

BIVOUAC FIELD BEHIND STATION

N193

GR20

TUNNEL STARTS

Gare de Vizzavona / Restaurant-Bar L'Altagna

Notre Dame des Neiges CHAPEL

La Foce

TO VIVARIO & CORTE

Hôtel Monte d'Oro

Le Col de Vizzavona

Bar-Restaurant de la Gare (ALSO GÎTE D'ÉTAPE

Hôtel I Laricci

SEE MAP 19

Vizzavona 920m

0   1km

0   1/2 mile

REFUGE DE L'ONDA 2 HOURS CRÊTE DE MURATELLO 2 HOURS CASCADES DES ANGLAIS 1 HOUR LA GARE DE VIZZAVONA

ROUTE GUIDE AND MAPS

START OF HIGH LEVEL VARIANT SUMMIT OF MONTE D'ORO 1 HR 30MINS BERGERIES DE POZZATELLI 1 HR 30 MINS LA GARE DE VIZZAVONA 2 HOURS you've descended through a leafy beech wood, the famous **Cascades des Anglais**. These falls, where the Agnone crashes through a series of beautiful turquoise pools, have been a major tourist attraction since the nineteenth century and people continue to flock here from the nearby main road for picnics in the summer.

A short way below the cascades, after scrambling through a steep and rocky section deep in the woods, the GR20 reaches a second **footbridge** which you should cross for Vizzavona. Anyone intending to spend the night in Hôtel Monte d'Oro (see p161) should head straight on here and follow the path until it meets a piste, where a right turn will bring you out after 10- to 15-minutes' level walking at the hamlet of La Foce (see Map 18, p157).

From the far (north) side of the footbridge the final section of the étape passes through some impressive old Laricio pine forest. Having followed a motorable piste for half a kilometre, you turn right onto a footpath, cross the Agnone for the last time and wind uphill to the **gare de Vizzavona**, reached a little over three hours after crossing the Crête de Muratello.

Monte d'Oro High-level *Variante* [Map 18, p157]

Scaling Monte d'Oro, this high-level *Variante* presents a challenging alternative to the long and somewhat monotonous descent of the Vallée de l'Agnone. The massif, a huge pyramid of blue-grey granite whose crags tower above the railway line at Vizzavona, is among the island's most distinctive peaks. Climbing it offers a memorable culmination to the GR20 if you're quitting at Vizzavona. From the Crête de Muratello, only 300m and a bit of tricky scrambling separate you from the summit. The descent to Vizzavona, however, involves a hefty drop of 1469m – longer even than the descent from the top of Monte Cinto to Asco.

Note that the **exposed position** of this peak means that it's particularly vulnerable to sudden changes in weather, so assess carefully the likelihood of a storm before you set off.

The first part of the *Variante* follows the red-and-white waymarked route from Onda up to the Crête de Muratello and down the other side across the head of the Vallée de l'Agnone to the point where the **yellow waymarks** begin. These, along with a chain of cairns that are fairly regular but peter out in places, indicate the route to the summit, which completes the traverse of the valley head to scale the western spur of Monte d'Oro at **Bocca di Porco** (2160m), where you turn right. Apart from the occasional foray into the boulders below it, the waymarks keep more or less to the ridge. The final approach to the summit involves a scramble up the north (left) side of a gully on a bouldery incline. Allow 1½ hours for the whole ascent from the Crête de Muratello.

The **descent** initially doubles back the way you came, across the boulder field to a point where the waymarks run off to the left. Having crossed a little grassy plateau on the east flank of the mountain known as **Pratu Scampicciolo**, it penetrates the gloomy ravine of **La Scala** where you'll almost certainly have to contend with a large névé. Once clear of the gully and past a distinctive rock pinnacle dubbed, for obvious reasons, 'La Cafetière', the route swings left to begin a steady, crisscrossing descent down the line of a stream over rough and rocky ground to the trees.

You should reach the ruined **Bergeries de Pozzatelli** around 90 minutes from the summit. Beyond there the path plunges into the forest proper, rounding the mountainside to reach the Speloncello stream. You cross a **piste** – part of a huge motorable track known as **La Grande Corniche** – shortly afterwards, and later join and follow the piste downhill for around 500m. A diagonal traverse through mature Laricio pine forest then takes you south across two of the Vecchio's main tributaries (via footbridges) to river level, where the yellow waymarks meet the red-and-white ones of the GR20 for the final half kilometre up to the gare de Vizzavona.

VIZZAVONA

Vizzavona has a scattering of hotels and tin-roofed forestry buildings littered around the col that divides Monte d'Oro and Punta dell'Oriente, where the main Ajaccio–Corte–Bastia artery crosses the Corsican watershed. Although long an important staging post on the journey across the mountains, the settlement only became a visitor attraction in its own right after the construction of the railway line at the end of the nineteenth century.

A significant proportion of the first tourists to venture up here from the coast were wealthy British aristocrats (among them Edward Lear) for whom Vizzavona became something of a low-key hill station renowned for its salubrious cool air and invigorating forest walks (the most famous of them to the falls that would become known as the 'Cascades des Anglais'). A handful of elegant Edwardian hotels sprang up to cater for this influx; one of them, the Monte d'Oro, still survives, its fin-de-siècle atmosphere lovingly preserved.

For most trekkers, however, Vizzavona means the little clearing in the forest around the railway station, 700m below the *route nationale*. As the de facto midway point of the GR20, the station (known in Corsica as the place where one of the island's most notorious bandits, Antoine Bellacoscia, gave himself up to police in 1892) is a major landmark of the route. Lots of people leave or join in here by train, while those aiming to complete all 16 stages often celebrate getting this far with a cooked meal and a few drinks at one of the terrace cafés outside the station.

If you're trekking on a tight budget, however, the Gare de Vizzavona may leave a less than positive impression. Apart from the inevitable inflated prices (particularly galling given the convenient rail connection), the main gripe is the absence of refuge facilities, or even a bloc sanitaire, near the station. The situation is compounded by the palpable reluctance of businesses at the station to allow walkers to use their toilets, or water sources. The politest solution if you're bent on staying here is, of course, to spend money as and where you're expected to.

Alternatively, peel off the GR20 at the bridge over the Agnone and head up to the hamlet of La Foce, near Col de Vizzavona, where the atmospheric Hôtel Monte d'Oro offers alternative accommodation, including a gîte d'étape (see p161).

Orientation and services

Four **trains** per day pass through Vizzavona in both directions on the line between Bastia, Corte and Ajaccio, two of them connecting with services to Calvi.

The next stop heading north down the valley is **Tattone**, site of the nearest **campsite** in the area; *Abri et Camping Savaggio* (☎ 04.95.47.22.14; May–Sep) has a couple of dozen well-shaded pitches and refuge accommodation for 22 people. It's close to the road and is used almost entirely by trekkers.

Trekkers arriving early in the day sometimes get on the train to **Vivario** to stock up with supplies at the village's excellent **shop**, or to call at the **post office**, the only one within easy reach of Vizzavona.

To change money or get to an ATM cashpoint, however, you'd have to continue on to Corte (see pp99-103), an hour's ride to the north.

ROUTE GUIDE AND MAPS

U Trinighellu (Micheline)

Even though few of them regularly use it, Corsicans love their narrow-gauge train line. When the government announced in 1972 that the coastal section between Ponte-Leccia and Calvi was to close, a massive public outcry blocked the plan. Bolstered by generous public funding and capacity tourist traffic in the summer, Le Chemin de Fer de la Corse (CFC) claims to transport nearly 800,000 passengers annually, many of them trekkers who use the line as a route to and from the heart of the island's mountains at Vizzavona.

Construction work began in 1855 but it wasn't until nearly 40 years later that Bastia, Ajaccio and Calvi were finally connected by rail. In all, 230km of track were laid, requiring a total of 32 tunnels. The longest, the 3916m Tunnel de Vizzavona through the watershed, took seven years to hollow out with pick-axes and, until the completion of the Mont Blanc tunnel, was the longest in Europe. The line also crosses 75 viaducts, including the 30m-high Pont de Vecchio at Vivario, engineered by no less than Gustav Eiffel (of Eiffel Tower fame).

Catching the *trinighellu* – or '*micheline*' as Corsica's pint-sized locomotives are known in French – can be a memorable if somewhat bone-shaking experience. The 1950s rolling stock and old diesel engines were recently replaced but the narrow-gauge track and typically Corsican speed at which the trains travel ensure a bouncy ride (whence the trinighellu's other, somewhat less felicitous nickname, the 'TGV' – Train de Grande Vibration).

The most scenic sections are between the Vizzavona tunnel and Corte, from where you get great views of Monte d'Oro and Monte Cardo, and the coastal stretch through the Balagne, which emerges from an olive-speckled hinterland to skirt one of the Mediterranean's most beautiful shorelines.

Where to stay and eat

A good range of food supplies and essential bits and bobs such as stove fuel, gas canisters, batteries, sticking plasters, blister pads and film (in short, the best selection of provisions on the GR20 between Calenzana and Conca) can be bought at Vizzavona's little **shop**, the Épicerie Rosy (open daily 7.30am-8pm) next to the station. It's run by the stationmaster and his wife, who also own the pleasant **Restaurant-Bar l'Altagna** next door, where you can order draught beer or a filling set-menu Corsican meal (14€ and 18.50€), served outdoors on a lively little terrace.

Far less appealing is **Bar-Restaurant de la Gare** (☎/🖳 04.95.47.22.20; open May to mid-Sep), directly opposite, whose meals, mostly dished up as part of their gîte's half-board deal, are poor value. Since

being handed on to the younger generation of the family, this place has gone decidedly downhill. The cramped six-bed dormitories and limited shower-toilet facilities of their **gîte d'étape** (34€ for obligatory half-board) also represent a worse deal than that offered by **Hôtel I Laricci** (☎ 04 95.47.21.12; open Apr-Oct), just up the lane from the station. Priced at 30€ per bed for (obligatory) half-board, dorms in this attractive period building, which has Alpine-style high-pitched roofs and a timber-lined interior, are much cleaner and airier, and there's the added attraction of a comfy lounge and garden to laze in.

You can also check into more comfortable double rooms here for 40€ per head half-board (plus 8€ for en suite); or 62€ single occupancy. The I Laricci's one failing is its food, which is little better than that served at Bar-Restaurant de la Gare.

If you're happy to be away from the train line a far better choice, whatever your budget, is **Hôtel Monte d'Oro** (☎ 04 95.47.21.06, 🖥 www.monteoro.com), 3km south-west along the route nationale towards the col. Dating from the late nineteenth century, when it was built to accommodate engineers working on the Vizzavona tunnel, the hotel epitomizes the genteel pre-war era when this area was popular with British aristos and a rich Parisian jet-set. Sepia photos of the building in its heyday, original hand-turned furniture and the pervasive scent of old-fashioned beeswax polish set the tone.

The rooms are spacious and most enjoy fine views of the forest. You also get the run of the lovely conservatory and terrace looking across the valley to the mountain. Rates range from 46€ to 75€ depend-ing on the season – very reasonable considering the location and atmosphere.

Hôtel Monte d'Oro has a small annexe offering basic but adequate gîte d'étape accommodation in three- or four-person dorms (15€ per bed, or 33€ for half-board) with a small kitchen for self-caterers. If you're staying in the refuge, where the dorms sleep only two people each (9.50€ per bed; no half-board), you can also use the kitchen but you'll need your own sleeping bags. All things considered, this is a more attractive budget option than the equivalent places near the station and you don't even have to walk here; phone from the station and they'll come and pick you up. The rates also include free transfer to the trailhead the following day after breakfast.

ROUTE GUIDE AND MAPS

The roving stones
The proprietors of Hôtel Monte d'Oro at Col de Vizzavona love to regale guests with a family yarn dating from WWII, when the building was requisitioned by the occupying Italians. Much to the consternation of the patronne, Mme Plaisant, some of the soldiers stabled their mules in the tiny chapel behind the hotel, dedicated to Our Lady of the Snows. 'War is war' was the only explanation offered by the Italians for this act of sacrilege.

However, luckily for Our Lady and Mme Plaisant and for all those travellers whose safe passage across the notoriously weather-prone pass depended on both women's goodwill, help was at hand in the form of the High Chaplain of the occupying army. When he found out from the disgruntled patronne how his troops had accommodated their animals, he made them stand to attention in front of the wooden chapel and ordered that it be 'purified by fire' and then rebuilt by the offenders. Stones were transferred for the purpose from the ruins of a nearby French fort (remnants of which still stand at the col) and the new shrine to Notre Dame des Neiges was consecrated on Ascension Day, August 15, of that year. It still stands next to the road, beside the Hôtel Monte d'Oro.

The locals see in this chain of events the settling of even older scores by the stones themselves. Village lore holds that the seventeenth-century French fort was erected using material pillaged from an earlier chapel dedicated to Saint Peter. Thus Vizzavona's protective deities deviously outwitted their occupier foes by means of the island's granite – an interpretation that has an unmistakably Corsican ring to it.

STAGE ELEVEN: VIZZAVONA → E'CAPANNELLE [MAP 19, opposite]

Overview

A relatively undemanding stage gets the southern portion of the GR20 under-way. From Vizzavona, the lowest point on the whole route, the inevitable ascent at the start of the étape follows old mule and foresters' tracks through deep, shady woodland. Easy gradients and springy, pine-needly paths make for a pleasant climb to the pass, Bocca Palmenti. From there an even gen-tler *sentier* contours around the west flank of the Fium' Orbu Valley and after a final short ascent reaches the ski sta-tion of E'Capannelle.

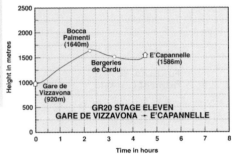

For once, water is plentiful throughout. From Vizzavona you'll only need enough to get you to the pass, just below which a gushing spring provides a perfect fill-up point. After that there is a string of bergeries and streams.

Anyone wishing to gain time and not intending to follow the high-level *Variante* over Monte Renoso (see p168) from E'Capannelle might consider dou-bling up this stage and pressing on to Bocca di Verdi (Col de Verde) or Prati. Either would make for a long day but would also present a far less arduous option than combining the next two étapes between E'Capannelle and Usciolu.

Route guide

From the Gare de Vizzavona the red-and-white waymarks lead you past Hôtel I Laricci and the roadside oratory of Notre Dame de la Forêt to cross a small bridge. Shortly after this they plunge to the right into the forest, emerging after 10 minutes at a sharp bend on the route nationale. A piste on the opposite side of the road, to the left of the ONF **Maison Forestière**, takes you north-east on a traversing ascent to a sequence of steeper zigzags that criss-cross up a spur and then veer south. Another series of zigzags at the head of the valley keep the trail on a fairly gentle incline despite the steepening hillside. By the time the Laricio pines thin out only a short climb across scrubby, over-grazed ground remains before the pass, although anyone who started out late from Vizzavona may find the final shadeless stretch hot going. Thankfully, the perennial **Funtana di Palmenti**, just off the left side of the path, spews deliciously cold water throughout the summer: a perfect spot from which to admire the impres-sive views of Monte d'Oro and Monte Rotondo to the south.

Bocca Palmenti, a broad, flat saddle, heavily denuded by flocks from the nearby bergeries, yields the first views of the Fium' Orbu Valley, which runs down to the east coast. Beyond the pass, the GR20 swings south into a gently

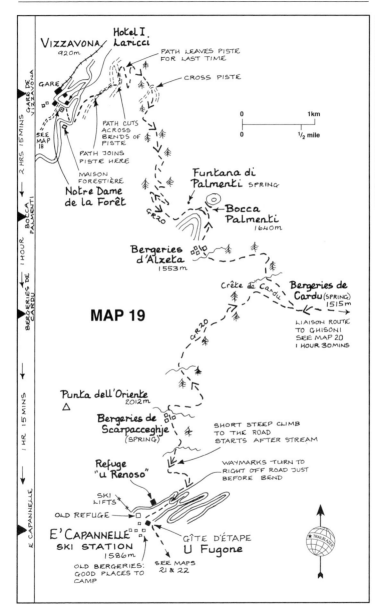

ROUTE GUIDE AND MAPS

Vizzavona 920m
Hotel I. Laricci
PATH LEAVES PISTE FOR LAST TIME
CROSS PISTE
GARE
GARE DE VIZZAVONA
2 HRS 15 MINS
SEE MAP 18
PATH CUTS ACROSS BENDS OF PISTE
PATH JOINS PISTE HERE
MAISON FORESTIÈRE
Notre Dame de la Forêt
0 ———— 1km
0 ———— ½ mile

Funtana di Palmenti SPRING
GR20
Bocca Palmenti 1640m
BOCCA PALMENTI
1 HOUR

Bergeries d'Alzeta 1553m
Crête de Cardu
Bergeries de Cardu (SPRING) 1515m
LIAISON ROUTE TO GHISONI SEE MAP 20 1 HOUR 30 MINS
BERGERIES DE CARDU

GR20

MAP 19

Punta dell'Oriente 2012m △
Bergeries de Scarpaceghje (SPRING)
SHORT STEEP CLIMB TO THE ROAD STARTS AFTER STREAM
1 HR. 15 MINS

Refuge "u Renoso"
WAYMARKS TURN TO RIGHT OFF ROAD JUST BEFORE BEND
SKI LIFTS
OLD REFUGE
E'CAPANNELLE SKI STATION 1586m
GÎTE D'ÉTAPE U Fugone
OLD BERGERIES: GOOD PLACES TO CAMP
SEE MAPS 21 & 22
E CAPANNELLE

TRAILBLAZER

descending traverse to the **Bergeries d'Alzeta** (1553m), where it crosses the Alzitone stream. The next landmark is the distinctive **Crête de Cardu** (1515m), where you get your first good view of Monte Renoso and the high ridges running south.

The GR20, meanwhile, turns west-north-west here to begin a long, sweeping traverse of Punta Dell'Oriente's lower eastern flanks. Passing through a series of minor stream hollows and scrub-filled breaks in the forest, you round a succession of smooth spurs to reach the tongue-twisting **Bergeries de Scarpacceghje**, site of another spring. Fifteen minutes' walk further south the waymarks strike uphill for the first significant ascent since Bocca Palmenti, gaining 150m in just over half a kilometre.

This short, steep climb takes you over the thinly wooded Crête de Chufidu, where you briefly meet a surfaced road before dipping into the maquis for the last drop down to the ski station.

E'CAPANNELLE [MAP 19, p163]

The run-down winter sports complex of E'Capannelle ranks among the GR20's least inspiring locations. Its buildings may be less intrusive than those at Asco Stagnu and Castel di Verghio, but its overall aspect is blighted by clanking ski lifts and eroded hillsides hemming it in.

E'Capannelle's only real plus is its bar-restaurant's rear terrace, which provides a congenial location to while away sunny afternoons over a beer and a hot meal. For trekkers whose budgets don't stretch to such luxuries there's also a new refuge just up the hill.

Orientation and services

E'Capannelle is connected to Ghisoni by a tarmac road but no public transport runs up here, even during peak season.

To cover the 42km from Vizzavona (or 38km from Vivario), **taxis** charge upwards of 80€; call Michel Salviani (☎ 04.95.46.04.88, or mobile ☎ 06.03.49.15.24).

Dorm beds, breakfast and supper are available at *Gîte d'étape 'U Fugone'* (☎ 04 95.57.01.81, 📠 04.95.56.39.34; open May-Sep), where obligatory half-board costs 33€. Meals are served in the lively downstairs bar.

The only other option is a recently opened refuge, *U Renoso*, whose rates considerably undercut those of the gîte. Hot showers, cooked meals and reasonably priced supplies are sold from the hut, which you can camp and bivouac around. To find it, turn right when you first hit the metalled road during the descent on E'Capannelle, and follow it uphill for five minutes; the refuge will be on your right.

Basic **supplies** are also sold from the bar of Gîte d'étape U Fugone. In the same room you'll also find a coin-operated **telephone** that accepts incoming calls. The most convenient source of **drinking water** is the dressed spring immediately outside the gîte.

Monte Renoso – ascent options

E'Capannelle is the traditional starting point for the ascent of Monte Renoso (2352m), the highest peak in southern Corsica. You can incorporate the ascent into the GR20 by following the **high-level** *Variante* route outlined on pp168-70, which descends from the summit via the massif's famous pozzines. A less strenuous approach would be to leave your gear at the ski station and make the climb with a light daypack, returning to E'Capannelle for lunch and heading south along the main path afterwards.

Liaison route to Ghisoni via the Bergeries de Cardu [Map 20, below]

At the ridge clearing on the Crête de Cardu, a PNRC signboard indicates the yellow-waymarked liaison route east down the crest to Ghisoni. Other than a small épicerie and hotel, the village holds little to detain trekkers; most people who stay here do so in order to complete the circular walk over Monte Renoso (described on pp168-70) without having to endure the relative discomforts of the station de ski at E'Capannelle.

Five minutes down the trail, the first landmark you come to is the **Bergeries de Cardu**, a cluster of shepherds' huts opposite conical Monte Calvi (1461m), which has a dependable **spring** and fine views down the Fium' Orbu Valley to the coast. Keeping to the ridge at the edge of the treeline you then drop down to a small saddle col, where the path divides, with the yellow waymarks leading to the right (east-south-east) around the side of Monte Cardu. At 1345m, this route then drifts off the ridge, crossing a small plateau and forestry plantation as it drops more steeply down to Ghisoni. The village centre lies five minutes' walk north of where the path meets the road. Allow around 1½ hours for this descent (and 2½ hours climbing in the other direction to rejoin the GR20).

Ghisoni Set against a grandiose backdrop of needle escarpments and Laricio pine woods, Ghisoni, the largest village in the upper Fium'Orbu, looks towards the east coast from its vantage point at a bend in the bottom of the valley. Dependent on pig rearing and forestry, it's an archetypal Corsican hill settle-

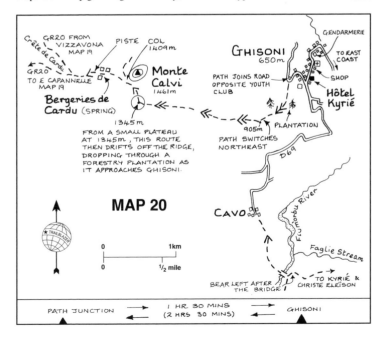

ment: severely depopulated and with a floundering economy. Hope of a renaissance came in the 1980s with the creation of the ski station at nearby E'Capannelle but the expected winter tourist trade never materialized.

These days the few visitors that come here tend to be walkers who use Ghisoni's self-assuredly old-fashioned *Hôtel Kyrié* (☎ 04.95.57.60.33, 📠 04 95.57.63.15; open April to mid-Oct) as a base for forays into the surrounding massifs. Situated on the main street near the centre of the village, this place has around 30 simple but clean, en suite rooms, the best of them at the rear of the building. The hotel's *restaurant* is the only place in the village to eat, which is unfortunate because the food is uninspiring.

Close to the church, **Libre-Service Micheli** (open year-round Mon-Sat 9am-noon and 4.30-6.45pm) is the best place for miles to stock up with supplies, though since the refuge at Bocca di Verdi (Col de Verde) opened few GR20 trekkers make the long detour just to shop here.

Ghisoni is not on a bus route. Other than hitching, the only way in or out is to phone **taxi** driver Michel Salviani (☎ 04.95.46.04.88, or mobile ☎ 06 03.49.15.24), who charges around 80€ one-way to Vizzavona.

Kyrié and Christe Eleïson

Kyrié and Christe Eleïson, the magnificent granite escarpments that dominate Ghisoni to the south-east on the opposite side of the Fium'Orbu Valley, are inextricably associated with the **Giovannali** sect, an heretic splinter group of the Franciscans who were persecuted in the fourteenth century by Pope Urban V. Accused of conducting orgies in their churches, members of the sect were hunted down by emissaries from Avignon and killed at their strongholds across the island in 1362. The most famous of these massacres took place at **Carbini** in the Alta Rocca region, but a large group of Giovannalis were also burned to death in a giant pyre on the banks of the river below Ghisoni. It is said, however, that the villagers took pity on the heretics and persuaded their priest to administer last rites before the fire was lit. As the flames rose, the onlookers drowned the cries of the dying by intoning verses of the prayer *Kyrié eleïson, Christe eleïson*, which reverberated through the crags on the far side of the river.

STAGE TWELVE: E'CAPANNELLE → BOCCA DI VERDI (COL DE VERDE) [MAP 21, p169; MAP 22, p171]

Overview

To reach the head of the Fium'Orbu Valley at Bocca di Verdi (or Col de Verde as it is marked on maps), where the GR20 begins its ascent to the Refuge de Prati, you've a choice of radically con-

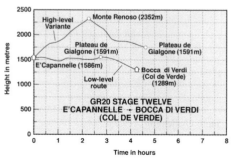

Vendetta and banditry in Corsica

Vendettas (blood feuds) are common to many traditional Mediterranean societies but in few regions of the world has eye-for-an-eye violence become as pervasive as in Corsica, where jealousy and mutual suspicion have always been defining traits of the island psyche.

References to *la vinditta* date back to the Roman era, but it was during the period of Genoese rule that internecine killing spiralled out of control. At one time in the sixteenth century the murder rate ran at around 900, for a population of only 12,000. Whole villages became locked in states of siege, their windows barricaded, with generations of families incarcerated under threat of death.

All manner of intended or perceived insults could ignite a blood feud: infringement of property rights was a common cause, as was petty theft. In a village in northern Corsica, for example, 36 people died in a dispute over ownership of a chestnut tree, while one of the longest-standing feuds in the south erupted after a donkey wandered into the wrong field.

Once a vinditta had kicked off it could take generations to run its course, drawing in ever greater numbers of protagonists. Traditional codes of honour required that blood be avenged with blood, and shame awaited any man and his family who failed to exact retribution. In this way, formerly peaceful, law-abiding individuals were forced to take up arms to uphold clan honour, giving rise to a particularly Corsican kind of hero, the *bandit d'honneur*. To avoid capture by the authorities or reprisal assassination, many men fled to the maquis after committing a vendetta murder, where they hid in remote regions.

Nineteenth-century France saw an extraordinary upsurge in public interest in bandits d'honneur, fuelled by a series of articles on the subject by journalists and wealthy adventurers. Some bandits even became national celebrities, posing for postcards and press calls with their flintlocks and characteristic broad-brimmed felt fedoras.

A spate of best-selling novels followed; the most famous, Prosper Mérimée's *Colomba*, was based on a real-life vendetta that had taken place in the village of Fozzano in the early nineteenth century. Its heroine, a raven-haired, passionate beauty drawn into a vendetta after losing a son in an ambush, was a far cry from the vicious, remorseless gang leader whom the author met in her old age, by which time the brutal reality of Fozzano's feud had been well and truly romanticized.

The last fully fledged Corsican vendetta officially ended in the 1950s, but the expression *reglements de compte* (literally 'settling of scores') is still frequently used to account for violence on the island. Many commentators regard the protracted bloodshed of the past two decades, in which dozens of murders were perpetrated by opposing factions of armed nationalists and Mafia clans, as essentially a modern manifestation of Corsica's most ingrained problem.

trasting routes. The conventional one is an uncharacteristically monotonous plod at mostly contour level around the forested eastern base of the Monte Renoso massif; this is the path to follow if you want to notch up several étapes in one day.

Alternatively, reacquaint yourself with the extremes of the watershed via a more challenging ridge trek over the rocky, névé-encrusted summit of Monte Renoso itself. Following the line of the watershed, this was the route originally envisaged by Michel Fabrikant: it's wilder, tougher and altogether truer to the spirit of the GR20. It's also more vulnerable to sudden changes in weather and can get exceptionally windy. The pay-offs are some unforgettable views over the island's southern summits, from Rotondo to Alcudina, and the experience of descending into an exquisite suspended valley carpeted with lush green pozzines.

Route guide

E'Capannelle → Plateau de Gialgone via Monte Renoso: the high-level *Variante*   [Map 21, opposite]

Stage twelve's high-level *Variante* represents a return to the kind of uncompromising mountain terrain you'll be familiar with if you've walked all the way from Calenzana. Cutting straight up the sharp side of Monte Renoso from E'Capannelle, the route arcs around the dividing ridge of the massif before shelving steeply down to a hanging valley on its southern side, lined with spongy pozzines. From there it veers east to rejoin the GR20 at the Plateau de Gialgone.

The only demanding section is the sheer descent from the summit ridge to the pozzines, which involves a stark drop over rugged, broken rock and alder scrub. The rest is surprisingly straightforward, following a well-worn, well-cairned route across rough but largely open ground. The views are superlative throughout.

Don't, however, attempt the high-level route in unstable conditions unless you have the compass skills to navigate in poor visibility. Exposed to strong winds off the sea, Monte Renoso sees a lot of wild weather and frequently gets misted up. If this happens, it's all too easy to wander off course and into one of the cwms that indent the east flank of the massif.

Allow around seven hours to reach Bocca di Verdi (Col de Verde) via the *Variante*, and as ever with high, exposed sections get a very early start so as to avoid the convection clouds that form in warm weather.

Zigzagging between the pylons of E'Capannelle's old chair lifts, the path scales the bare, steep hillside directly opposite Gîte d'étape U Fugone, reaching the shoulder of the ridge at 1725m in just over half a kilometre. The cairns then lead you up the crest, with a rocky outcrop looming to the right, as far as a grassy depression where the route levels off briefly before tackling a more gradual, bouldery ascent. Shortly after crossing the 2000m contour line you round a rise and see **Lac de Bastiani** (2092m) for the first time, with the summit of Monte Renoso, which rises dramatically behind, reflected in its water.

The cairns skirt the north shore of the lake and begin a steeply ascending traverse of its rocky cwm to reach the ridge at roughly 2050m. From there a distinct path winds southwards across a huge, gently shelving crest strewn with boulders and broken rock, swinging gradually to the left as it approaches the summit.

From the top of **Monte Renoso** (2352m), a fine view extends north as far as Monte Cinto and south to Alcudina, with Monte d'Oro and Monte Rotondo dominating the mid-horizon. You can also see both the Golfe d'Ajaccio and the east coast on clear days.

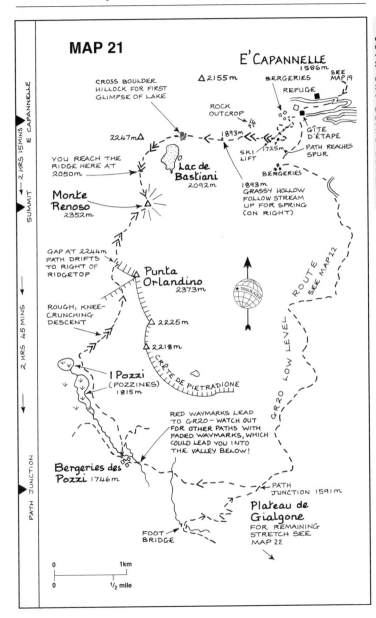

MAP 21

E'CAPANNELLE 1586m

SEE MAP 19

△2155m   BERGERIES
REFUGE

CROSS BOULDER HILLOCK FOR FIRST GLIMPSE OF LAKE

ROCK OUTCROP

GÎTE D'ÉTAPE

2247m△   1893m

SKI LIFT   1725m   PATH REACHES SPUR

YOU REACH THE RIDGE HERE AT 2050m

Lac de Bastiani 2092m

BERGERIES

Monke Renoso 2352m

1893m GRASSY HOLLOW FOLLOW STREAM UP FOR SPRING (ON RIGHT)

GAP AT 2244m PATH DRIFTS TO RIGHT OF RIDGETOP

Punta Orlandino 2373m

ROUTE SEE MAP 22

TRAILBLAZER

ROUGH, KNEE-CRUNCHING DESCENT

△ 2225m

△ 2218m

CRÊTE DE PIETRADIONE

GR20 LOW LEVEL ROUTE

I Pozzi (POZZINES) 1815m

RED WAYMARKS LEAD TO GR20 – WATCH OUT FOR OTHER PATHS WITH FADED WAYMARKS, WHICH COULD LEAD YOU INTO THE VALLEY BELOW!

Bergeries des Pozzi 1746m

PATH JUNCTION 1591m

Plateau de Gialgone FOR REMAINING STRETCH SEE MAP 22

FOOT BRIDGE

0   1km
0   ½ mile

E'CAPANNELLE – 2 HRS 15 MINS – SUMMIT – 2 HRS 45 MINS – PATH JUNCTION

The descent sticks close to the ridge for another kilometre until you reach a **gap at 2244m,** where the cairns swing right onto the more level dip slope of Punta Orlandino. Below you a *thalweg* (the line of steepest descent down a hillside) plunges due south down the line of the mountain to I Pozzi, a tangle of sinuous water channels and pools lining the base of a beautiful suspended valley. The ensuing drop of 250 metres or so, where the cairns lead you through a mess of alder, juniper scrub and rock, is the trickiest section of the day.

The springy turf of I Pozzi comes as a relief after the rough descent and you'll probably be tempted to kick back for half an hour with the pigs and cows who graze these pastures in the summer. Shortly after them you arrive at a **path junction** where you should ignore the waymarks heading left and those veering sharply back to the right, and continue instead straight on to the **Bergeries des Pozzi.** Once clear of the bergeries, the route, marked with red paint blobs, bends east and crosses two streams on its gentle descending traverse to the **Plateau de Gialgone,** where it intersects the GR20. See below for the remaining section to Bocca di Verdi.

E'Capannelle → Plateau de Gialgone: the low-level route
[Map 22, opposite]

The bulk of this étape is very much in the mould of the previous stretch from Bocca Palmenti, with a well-defined path that winds around a succession of shallow stream valleys and blunt spurs. It's well shaded throughout, and punctuated at regular intervals with water sources.

From E'Capannelle the red-and-white waymarks strike steeply up the mountainside initially, bearing left after the second ski-lift tower to cross a spur. Beyond the ridge you descend abruptly down a rugged path flanked by mature Laricio pines to the **Bergeries d'E Traghjete,** whose immaculately restored stone cottages nestle beneath the open crags of Renoso. The path continues to descend on the left side of a stream from the bergeries, emerging after 15 minutes or so at the **Pont d'E Casaccie** on the D169, which you follow briefly before the route peels away to the right of the road.

The ensuing 2^1/$_2$ hours comprise a long traverse that's interrupted by a succession of easy ascents and descents to and from stream level, most of it through fragrant stands of pine and beech. Having forded the Cannareccia and Lischetto, and rounded the Crête de Scopina, the traverse comes to an end at the **Plateau de Gialgone,** an expanse of gently shelving grassland where a signboard marks the route up to the pozzines and Monte Renoso. To the south-west you can trace the GR20 as it winds up the watershed and Bocca d'Oro, and then presses south along the ridgetops.

Plateau de Gialgone → Bocca di Verdi (Col de Verde)
[Map 22, opposite]

The high-level *Variante* rejoins the GR20 at Gialgone; shortly after this it begins a pronounced, zigzagging descent to the Marmano stream. At the **footbridge** the path swings sharply to the left (east). The giant spruce trees lining the route here are reputedly some of the most ancient in the Mediterranean;

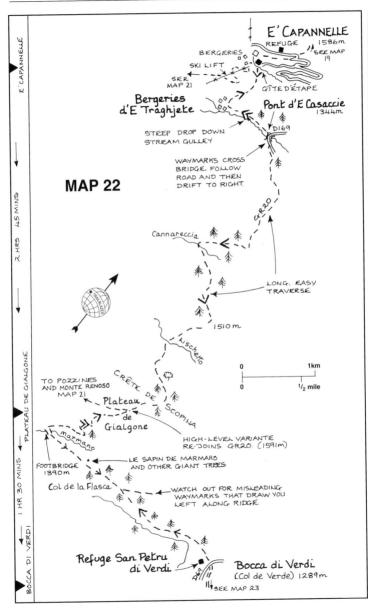

MAP 22

E' CAPANNELLE

REFUGE 1586m
SEE MAP 19
BERGERIES
SKI LIFT
SEE MAP 21
GÎTE D'ÉTAPE
Bergeries d'E Traghjete
Pont d'E Casaccie 1344m
D169
STEEP DROP DOWN STREAM GULLEY
WAYMARKS CROSS BRIDGE. FOLLOW ROAD AND THEN DRIFT TO RIGHT.

GR20

Cannareccia

LONG, EASY TRAVERSE

1510m

Kischeto

TRUE NORTH

0   1km
0   ½ mile

Crête de Scopina

TO POZZINES AND MONTE RENOSO MAP 21

Plateau de Gialgone

HIGH-LEVEL VARIANTE RE-JOINS GR20. (1591m)

marmano

LE SAPIN DE MARMARO AND OTHER GIANT TREES

FOOTBRIDGE 1390m

WATCH OUT FOR MISLEADING WAYMARKS THAT DRAW YOU LEFT ALONG RIDGE

Col de la Flasca

Refuge San Petru di Verdi

Bocca di Verdi (Col de Verde) 1289m

SEE MAP 23

E' CAPANNELLE   2 HRS 45 MINS   PLATEAU DE GIALGONE   1 HR 30 MINS   BOCCA DI VERDI some are about 500 years old. A rusty plaque pinned to one especially grand specimen distinguishes it as the tallest tree in Europe. Until 2.8m was chopped off its top by lightning a few years back, the **Sapin de Marmaro** measured a staggering 56m with a circumference of 6.3m.

After a gradual ascent to the **Col de la Flasca** the path starts to give ground, winding down to a stream which it follows by means of a piste. However, the route becomes repeatedly confused with other red-and-white waymarked paths (the most misleading of which takes you left from the Col de la Flasca along the line of the ridge to approach Bocca di Verdi from the north). Stay close to the stream, though, and you'll be led along a clear piste most of the way to the col.

Bocca di Verdi (Col de Verde)

Flanked by windy 2000m ridgetops and swaths of dense coniferous forest, Bocca di Verdi forms a low pass through the watershed mountain range between the Fium'Orbu and Taravo valleys.

From here the rivers flow in opposite directions, debouching into the sea on the east and west coasts respectively. Although hidden from view by only a single curtain of hills, the sea feels far off (you'll be seeing it again in the course of the next étape, once over the Bocca d'Oro).

For GR20 trekkers Bocca di Verdi is significant as the place where the route makes its penultimate descent to road level. On hand to help you make the most of your relative proximity to civilization is a well-kept bar-cum-refuge, the *Refuge San Petru di Verdi* (☎ 04.95.24.46.82; open late May to mid-Oct), whose shady garden terrace is a very pleasant spot to eat, drink and laze around on, contemplating the stiff hike ahead.

The convivial atmosphere makes this one of the most pleasant stops on the GR20. You can sleep in clean, wood-panelled dorms (11€ per bed). Campers are charged 5€ to pitch in the garden (bivouacking is free); rates include the use of a bathroom equipped with piping-hot, solar-heated showers (bivouackers pay 2€ for these). Half-board is decent value at 32€ per head; copious Corsican meals, based on produce from the Taravo Valley, are served on the terrace or in the cosy dining room. Note that it is possible to make **reservations** by telephone and that basic **provisions**, including quality charcuterie and ewe's cheese, are sold from the bar.

No public transport runs to Bocca di Verdi. The nearest village with a bus service is Cozzano (see pp178-9), 18km to the south. In July and August only you can arrange a **taxi** through the owner of the refuge.

STAGE THIRTEEN: BOCCA DI VERDI → REFUGE D'USCIOLU
[MAP 23, p174]

Overview

After an initial climb of 550m, stage thirteen of the GR20 settles into a long but highly varied ridge walk following the rocky spine of the watershed due south. To avoid the more problematic *puntas* and sheer rock outcrops that punctuate the crest, the waymarks regularly switch from one side to the other. The route thus affords constantly changing views of both the spectacular Taravo Valley to the west (right) and the east coast to your left.

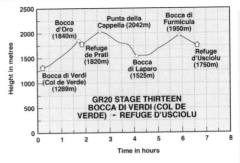

Don't, however, be lulled by the comparative lack of sustained ascents into thinking this is an easy day's walk. Some of the rockier passages are quite physical and the stage is long (16km), with a total of more than 2100m of altitude change. For this reason it isn't advisable to double up stage thirteen; lots of trekkers do walk to Usciolu from E'Capannelle in a day but they invariably regret it.

A refuge run by the PNRC provides shelter and supplies along the way. It's also virtually the only place on the étape where you can refill your water bottles. This stage, perhaps more than any other, underlines the fact that the GR20 is essentially a ridge walk along the island's parched *partage des eaux*.

Route guide

The stage kicks off with a climb through shady mixed beech and pine woodland. From Bocca di Verdi (Col de Verde) you cross the road and follow the forestry piste to the right as it traverses the hillside at a gentle angle and later swings east into a much steeper gradient, zigzagging up the line of a shallow stream valley. Once clear of the tree line, with impressive views of the Renoso massif opening up to the west, you pick your way around a valley head via a succession of seasonal streams. Later the waymarks cut more decisively uphill to crest a shoulder beyond which the GR20 begins its steep approach across a bouldery slope to the pass, visible to the right of a towering rock outcrop.

A rounded gap scattered with boulders and clumps of heavily grazed vegetation, the **Bocca d'Oro** (1840m), around 1½ hours from Bocca di Verdi, is marked with a large cairn and a PNRC signboard. Looking north-west you can see back along the route of the GR20, dominated by Monte d'Oro and Monte Renoso, while an equally amazing view of the eastern plain is revealed in front. Far to the north-east, Elba rises from the Tyrrhenian Sea and on a clear day you might be able to pick out the shadowy profile of the Tuscan coast.

Refuge de Prati

A leisurely 15-minute stroll down from the pass brings you to the superbly sited Refuge de Prati, from whose sunny deck you have a wonderful panoramic view over the island's coastal plain. After being damaged by lightning, the hut was entirely rebuilt by the PNRC in 2000 and it's now a well-set-up place with 22 beds. If you sleep inside you can use the kitchen, which has a good range of utensils and a large wooden dining table; bivouackers, however, have to make do with the gas hob in the shelter next to the main hut. People who are just passing through technically don't have the right to use any of these facilities.

ROUTE GUIDE AND MAPS

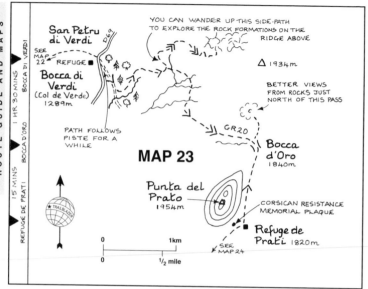

YOU CAN WANDER UP THIS SIDE-PATH TO EXPLORE THE ROCK FORMATIONS ON THE RIDGE ABOVE

San Petru di Verdi

SEE MAP 22

REFUGE ■

Bocca di Verdi
(Col de Verde)
1289m

△ 1934m

BETTER VIEWS FROM ROCKS JUST NORTH OF THIS PASS

PATH FOLLOWS PISTE FOR A WHILE

GR20

MAP 23

Bocca d'Oro
1840m

Punta del Prato
1954m

CORSICAN RESISTANCE MEMORIAL PLAQUE

Refuge de Prati 1820m

SEE MAP 24

0 ——— 1km
0 ——— 1/2 mile

TRAILBLAZER

SEE MAP 22 BOCCA DI VERDI 1 HR 30 MINS BOCCA DI VERDI BOCCA D'ORO 15 MINS REFUGE DE PRATI

A scenic spot this might be but it's not a great place to sleep outside as there's precious little cover, so peg in your tent well and expect a strong wind off the sea in the night. The spread of open ground along this stretch of the ridge made a perfect site for parachute drops to the Corsican Resistance in the WWII, as a nearby plaque recalls. British and American planes, guided in by fires lit by local shepherds, landed supplies of arms, ammunition and money that were hidden and later deployed to harass the German retreat along the east coast in September 1943.

Prati → Refuge d'Usciolu   [Map 24, opposite; Map 25, p177]
Following the waymarks south-west from the refuge, a short walk across closely cropped turf takes you back to the ridgeline, which you follow through a steepening ascent. At the 1788m mark the GR drifts left onto the rim of a small cirque where you might find patches of snow clinging to the shadier crevices. The peak above, **Punta della Cappella** (2042m), is bypassed by the route, which cuts across a shoulder on its east flank, but you can easily scramble up to the bouldery summit for a superb view of the Taravo Valley and the watershed tapering south. Apart from Monte Alcudina, crossed a couple of étapes further on, this is the final point above 2000 metres on the GR20 and a good place to get your bearings for the day ahead.

Dipping down the south-east side of the punta, the path rejoins the ridge at a small rocky depression known as the **Bocca di Campitello**. From there it

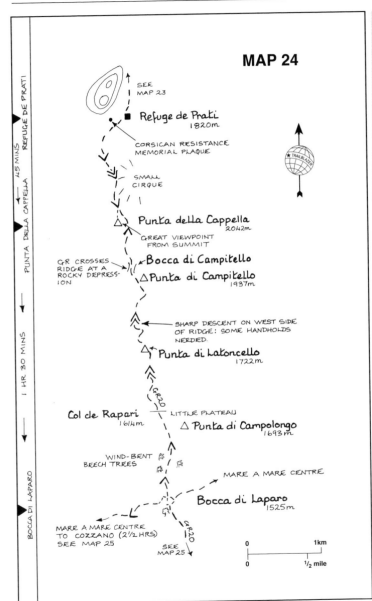

MAP 24

SEE MAP 23

■ Refuge de Prati 1820m

CORSICAN RESISTANCE MEMORIAL PLAQUE

SMALL CIRQUE

△ Punta della Cappella 2042m

GREAT VIEWPOINT FROM SUMMIT

GR CROSSES RIDGE AT A ROCKY DEPRESSION

✕ Bocca di Campitello

△ Punta di Campitello 1937m

SHARP DESCENT ON WEST SIDE OF RIDGE: SOME HANDHOLDS NEEDED.

△ Punta di Latoncello 1722m

GR20

Col de Rapari 1614m   LITTLE PLATEAU

△ Punta di Campolongo 1693m

WIND-BENT BEECH TREES

MARE A MARE CENTRE

Bocca di Laparo 1525m

GR20

MARE A MARE CENTRE TO COZZANO (2½ HRS) SEE MAP 25

SEE MAP 25

0   1km
0   ½ mile

REFUGE DE PRATI
PUNTA DELLA CAPPELLA   45 MINS
1 HR. 30 MINS
BOCCA DI LAPARO

skirts the side of another peak to begin a steep 200m descent over exposed granite, most of it on the west side of the crest. There are a few tricky passages along this stretch. At **Punta di Latoncello** the route briefly levels off then continues downhill through clumps of stunted beech trees on its approach, via the east side of the ridge, to **Col de Rapari** (1614m), a broad, open pass that looks directly down onto the village of Palneca on the floor of the Taravo Valley. From the col another steady traverse across the eastern flank of the mountain brings you to a saddle pass below **Punta di Campolongo**, where the GR switches to the west side of the ridge and falls sharply through a wood of ancient beech trees, wonderfully contorted by the wind.

At **Bocca di Laparo** (1525m), the lowest point of the étape, the GR20 intersects the Mare a Mare Centre, by means of which you can reach **Cozzano** in 2½ hours of easy downhill walking. For more on Cozzano and this liaison route see pp178-9. Once clear of Bocca di Laparo, the GR20 takes on a completely different aspect as it penetrates a gloomy beech wood lined with mossy boulders. A gradually ascending traverse through the forest, which avoids the craggy summit of Punta Mozza, comes to an abrupt end just under one kilometre beyond the refuge when the path cuts into the line of the hillside to begin a steep, zigzagging ascent. Pestered by clouds of flies, many trekkers find this leg along an old mule path the toughest of the day despite most of it being in shade by mid-morning.

Roughly halfway through the climb you get a short breathing space at a magical little hollow dotted with asphodel and wizened trees, after which the final steep stretch begins.

A series of endless switchbacks takes you rapidly back to the ridge at **Bocca Punta Mozza**, but the ascent continues in earnest after the col, only levelling off when it reaches a bare saddle just below the peak of **Punta Bianca**. The views from this point are wonderful, encompassing the Taravo Valley all the way up to Bocca di Verdi and beyond; it's a particularly atmospheric spot late in the day, with the sun setting over the ridge opposite.

The remaining ascent to the last pass of the étape is an easy amble over eroded, grazed ground. Fabrikant dubbed the **Bocca di Furmicula** (1950m) the 'Fog Pass' with good reason: the whole ridge section from here to the Plateau de Coscione is often shrouded in mist and cloud or else scoured by incredibly strong winds.

With the bouldery summit of Monte Furmicula on your right, you begin a steady traverse across the east flank of the mountain towards the head of a sheer gully, the ravin d'Acqua Acelli. Close to its edge the GR intersects another path, waymarked in orange, which runs left (east) in a tortuous descent to the village of Chisa. The red-and-white paint blobs, however, fall steeply downhill in the opposite direction towards the Refuge d'Usciolu, reached after a tumbling drop of nearly 200m across loose stone and messy rocks.

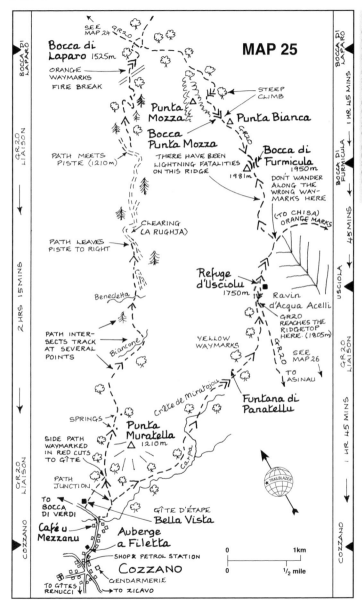

MAP 25

Bocca di Laparo 1525m
ORANGE WAYMARKS FIRE BREAK

SEE MAP 24

GR20

STEEP CLIMB

Punta Mozza

Punta Bianca

Bocca Punta Mozza

GR20

PATH MEETS PISTE (1210m)

THERE HAVE BEEN LIGHTNING FATALITIES ON THIS RIDGE

Bocca di Furmicula 1950m

DON'T WANDER ALONG THE WRONG WAYMARKS HERE

1981m

(TO CHISA) ORANGE MARKS

CLEARING (LA RUGHJA)

PATH LEAVES PISTE TO RIGHT

Refuge d'Usciolu 1750m

Ravin d'Acqua Acelli

Benedetta

GR20 REACHES THE RIDGETOP HERE (1805m)

PATH INTERSECTS TRACK AT SEVERAL POINTS

Biancone

YELLOW WAYMARKS

GR20

SEE MAP 26

TO ASINAU

Crête de Miratojou

Funtana di Panatellu

SPRINGS

Punta Muratella △ 1210m

SIDE PATH WAYMARKED IN RED CUTS TO GÎTE

Cara

PATH JUNCTION

TO BOCCA DI VERDI

GÎTE D'ÉTAPE
Bella Vista

Café u Mezzanu

Auberge a Filetta

SHOP & PETROL STATION

COZZANO

GENDARMERIE

TO GÎTES RENUCCI

TO ZICAVO

TRAILBLAZER

0   1km
0   ½ mile

BOCCA DI LAPARO

GR20 LIAISON

2 HRS 15 MINS

GR20 LIAISON

COZZANO

BOCCA DI LAPARO 1 HR 45 MINS

BOCCA DI FURMICULA 45 MINS

USCIOLA

GR20 LIAISON 1 HR 45 MINS

COZZANO

ROUTE GUIDE AND MAPS

Refuge d'Usciolu

Usciolu ranks among the PNRC's best-run refuges, thanks to the efforts of its long-time gardien (Frances Pantalacce), whose marathon mule treks to and from Cozzano each day ensure the hut is outstandingly well provisioned. Its shop stocks an amazing range of supplies (including fresh bread) at fair prices. You can even buy postcards and stamps here, franked with a special 'Refuge d'Usciolu GR20' postmark, which will be delivered to the post office down in the valley the next day. Copious mixed vegetable pasta stews are also served up each evening (8€ per portion); if you want one, order it in advance on arrival.

The only catch is the shortage of space. The hut, which has room for 32 people, is comfortable enough but the bivouac and camping area below it strain to accommodate the crowds in summer. Most tents end up pitched cheek-by-jowl on the grassy patches between rocks.

However, the welcoming personality of the gardien, who likes to serenade trekkers with stirring Corsican polyphonic music from his solar-powered hi-fi at dusk, is ample compensation, as are the superb views of Alcudina to the south. If you feel like stretching your legs before bedding down, a good incentive is the panorama from the ridge above the refuge, from where the sunsets over the Taravo Valley and distant Golfe d'Ajaccio are magnificent.

Liaison route: Bocca di Laparo → Cozzano   [Map 25, p177]

Trekkers sometimes use the Mare a Mare Centre, which cuts across the GR20 at Bocca di Laparo, to escape the high ridge if bad weather suddenly halts progress towards Usciolu. The pharmacy at Cozzano, on this liaison route, is also the region's most accessible source of medical supplies.

The route, clearly waymarked with blobs of orange paint, follows a gently descending traverse through a dense forest of mature pine and beech, crossing a succession of streams before it meets a *piste forestière* at 1210m. The waymarks follow this for nearly 2km until the track, bending sharply to the left around a spur, arrives at a large clearing known locally as **A Rughja** (1240m). Immediately after this, look out for the orange paint marks leading to the right, back into the forest. The long, gradual descent along a clear path continues from there, passing two perennial streams – the Benedetta and the Biancone – and two springs as it drops below the rocky peak of Punta Muratella. Ten minutes before Cozzano, in an old chestnut forest, you join the GR20's liaison path from Usciolu (see opposite). This takes you onto the D69 where you should turn left for the village or right for the gîte d'étape. The descent of around 800 metres shouldn't take more than 2¹/₂ hours in normal conditions.

Cozzano, clustered on a spur overlooking the Taravo River, is a pretty granite village that sees a good deal of trekking traffic thanks to its prominence as a staging point for the Mare a Mare Centre. Most people who pass through stay in *Gîte d'étape Bella Vista* (☎ 04.95.24.41.59; open April-Sep), on the north-east outskirts of the village. The gîte has 36 beds (10€ per person), a couple of double rooms (27€ for two people) and camping space (5€ per person, including use of the kitchen). They also offer evening meals (15€) and half-board for 29€ per person.

A more comfortable option, and the only other place to stay in Cozzano, is the bright and cheerful *Auberge A Filetta* (☎ 04.95.24.45.61, 🖳 www.pour-les-vacances.com/filetta), on your right as you enter the village. The hospitable owners, M and Mme Renucci, have six double rooms costing 45€ for two persons (plus 10€ for extra beds). They also do evening meals of quality local cuisine for only 18€ per head (80€ half-board for two people).

Cozzano's **pharmacy**, on the square, is open Monday to Saturday. You can buy groceries at the **shop** nearby (Mon-Sat plus Sunday mornings in summer). The village also boasts a year-round **bus** service (☎ 04.95.22.64.44 or 04.95.24.51.56, 🖳 www.autocars-santoni.com) to Ajaccio, which leaves at 6.50am (Mon-Sat) arriving one hour and forty minutes later.

Liaison route: Usciolu → Cozzano [Map 25, p177]
It's possible to reach the village of Cozzano in around 1¾ hours from Refuge d'Usciolu. To pick up the path follow the GR20 in the direction of Asinau to the ridgetop above the refuge, where a PNRC signboard indicates the liaison route; the first part comprises a steep, sustained descent through old beech forest. At the end of a long thin clearing the path passes the **Funtana di Panatellu** (on your right) and drops straight down a ridge called the Crête de Miratojou to cross a second clearing.

Shortly after this you twice ford the **Carpa stream**, which the route then follows at a gradually levelling gradient as far as its intersection with the Mare a Mare Centre, arriving from the north-east. When you reach the road turn left for the village or right for the gîte. For more details of accommodation and services available in Cozzano see opposite.

STAGE FOURTEEN: REFUGE D'USCIOLU → REFUGE D'ASINAU
[MAP 26, p181; MAP 29, p187]
Overview
Stage fourteen comprises three wildly contrasting sections. The first, a sustained ridge trek along the famous Arête a Monda, takes you through a jumble of wind-eroded outcrops that are fully exposed to the vagaries of the Corsican weather: if you get caught in cloud or by a storm anywhere on the GR20 it'll probably be here. Once off the ridge, however, you cross much less harsh, undulating moorland, the Plateau de Coscione, which is grazed by cows and sheep in the summer. The third part is the traverse of Monte Alcudina (2134m; Monte Incudine in French), the last of the 2000m+ peaks along the route, which involves what might be your final protracted ascent of the walk. The climb takes you to the surreal, bouldery world of the mountain's domed summit, a superb vantage point marked by a crucifix, from where southern Corsica's rolling maquis and oak woods are revealed for the first time.

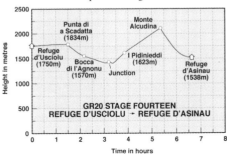

A long étape requiring a total of 1900m of altitude change, stage fourteen is usually more than enough of a day's work for most trekkers. However, with an early start and short rest breaks it is possible to double up and reach Bavella by nightfall, especially if you take the shorter *Variante Alpine* over the needles (see p190). For once, water isn't a problem – at least once you're clear of the ridge section. There are two perennial springs on the route: one on the north edge of Coscione and the other at the foot of Alcudina, perfectly placed for a top-up ahead of the climb.

Before the era when most refuges stocked supplies, many trekkers would quit the GR20 during this stage for a re-provisioning detour to Zicavo, two hours' walk down a side valley. Comparatively few do so these days but the path, which peels away from the main route at the end of the ridge traverse, provides a quick way to one of the region's larger mountain settlements, where you can enjoy the comforts of Corsican village life before getting stuck into the ascent of Alcudina.

Route guide
Usciolu to Plateau de Coscione   [Map 26, opposite]
The stage begins with a short but gritty climb to the ridgetop followed by the first of the day's real challenges: the traverse of the **Arête a Monda** (also called the 'Arête des Statues' after the spooky rock formations punctuating it). The giant, ribbon-thin outcrop lining the ridge, a mass of smooth-backed boulders, steeply angled slabs and pinnacles sculpted into weird shapes by the wind, would be a formidable obstacle were it not for some clever waymarking. The path traced by the paint blobs along the arête, which snake continually from one side of the ridge to the other by means of open rock, narrow gullies and gangways, is a vivid testimony to the ingenuity of the GR20's originators.

The end of the ridge section comes quite abruptly. Having rounded the arête's highest point, **Punta di a Scadatta** (1834m), the waymarks squeeze through a distinctively shaped gap (known as **Brêche di a Petra di Leva**) to the east side of the ridge, and from there drop sharply downhill, passing through the treeline into a depression lined by twisted old beech trees. At the point where the path more or less levels off, a sign points out the site (to your right) of a welcome **spring** where you can refill your bottle for the crossing of Coscione. Another sharp drop through the trees brings you to a second, much larger wooded hollow, called the **Bocca di l'Agnonu**, where a prominent PNRC signboard marks the start of the **liaison route to Zicavo**, heading down the valley to the right.

The main route, meanwhile, veers left over a rise covered in more fairy-tale beech forest. By the time you've crossed it you're technically in the Coscione basin proper, but the defining feel of the plateau doesn't become apparent until you emerge from the trees, from where the grassland rolls south to the foot of Monte Alcudina, interrupted by pozzines and winding brooks.

The enjoyable plod across the heart of the **Plateau de Coscione** (see box p182), in the course of which you cross a succession of shallow streams and grassy gullies, takes around one hour. You'll know you're nearing the edge of it when you arrive at a second PNRC signboard for Zicavo; where the liaison route (see p183) rejoins the GR20.

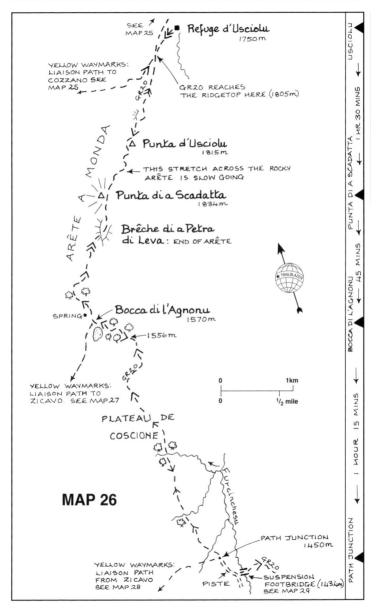

SEE MAP 25

■ Refuge d'Usciolu
1750m

YELLOW WAYMARKS:
LIAISON PATH TO
COZZANO SEE
MAP 25

GR20 REACHES
THE RIDGETOP HERE (1805m)

△ Punta d'Usciolu
1815m

← THIS STRETCH ACROSS THE ROCKY
ARÊTE IS SLOW GOING

△ Punta di a Scadatta
1834m

Brêche di a Petra
di Leva : END OF ARÊTE

ARÊTE A MONDA

SPRING ●

Bocca di l'Agnonu
1570m

←1556m

★ TRAILBLAZER

YELLOW WAYMARKS:
LIAISON PATH TO
ZICAVO. SEE MAP 27

GR20

0   1km
0   ½ mile

PLATEAU DE
COSCIONE

MAP 26

Furcinchesu

PATH JUNCTION
1450m

YELLOW WAYMARKS:
LIAISON PATH
FROM ZICAVO
SEE MAP 28

PISTE

GR20

SUSPENSION
FOOTBRIDGE (1434m)
SEE MAP 29

ROUTE GUIDE AND MAPS

USCIOLU
↓
1 HR 30 MINS
↓
PUNTA DI A SCADATTA
↓
45 MINS
↓
BOCCA DI L'AGNONU
↓
1 HOUR 15 MINS
↓
PATH JUNCTION

Plateau de Coscione

The Plateau de Coscione, which the GR20 traverses between Bocca di l'Agnonu and Monte Alcudina, provides a rare grassy interlude along this relentlessly rocky route. For northern European walkers, trekking over its rolling moorland, riddled by hundreds of small streams, will feel an oddly familiar experience, especially when the mist and drizzle is down and the typically Corsican summits and ridges that surround it are shrouded in cloud.

Known locally as 'U Pianu' ('the table'), the lush depression hidden at the heart of the island was the linchpin of the local economy for many centuries. During the summer months, 600 to 700 shepherds used to live up here, tending their flocks and herds of cattle as they fed on the lush pasture. Nowadays, however, only a handful of working bergeries remain inhabited. The decline of transhumance in the region at the beginning of the twentieth century (see box p138) became terminal after WWII, when a large timber company moved in to harvest the beech in order to replace railway sleepers damaged by the fighting on the continent. When it pulled out, hundreds of men found themselves without work and were forced to emigrate, having allowed their ancestral flocks to dwindle.

The few shepherds that still work Coscione tend to do so using pick-up trucks, travelling up here once or twice a week from the villages of the Taravo Valley to check on their animals. EU subsidies rather than sales of brocciu account for the bulk of their income but you can still buy top-quality cheese made in the traditional way (with milk from the plateau) at the bergeries along the liaison path to Zicavo (see below).

Apart from mid-summer when Coscione is crossed by an unending stream of GR20 trekkers, the only time of year when the plateau sees visitors is after heavy snow when it becomes a paradise for cross-country skiers.

Liaison route: Bocca di l'Agnonu → Zicavo [Map 27, p184]

One of the more worthwhile forays off the GR20 begins at Bocca di l'Agnonu, from where an easy, well-shaded path winds down the mountainside to Zicavo. If you're not in a hurry this detour warrants consideration not only because it provides an opportunity to visit a very pretty, unspoilt Corsican village (of which there are few within easy reach of the route) but also for the chance to trek across the most scenic corner of the Plateau de Coscione on your return via the second liaison path.

At Boccia di l'Agnonu a PNRC sign points the way to the right off the GR down the Padulelli Valley; the route is waymarked with **yellow** paint flashes. After half an hour following these through beech woods you emerge at a clearing where the route swings north-west and crosses a stream flowing off Monte Ucchjatu, whose crags rise to the north. Running alongside an old dry-stone wall for a while, the path then penetrates oak forest and, shortly after intersecting a waymarked path from Cozzano, a large wood of chestnut trees. Allow two hours to cover this stretch from Bocca di l'Agnonu, which brings you out at the north side of the village.

Zicavo With over 300 permanent residents, Zicavo, *chef-lieu* of the upper Taravo Valley, remains one of the few populous villages in this remote corner of the island. The source of its relative prosperity are the legions of semi-wild pigs you'll doubtless have encountered on the way down here. They fatten on windfall chestnuts in the surrounding forest in the autumn and are then slaughtered in prodigious numbers during December. The result is outstanding charcuterie, and aficionados shouldn't miss the opportunity to sample the local figatellu.

The Zicavais long-standing association with the bloody art of sausage-making may in part account for the other phenomenon for which the village is renowned. On foggy nights it is said that female **vampires**, or *streghe*, swoop down in search of infants' blood. Another word for them is *gramantis*, which probably derives from the name of a much-feared Saracen pirate, d'Agramante, who terrorized the region in the fourteenth century from his base on the coast. Lone trekkers should also beware of the Zicavais zombies – *i acciaciatori* – who are said to crush the skulls of solitary travellers.

If you can forget its tongue-twisting occult associations, Zicavo is a great place to relax and recover from the travails of life on the GR. Among its picturesque huddle of old granite houses (many of them over 500 years old) are a handful of pleasant **places to stay**. The cheapest and most welcoming is the *Gîte d'étape Le Paradis* (☎ 04.95.24.41.20; open May-Oct, and out of season with advance booking), just north of where the yellow GR20-liaison waymarks hit the D69. Taking its name from the cemetery next door (home of the aforementioned acciaciatori, one imagines), the gîte is impeccably managed by its friendly patronne, Mme Pirany, who uses home-grown produce to create sumptuous Mediterranean cuisine for guests in the evening. Her breakfasts are equally copious, comprising some 10 different kinds of jam and bread fresh from the bakery. Double rooms cost from 35€ to 40€, depending on the level of comfort, and there are beds in four-person dorms (11€). Book in advance if you can as the gîte is very popular with trekkers.

Next door to Le Paradis, *Hôtel Le Florida* (☎ 04.95.23.49.40; open all year) is another inviting option with en suite single/double rooms for 45/50€. Otherwise there's the homely *Hôtel-Restaurant du Tourisme* (☎ 04.95 24.40.06), a short way below the chapel San Roccu, where doubles with shower and toilet are good value at 40€. Next door, the *Prestige Club* is a cheap and cheerful pizzeria where you can eat al fresco with views over the valley for under 8€. Zicavo's **shop**, which stocks a good range of trekker-friendly food (including delicious, locally made chestnut-flour biscuits), stands at the south side of the village on the Ajaccio road.

For anyone wishing to leave the GR20 at this point, an Autocars Santoni **bus** (☎ 04.95.22.64.44 or 04.95.24.51.56, 🖳 www.autocars-santoni.com) departs for Ajaccio each morning except Sunday.

Returning to the GR20 [Map 28, p185]

The only drawback with dipping down to Zicavo is that you have to slog all the way back up to Coscione afterwards. Rather than retrace your steps to Bocca di l'Agnonu, however, it is possible to follow another liaison path that arcs south from the village to rejoin the GR20 at the foot of Monte Alcudina – a hike of around 3¹/₂ hours.

The first stretch of the path is, it has to be said, an extremely dull plod by the standards of the GR20. You'd do well to avoid it by hitching a lift up the mountain with one of the owners of the bergerie who make the journey by jeep most days during the summer: ask at the village shop or phone ☎ 04.95 25.74.20. If you don't manage to arrange a ride you'll have to follow the D69 south towards Aullène/Ajaccio, past the shop and on for another 1.5km until you reach a PNRC signboard on the left side of the road.

(continued on p186)

ROUTE GUIDE AND MAPS

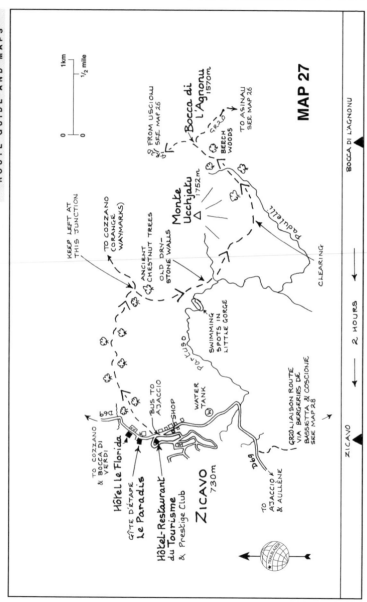

MAP 27

1km
½ mile
0
0

Bocca di L'Agnonu
1570m

FROM USCIOLU
SEE MAP 26

TO ASINAU
SEE MAP 26

BEECH WOODS

Monte Ucchjatu
△ 1752m

Paduledu

CLEARING

KEEP LEFT AT THIS JUNCTION

TO COZZANO (ORANGE WAYMARKS)

ANCIENT CHESTNUT TREES

OLD DRY-STONE WALLS

SWIMMING SPOTS IN LITTLE GORGE

Pè d'Usso

BUS TO AJACCIO

SHOP

WATER TANK

GR20 LIAISON ROUTE VIA BERGERIES DE BASSETTA & COSCIONE SEE MAP 28

TO COZZANO & BOCCA DI VERDI

D69

GITE D'ÉTAPE le Paradis

Hôtel le Florida

Hôtel-Restaurant du Tourisme & Prestige Club

ZICAVO 730m

TO AJACCIO & AULLÈNE

D69

ZICAVO   2 HOURS   BOCCA DI LAGNONU

TRAILBLAZER

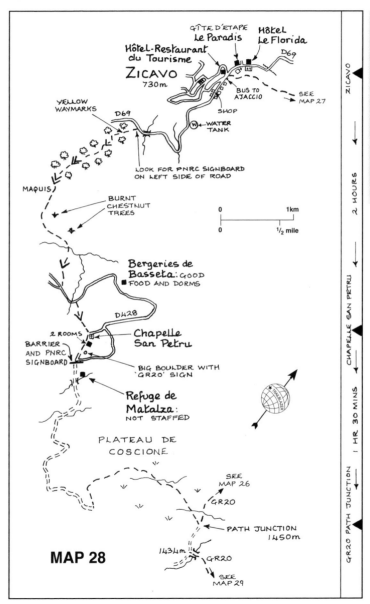

GÎTE D'ÉTAPE
Le Paradis

Hôtel
Le Florida

Hôtel-Restaurant
du Tourisme

ZICAVO
730m

D69

BUS TO
AJACCIO

SEE
MAP 27

YELLOW
WAYMARKS

D69

SHOP

WATER
TANK

LOOK FOR PNRC SIGNBOARD
ON LEFT SIDE OF ROAD

MAQUIS

BURNT
CHESTNUT
TREES

0   1km

0   ½ mile

Bergeries de
Basseta: GOOD
FOOD AND DORMS

D428

2 ROOMS

Chapelle
San Petru

BARRIER
AND PNRC
SIGNBOARD

BIG BOULDER WITH
'GR20' SIGN

Refuge de
Matalza:
NOT STAFFED

PLATEAU DE
COSCIONE

SEE
MAP 26

GR20

PATH JUNCTION
1450m

1434m

GR20

SEE
MAP 29

MAP 28

ROUTE GUIDE AND MAPS

ZICAVO

2 HOURS

CHAPELLE SAN PETRU

1 HR. 30 MINS

GR20 PATH JUNCTION

(continued from p183) **Yellow waymarks** lead into the forest, striking steeply uphill through the woods and later swinging over open, flatter ground around the foot of Punta di l'Erta.

Shortly after crossing a stream, you arrive at the D428 which has zig-zagged up here from its junction with the D69 14km below. Where it bends to the left the waymarks head straight on up the line of a stream but if you're feeling peckish, follow the road instead to the **Bergeries de Basseta** (☎ 04.95 25.74.20), which serves top-notch Corsican-speciality meals of Zicavais charcuterie and Coscione cheese (count on 18€ for three courses). They also offer simpler *plats du jour* such as mint-and-brocciu omelettes or bowls of filling pork stew flavoured with herbes du maquis for around 9€. Set in an idyllic spot on the edge of the Coscione plateau, the converted bergerie makes a great place to stay the night: a bed in one of the impeccably maintained dorms costs 30-35€ per head for half-board.

From Basseta the quickest way back to the path is to retrace your steps to the bend in the D428 and from there continue south-west along the yellow waymarks to the **Chapelle San Petru**. This tiny church is said to have been built in fulfilment of a vow by three brothers from Sartène who were locked in a bloody vendetta with a rival family.

While hiding out in the woods above Zicavo, Saint Peter appeared to them in a dream to tell them their pursuers were approaching. Thus warned, they escaped and ultimately survived the feud, which was resolved some years later. Saint Peter, however, made a second nocturnal appearance to demand that the brothers, by way of thanks for his having saved their skins, erect a chapel at a spot on the Plateau de Coscione where an 'iron stake sprouted from a boulder'. After its legendary foundation in the sixteenth century, the Chapelle San Petru became the patron shrine of the region's shepherds, who traditionally gather here for a festival on 1st August each year. Two simple rooms provide basic *shelter*.

Pressing on south-west up a stony slope, you soon pass a large boulder pointing the way to the GR20. Beyond this a PNRC signboard and vehicle barrier herald your arrival at the unstaffed **Refuge de Matalza** which has two dingy rooms but no water source. From this point you're on the Plateau de Coscione proper as the path crosses a succession of streams and hollows drained by beautiful little pozzines. Cairns and intermittent yellow paint flashes reassure you that you're on the correct track which, around $1^{1}/_{2}$ hours after the Chapelle San Petru, intersects the GR20, as indicated by a prominent PNRC sign. The route onwards to Asinau is described below.

Plateau di Coscione to Refuge d'Asinau   [Map 29, opposite]

Ten minutes further along the trail, after following a piste for a short way, the waymarks drop down to the Furcinchesu stream, crossed by means of a suspension **footbridge**. From the far bank they zigzag quite steeply uphill through the woods, emerging 20 to 30 minutes later at a denuded hollow known as **I Pidinieddi** (1623m), site of a long-disused refuge. Bivouacking and camping are allowed but in practice few trekkers spend the night here unless bad weather blocks the route over Alcudina.

Another five minutes or so uphill from the ruined refuge, a **spring** sheltered by a coppice of trees is your last dependable water source before Asinau. Beyond it the GR20 presses on across more denuded hillside to a sharp ridge,

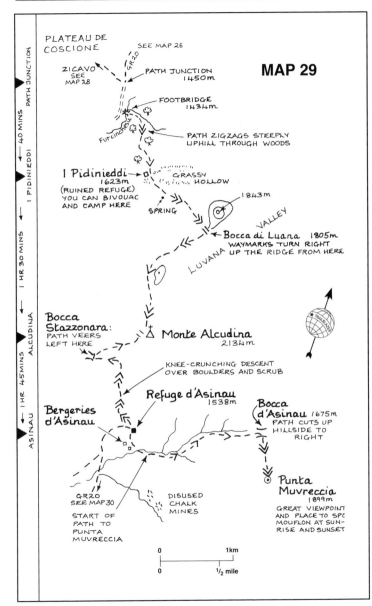

MAP 29

PLATEAU DE COSCIONE

SEE MAP 28

GR 20

ZICAVO SEE MAP 28

PATH JUNCTION 1450m

FOOTBRIDGE 1434m

PATH ZIGZAGS STEEPLY UPHILL THROUGH WOODS

Furcione

I Pidinieddi 1623m (RUINED REFUGE) YOU CAN BIVOUAC AND CAMP HERE

GRASSY HOLLOW

SPRING

1843m

VALLEY

Bocca di Luana 1805m WAYMARKS TURN RIGHT UP THE RIDGE FROM HERE

LUVANA

Bocca Stazzonara: PATH VEERS LEFT HERE

Monte Alcudina 2134m

KNEE-CRUNCHING DESCENT OVER BOULDERS AND SCRUB

Refuge d'Asinau 1538m

Bocca d'Asinau 1675m PATH CUTS UP HILLSIDE TO RIGHT

Bergeries d'Asinau

DISUSED CHALK MINES

Punta Muvreccia 1899m

GREAT VIEWPOINT AND PLACE TO SPOT MOUFLON AT SUNRISE AND SUNSET

GR20 SEE MAP 30

START OF PATH TO PUNTA MUVRECCIA

0   1km
0   1/2 mile

PATH JUNCTION

40 MINS

I PIDINIEDDI

1 HR 30 MINS

ALCUDINA

1 HR 45 MINS

ASINAU

reached at a point known as the **Bocca di Luana**, where the waymarks switch southwards to tackle the crux of the climb. This comprises a long, steady ascent up a stony path, with an occasional easy clamber over outcrops. Above you, Alcudina's twin forepeaks bring the wild head of the Luvana Valley to an abrupt, dramatic end.

The final haul to the top starts after the path drifts temporarily to the right of the ridgeline and then back towards it again. Crowned with a large crucifix, the summit of **Monte Alcudina**, reached around $1^1/2$ hours after leaving the I Pidinieddi, rises from the middle of a smooth granite dome, surrounded by a mass of gently tilting slabs. In good weather it provides one of Corsica's most extraordinary viewpoints. To the south-east the spectacular Aiguilles de Bavella, seen here for the first time, dominate the landscape, while beyond them you might be able to make out the east coast running down to the Golfe de Porto-Vecchio, and in the opposite direction, the Golfe de Valinco on the island's west side. Between them the dark oak woods and ridges of the Alta Rocca region ripple away towards Sardinia, obscured by the massif of Uomo di Cagni.

Explore the fringes of the summit area and you might be lucky enough to spot a herd of mouflon scouring the rocky slopes for vegetation. This is also a good spot for sighting lammergeier vultures (see box p136) and golden eagles, who exploit the hot thermals rising from the granite slabs lining the mountain.

The descent starts with a gentle drop through rocky outcrops along the ridge running south-west from the summit. At a niche known as **Bocca Stazzonara** (2025m) it cuts sharply back to traverse Alcudina's southern flank, a mass of sharp-edged boulders and scrub. Seeming to lose interest in their leisurely course, the waymarks then plunge straight down the line of the mountain – an exceptionally abrupt descent (the steepest part of the GR20's southern section). In dry conditions you should reach Asinau between 60 and 75 minutes after leaving the summit.

Refuge d'Asinau

Asinau clings to the hem of Alcudina's southern skirts, at the head of a wonderfully wild valley. Enfolded by ridges, it's the last of the GR20's refuges situated amid high-mountain terrain. Once again, bivouackers and campers will find little flat ground to pitch on at the height of the season, an inconvenience that prompts many trekkers to press on towards Bavella. Nevertheless the hut, with bunks for 30 people and a large kitchen area, makes a good base from which to savour the atmosphere of the watershed. From the wooden deck, which looks south down the valley towards the majestic Aiguilles de Bavella, you may glimpse a mouflon (see opposite) or two grazing on the ridgetops opposite. The refuge facilities are adequate, but a much more convivial atmosphere prevails at **Bergeries d'Asinau** (☎ 06.17.53.98.92), ten minutes' walk below it. This is a working sheepfold, complete with pens of bleating ewes and lambs, but the affable patronne finds time to whip up fine Corsican mountain cooking. You can also sleep here in rustic wooden bunks: half board costs 33€, full board 40€.

Mouflon-spotting walk from Asinau [Map 29, p187]

Refuge d'Asinau stands less than an hour's walk from one of Corsica's top mouflon-spotting locations. If you haven't yet seen one of the island's rare mountain sheep (see box p128) consider slotting in the following walk as it takes you to a viewpoint from where you get an unrivalled (and rarely seen) vista of the Alcudina massif and Bavella crags.

Rather than following the red-and-white waymarks to the right (west) of the hut, drop straight down the line of the mountain to **Bergeries d'Asinau**. From there, a cairned path drifts left to cross the stream at the base of the valley and then winds along its true left (south-east) bank towards the **Bocca d'Asinau** (1675m), which you should reach in around half an hour from the bergeries. Once at the col, turn 90° to your right and keep to the ridgeline as it climbs more steeply south-east across denuded ground to the **Punta Muvreccia** (1899m), a superb vantage point overlooking the mass of cliffs and crags on the north rim of the Fiumicelli Valley. Below you can trace the line of the D268 – which many claim to be Corsica's most scenic road – as it winds from Bavella down to the east coast.

The far (south-east) side of the ridge running from the Punta Muvreccia is where you're almost certain to sight mouflon if you reach it early enough on a summer's morning. The crête runs along the top of a row of spectacularly rugged little cirques, sliced by narrow stream ravines by means of which the animals ascend to these high pastures. It's best to start the hike from the refuge at first light, not only because dawn and dusk are the most promising times for wildlife watching but because in good weather you'll be able to catch the extraordinary spectacle of the sun's first rays illuminating the rocky summit of Alcudina.

STAGE FIFTEEN: ASINAU → BAVELLA → PALIRI
[MAP 30, p191; MAP 31, p195]

Overview

Whether you trek around their base or scramble over the top of them on the *Variante Alpine*, the Herculean pinnacles of the Aiguilles de Bavella, which soar from an undulating sea of maquis, form the defining feature of Stage Fifteen and are the GR20's last major cadence before Conca. Once past them the watershed disintegrates into a chaos of bizarrely eroded orange cliffs. The GR, however, is far from over, especially for those who opt to reach the Col de Bavella the hard way, by clambering over the crags of the Aiguilles. Some imposing landscape stands between you and a late breakfast at the pass. That said, the *Variante Alpine* is a far less intimidating proposition than it might look from Asinau. There's a fair

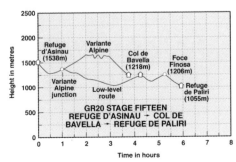

bit of scrambling over steep rock to contend with but in dry conditions the high-level route poses no obstacles that anyone who's made it this far should shy away from. Apart from the stupendous views and intense feeling of wilderness you get from the needles, a further incentive to take the *Variante* is that the low-level route is basically a monotonous yomp with little to recommend it unless you're mad for pine forest. Winding around the base of the Aiguilles in a huge semi-circle, it's also a much longer route to the col.

However you get there, the seasonally inhabited village that spills from the far side of the pass comes as a bit of a shock if you've not seen a café since Bocca di Verdi. A popular target for bus tours and car trippers, it is usually swarming by mid-morning, although compensation comes in the form of fresh croissants and real coffee at the sunny roadside terraces, and you can pen a few last-minute postcards while bracing yourself for the final leg.

Route guide
Asinau → Variante Alpine Junction   [Map 30, opposite]
It's hard to be enthusiastic about this stretch, which seems to drag on far longer than it should, but it does offer some pleasantly level walking through what, if you hadn't just spent a week or two high on the Corsican watershed, would be an impressive valley. The forest covering much of the route offers plenty of shade and water sources but the last half of the étape, where the well-worn path winds through maquis carpeting the south-west base of the Aiguilles, is exposed to the full glare of the afternoon sun and should thus be avoided during hot weather.

After a level stretch across boulders and scrub from Refuge d'Asinau, the red-and-white waymarks turn at a gradually steepening gradient down the line of the hillside to a **path junction**, where a liaison route peels off the GR20 to the village of Quenza. Shortly below this point you cross the Asinau and begin a steady climb up the opposite flank of the valley through shady silver-birch woods. At the **1382m mark** (only 70m higher than the river crossing) the path, having traversed up a series of stream thalwegs, hits a level that it sticks to for most of the remaining route to the mouth of the valley.

The first major landmark beyond the river, after around 45 minutes, is the point where the *Variante Alpine* turns left off the main path, as indicated by a PNRC signboard.

Variante Junction → Bavella: the low-level route [Map 30, opposite]
Once past the junction, the route emerges from the birch trees to cross a broad band of deforested hillside, rising and falling slightly as it winds in and out of shallow side valleys.

The definitive change of direction comes after a long, very gradual descent, at the end of which the GR20 crosses the **Crête di Pargulu**, the spine of the Bavella ridge, to reach a small maquis-covered plateau known as the **Pianu di a Pulvara** (1046m). Look out for the **spring** to the left of the path here. Beyond it the maquis, dotted with the odd maritime pine, closes in as the waymarks swing north-east to enter the Caracutu ravine. From there they turn south-east and zigzag steeply uphill for 50 metres or so to a new contour level.

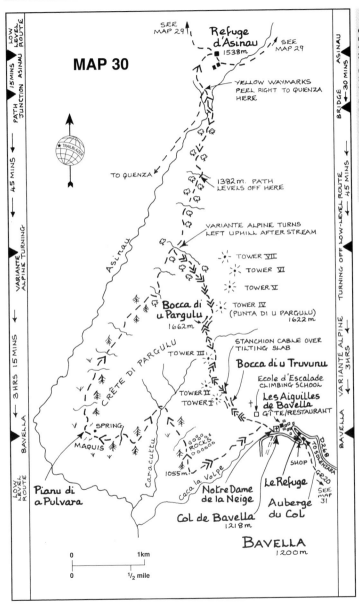

MAP 30

SEE MAP 29

Refuge d'Asinau 1538m

SEE MAP 29

YELLOW WAYMARKS PEEL RIGHT TO QUENZA HERE

TO QUENZA

1382m. PATH LEVELS OFF HERE

Asinau

VARIANTE ALPINE TURNS LEFT UPHILL AFTER STREAM

TOWER VII
TOWER VI
TOWER V

Bocca di u Pargulu 1662m

TOWER IV (PUNTA DI U PARGULU) 1622m

CRÊTE DI PARGULU

TOWER III

STANCHION CABLE OVER TILTING SLAB

Bocca di u Truvunu

Ecole d'Escalade CLIMBING SCHOOL

Les Aiguilles de Bavella
GÎTE/RESTAURANT

TOWER II
TOWER I

SPRING

MAQUIS

Capacutellu

GORGO ROCKS

1055m

Caca la Volpe

SHOP

Pianu di a Pulvara

Notre Dame de la Neige

Le Refuge

D268 TO SOLENZARA

GR20 SEE MAP 31

Col de Bavella 1218m

Auberge du Col

BAVELLA 1200m

TRAILBLAZER

LOW LEVEL ROUTE

PATH /15MINS JUNCTION ASINAU

45 MINS

VARIANTE ALPINE TURNING

3 HRS 15 MINS

BAVELLA

LOW LEVEL ROUTE

BRIDGE ASINAU /30 MINS

TURNING OFF LOW-LEVEL ROUTE /45 MINS

VARIANTE ALPINE 3 HRS

BAVELLA

0   1km
0   ½ mile

With the cliffs of the Aiguilles towering above, you then enter a much rockier landscape where the path begins its approach to the col along the side of the Ceca la Volpe stream valley. This is one stretch where you should keep an eye on the waymarks; lose your concentration and you could find yourself following one of the many sheep trails that run down to stream level.

The final ascent over rock and scrub takes you up just under 200m. Towards its end, the *Variante Alpine* rejoins the main route at a small forested plateau from where you can see the statue of Notre Dame de la Neige through the trees.

Variante Junction → Bavella: the high-level *Variante Alpine*
[Map 30, p191]

The final yellow-waymarked portion of the GR20, dubbed the *Variante Alpine*, marks a radical shift in tone after the restrained scenery of Coscione and the Asinau Valley. Don't be put off by its nickname. Some of the gradients (notably the initial approach section) are undeniably strenuous and the terrain as harsh as any on the GR but none of the passages is any more technical or vertigo-inducing than those of the first three days. Threading around the base of the immense Bavella needles, this portion offers the last real thrills of the walk, and some dramatic views. The only reason you'd regret choosing it is if the weather took a nasty turn; some of the steep, exposed rock around the *aiguilles* can get very slippery when wet.

The *Variante*, clearly marked with conspicuous yellow flashes, begins 45 minutes into the étape, zigzagging steeply to the left of the main path through a long ribbon of silver birch. The gradient eases up once you're clear of the trees as the route drifts to the right (south) into a long traverse across boulders and juniper scrub below towers VII, VI and V of the Aiguilles.

Having skirted the base of tower IV (Punta di u Pargulu) you reach the precise line of the watershed at a spectacular pass called **Bocca di u Pargulu** (1662m). From there the yellow flashes descend steadily to the south, past the east side of towers III and II. An especially steep stretch over an awkwardly tilting slab, negotiated with the help of a 10m **chain** secured to posts, is followed by a short, stepped descent and then an easier passage up a pine-covered boulder slope to a second pass, **Bocca di u Truvunu**, below tower I. From there a sustained, rocky scramble down a sheer-walled gully takes you back to the tree-line at the Col de Bavella.

BAVELLA   [MAP 30, p191]

With its parking lot full of hire cars, camper vans and luxury coaches, Bavella can come as a disappointment after the trek from Asinau. The bulk of the day-tripper traffic congregates at the **col**, where a large white statue of **Notre Dame de la Neige** looks benignly down on the main road from her boulder pedestal, scattered with miniature effigies of tin limbs and red plastic candle offerings.

Bavella itself lies 300m beyond the rise. The settlement, a scattering of corrugated-iron and felt-roofed huts that nestle in the shade of huge Laricio pines, has served as an escape from the summer heat for the

---

(Opposite) Top: Notre Dame de la Neige (Our Lady of the Snow), Col de Bavella.
Bottom: Morilles – tastiest mushrooms in the Corsican forests. (Photos © David Abram).

villagers of Conca since the land was gifted to the commune by Napoléon III in the nineteenth century. Deserted for six months of the year because of its position at the head of the D268, it sees an overwhelming amount of through traffic in the summer months to Solenzara on the east coast; tourist literature loves to call this 'Corsica's most beautiful road', an accolade it thoroughly deserves. Flanked by spectacular cliffs and rock formations, the entire area is a paradise for climbers.

Where to stay and eat

Among GR20 trekkers not desperate to get onto the rock, opinion is divided over whether Bavella warrants a stopover, but most people take the opportunity to buy provisions for the last leg to Conca. A single **shop**, on the left just past the bend in the road, sells top-grade charcuterie, cheese and other edible supplies (at inflated tourist prices) but little else. The boulanger's van from nearby Zonza doesn't make it this far but you might be able to rustle up a baguette at the friendly *Les Aiguilles de Bavella* (☎ 04.95.72.01.88), next to the car park. Although the café gets swamped with tour groups around lunch time, behind it there's a pleasant 24-bunk **gîte d'étape** (15€ per dorm bed, 30€ half board). The restaurant serves menus of Corsican spe-

cialities, such as wild board stew with myrtle, from 14€ to 21€. Down the hill from the col in the village proper, the *Auberge du Col* (☎ 04.95.72.09.87, www.auberge-bavella.com; open April-Oct), opposite the shop, also does filling *menus corses* (from 14€ to 22€), in addition to an exhaustive à la carte selection. House specialities include local-style lasagna made with fresh brocciu, lamb aux herbes du maquis, and sweet chestnut flan. Around the back of the restaurant, an annexe of six-berth dorms provides basic **gîte d'étape accommodation** for 13€ per bed (30€ for half-board).

The only other place to stay is *Le Refuge* (☎ 04.95.70.00.39; open May-Sep) a couple of doors down, which also has a handful of simple dorms (with shared showers and toilets) costing the same as those at the Auberge. You can order wood-fired pizzas in their small restaurant, as well as a range of inexpensive snacks.

For those who can't face the last étape and a half to Conca it's worth knowing that a **bus** departs from Bavella for Ajaccio via Levie, Propriano and other villages in the Alta Rocca. The service, run by Autocars Ricci (☎ 04.95.51.08.19 or ☎ 04.95.76 25.59), operates daily (including holidays) from July 1 until September 15; outside these dates it starts from Zonza, 7km south-west down the D268, and operates Mon-Sat only.

Bavella → Paliri [Map 31, p195]

The GR20 leaves Bavella on the piste behind the Auberge du Col. Once you've filled up your water bottle at the **spring** (Funtana di u Canone), follow the track at contour level for 450m to where the orange waymarked trail to Trou de la Bombe (a popular picnic spot) peels away to the right. The red-and-white flashes drop quite steeply downhill from here to cross a stream and, after another short descent down a wooded spur, meet a motorable piste forestière. This crosses the Ravin de Volpajola via a **bridge** from which a right turn and a five-minute detour upstream take you to a beautiful but little-known bathing spot.

Thus refreshed, you can look forward to the last climb of the day, which strikes uphill to the right of the piste, 20m after the bridge. From here to Conca you'll be following an ancient transhumant path along which shepherds used to

---

(Opposite) Top: The phantasmagorical Aiguilles de Bavella. **Bottom**: Sea views from snow fields: a Corsican speciality. The watershed approaches the coast at Bocca d'Oro (1840m, see p173), with the eastern plain below and hills of Tuscany visible across the Tyrrhenian Sea. (Photos © David Abram).

drive their flocks from the coastal plains north of Porto-Vecchio to the high valleys around Alcudina and the Plateau de Coscione. Much of the well-engineered route has retained its original, time-worn paving slabs and buttressed bends, now maintained by the PNRC.

Winding north-east from the piste at a gradually steepening gradient, the old path crests the Crête de Punta Tafonata ('Pierced Peak Ridge') at the **Foce Finosa** (1206m) where a superb view south-west over the wild valleys below greets you. Beyond it the stream-eroded route drops sharply down, switching first to the right and then to the left to begin a descending traverse of a hillside that's dwarfed by the massive cliffs of Punta Tafonata di Paliri.

Refuge de Paliri

Less than five hours from Conca, Paliri is often leapfrogged by trekkers eager to polish off the last, easy stage of the GR20. But the hut, which stands on a beautiful belvédère dominated by the awesome east wall of Punta Tafonata, makes an ideal base for exploring one of the island's truly unique landscapes. With your pack stashed in the hut you can amble unencumbered up the approach trail through maritime pine forests to the mighty pierced peak itself (whose amazing hole is visible high above at the head of the cliffs), or simply laze around enjoying the sublime views over the Vallée du Carciara.

The refuge is a small one, with bunks for only 20 people, but the bivouac area is spacious and superbly sited. To reach the water source you've a bit of a trek back down the path, where a sign points the way to a spring and shower area.

STAGE SIXTEEN: PALIRI → CONCA
[MAP 31, opposite; MAP 32, p197]

Overview

The concluding stage of the GR20 holds no unpleasant surprises. With the splendour of Bavella receding behind you, resinous maritime pine forest gives way to a landscape of blasted, orange-tinted rock, charred trees and brittle, spiny maquis. Underfoot, the crystalline gravel of the Corsican coast begins to reassert itself as you press through a belt of rock outcrops eroded into phantasmagorical shapes. By the time the door-sized niche of the Bocca d'Usciolu heralds the start of the final descent to Conca, the high peaks will seem like a distant memory and you'll probably have your mind fixed firmly on the prospect of a hot shower.

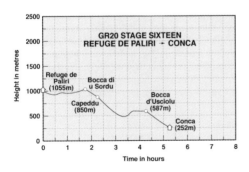

The one danger you really do have to be aware of on this leg is the **heat**. Most of the path

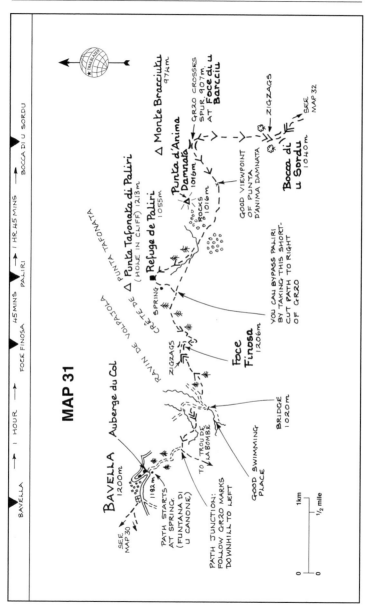

MAP 31

BAVELLA 1200m
Auberge du Col

BAVELLA
1182m

SEE MAP 30

PATH STARTS AT SPRING (FUNTANA DI U CANONE)

PATH JUNCTION: FOLLOW GR20 MARKS DOWNHILL TO LEFT

GOOD SWIMMING PLACE

TO TROU DE LA BOMBE

BRIDGE 1020m

RAVIN DE VOLPAJOLA

CRETE DE △ PUNTA TAFONATA

ZIGZAGS

Foce Finosa 1206m

ZIGZAGS

SPRING

△ Punta Tafonata di Paliri 1213m (HOLE IN CLIFF)

■ Refuge de Paliri 1055m

ROCKS 1016m

△ Monte Bracciutu 974m

△ Punta d'Anima Damnata 1016m

GR20 CROSSES SPUR. 907m AT Foce di u Barcciu

YOU CAN BYPASS PALIRI BY TAKING THIS SHORT-CUT PATH TO RIGHT OF GR20

GOOD VIEWPOINT OF PUNTA D'ANIMA DAMNATA

ZIGZAGS

Bocca di u Sordu 1040m

SEE MAP 32

1 km
0
½ mile
0

BAVELLA → 1 HOUR → FOCE FINOSA → 45 MINS → PALIRI → 1 HR 45 MINS → BOCCA DI U SORDU

TRAILBLAZER

from Paliri faces south-east and is thus exposed to the full glare of the morning sun – a force to be reckoned with from June onwards. After the cooler climes of the interior, the temperatures here can come as a surprise. With only one (easily missed) source of drinking water on the route, the risk of **dehydration** is significant. Bear in mind that if you're hit by sunstroke you'll have a very long, dry and shadeless walk to safety. So, if the weather's hot, force down as much liquid as you can and carry at least two litres with you.

Route guide

A steepish descent through the narrow, pine-forested stream valley that runs south-east from Refuge de Paliri is followed by a short ascent to a rocky gap from where you have an impressive view of the witch's-hat-shaped **Punta d'Anima Damnata** ('Peak of the Damned Soul'; 1016m), a renowned climbing spot. Having crossed through the gap in the rocks above, you penetrate the edge of a broad cirque, dominated by the mass of Monte Bracciutu (974m) that rises from the centre of the amphitheatre.

The old transhumant path keeps faithfully to contour level as it swings north around the flank of the basin to round a sharp shoulder at a pass called **Foce di u Barcciu** (907m). Once around the spur the waymarks veer decisively south into an ascending traverse that culminates with a strenuous, zigzagging climb to **Bocca di u Sordu** (1040m), the last serious climb of the GR20. From the top you can see the sea and trace most of the onward route, which descends from here across a large depression cluttered by eroded slabs of white granite. Clinging to the sandy soil between them are the first of many scorched trees – the result of the fire that laid waste to much of Conca's deserted hinterland in 1985. At the end of a fairly long, steep descent through maquis on a rain-rutted, gravelly path the trail cuts past ruined stone huts at **Capeddu**, where a sign points the way through the bushes to the only **spring** of the étape. There's also a rubbish point here, installed primarily for walkers heading north on the GR20, that's periodically emptied by helicopter (and rummaged by stray dogs and pigs). From Capeddu the descent continues in earnest down the side of a shallow valley, over a low, broad ridge and thence more steeply down the side of another valley to cross the **Punta Pinzuta** stream, beyond which the path swings right to follow the bank southwards. This whole section of former Laricio pine forest is blighted by ghoulish fire-blackened trees.

After fording the stream a second time the GR20 climbs in a short series of tight switchbacks to another pass, beyond which it contours through more dense maquis around the lower north-eastern slopes of a hill called **Alzu di Lanu** (769m). Ahead of you to the south-east you can make out at last the niche of **Bocca d'Usciolu** (587m), a gap in the ridge that feels like a ceremonial gateway marking the end of the GR20. Once through it, you'll finally lose sight of the high mountains. From here on it's downhill all the way to Conca.

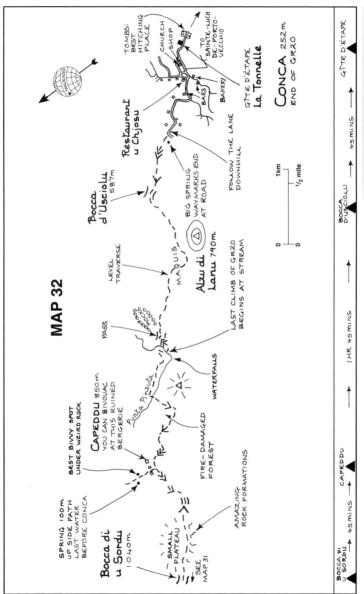

MAP 32

Bocca di u Sordu 1040m.

SPRING 100m. UP SIDE PATH LAST WATER. BEFORE CONCA

BEST BIVVY SPOT UNDER WEIRD ROCK

CAPEDDU 850m. YOU CAN BIVOUAC AT THIS RUINED BERGERIE.

SMALL PLATEAU

SEE MAP 31

AMAZING ROCK FORMATIONS

FIRE-DAMAGED FOREST

Punta Pinzuta

WATERFALLS

PASS

LEVEL TRAVERSE

MAQUIS

LAST CLIMB OF GR20 BEGINS AT STREAM

Alzu di Lanu 790m.

Bocca d'Usciolu 587m.

BIG SPRING WAYMARKS END AT ROAD

FOLLOW THE LANE DOWNHILL

Restaurant u Chjosu

TOMBS: BEST HITCHING PLACE

CHURCH

SHOP

TO SAINTE-LUCIE-DE-PORTO-VECCHIO

BARS

BAKERY

GÎTE D'ÉTAPE La Tonnelle

CONCA 252m. END OF GR20

0 ——— 1km
0 ——— ½ mile

CONCA   [MAP 32, p197]

Were it not at the end of the big GR, Conca, spread around the head of a valley below an amphitheatre of crags and maquis, would be a largely undistinguished place – picturesque enough but not somewhere you'd go out of your way to visit.

As it is, though, thousands of trekkers pour through here annually, most of them via the gîte d'étape at the bottom of the village, which benefits from a remarkable (although typically Corsican) absence of competition.

Once you've showered off, had a nose around the centre and swapped a few yarns with fellow GR veterans, there's precious little to do other than savour the prospect of a dip in the sea, only 9km down the valley.

Where to stay and eat

Trekking traffic through Conca is all but monopolized by the large *Gîte d'étape La Tonnelle* (☎ 04.95.71.46.55; open Apr-Nov), a one-stop establishment which, with well-oiled efficiency, provides for the specific needs of *nouveaux arrivées* off the GR. Rates range from 15€ for a dorm bunk to 19€ for a bed in a double room. You can also camp in their very large, well-shaded garden for 5€. The rates include access to hot showers.

Most people who stay here celebrate with a slap-up meal; the cheapest way to do this is to opt for half-board (an extra 19€ on top of your accommodation, and **obligatory in July and August**), which buys you a three-course supper and French breakfast with fresh bread, jam and croissants. The

---

Les Faux Éleveurs

The kind of fire damage encountered on the GR20 in the hills above Conca is sadly typical of the landscape in Corsica these days; each year upwards of 15,000 hectares of forest and maquis are consumed by flames. This calamity appears all the more shocking when you realize that the vast majority of fires are started intentionally – not by lone pyromaniacs or thoughtless trekkers but by ordinary Corsicans.

The truth behind the annual infernos, which together account for one-fifth of all the land laid waste by fire in France, was exposed by a visionary (some would say reckless) fire-service chief in 1994 after he noticed that a disproportionate number of the blazes occurred on common land near villages. By cross-referencing his statistics with farming patterns he showed that the most likely culprits were the owners of cattle.

Fire has for centuries been used on the island as a means of clearing unproductive land so that green shoots may grow back to provide fodder for animals. But this ancient transhumant practice spiralled out of control in the 1990s following the introduction of dairy **subsidies**, since when Corsican villagers have acquired more cows than they know what to do with. Rather than dip into the 1250€ most receive each month from Brussels to buy in fodder, the so-called 'Faux Éleveurs' ('Fake Cattle Rearers') simply torch the hillsides around their villages where the animals that nominally belong to them roam free.

When the EU was informed about this destructive abuse of the Common Agricultural Policy it suspended all aid to Corsica. The move slashed the incidence of wild fires almost overnight. Payments have since been re-instated but the problem persists, not least because of the wide-ranging economic benefits fires bring to an island plagued by unemployment for most of the year. When a mountain burns in Corsica, firemen, foresters, builders, council workers and Canadair pilots (who douse the flames with water from specially converted tanker planes) all get a lot of overtime pay.

Which beach?

If you've walked all the way to Conca from Calenzana, you can pride your-self on having covered 140km across some of the most rugged mountain terrain in Europe, notching up 19,000m of ascent and descent over the 16 stages. After such a mammoth trek, few can resist the lure of the beaches that line the near-by coast, which comprise some of the most beautiful shorelines in the entire Mediterranean.

Unfortunately, without your own transport little of it is easily accessible unless you've got time to spare. You'd need at least a day to reach the pick of the beaches **south of Porto-Vecchio** (see box p104).

All things considered your quickest route to pearl-white sand and turquoise water is to head 4km south-east of Sainte-Lucie-de-Porto-Vecchio on the main N198, to the **plage de Pinarellu**. A long, gently curving bay enfolded by headlands and overlooked by a Genoan watchtower, it has ticks in all the right boxes and is large enough to soak up the crowds of holidaymakers and the campers from the site behind it who descend there in July and August. Best of all, the owner of Conca's gîte d'é-tape 'La Tonnelle' will drop you slap on the beach in his minibus.

Further north, the bays of the **Côte des Nacres** – Solenara and Anse de Favone – are mediocre by Corsican standards and really not worth breaking the journey to Bastia for.

If, on the other hand, you're heading up the other side of the island towards Ajaccio, one more option stands out. You'll have to walk 4km from the main road to reach it, but **Roccapina** is a real gem. The simplest way to get there is to jump on any Eurocorse Voyage bus heading between Porto-Vecchio and the capital Ajaccio, and ask to be dropped off at the turning for the beach, exactly 42km south-west along the N196. A piste leads from the main road past a pleasant little campsite to a bay backed by a band of shell sand that's easily one of the most spectacular and undeveloped beaches in southern Corsica.

food is nothing special but the portions are generous and the atmosphere well worth shelling out for, even if this would normal-ly be beyond your budget.

The only other place to eat in the vil-lage is the old-fashioned *Restaurant U Chjosu*, on the main street, whose 20€ *menu corse* is a notch above the cheap and cheerful food dished up in the gîte d'étape.

Conca also has a couple of **grocery shops** (in summer the one just below the church near the gîte stays open the latest) and a **bakery**.

Onward transport

Predictably, the only public transport between Conca and the coast road is laid on by the gîte d'étape, which boasts of never

leaving anyone stranded in the village. Straight after breakfast, the **gîte minibus** begins to shuttle trekkers down the valley to Sainte-Lucie-de-Porto-Vecchio (4€), from where you can pick up one of Rapides Bleue's two daily services up the east coast to Bastia via Solenzara and Aléria. Timetables for this route may be consulted in the gîte. Alternatively, pay a bit more to be driven all the way to Porto-Vecchio (7€) where buses leave for Ajaccio, stopping at Sartène and Propriano en route. They'll deliver two people to Ajaccio for 30€ (dropping to 12€ per head if there are more than two).

For more details on transport, accom-modation and services in Porto-Vecchio, see pp104-7.

APPENDIX A: FRENCH/CORSICAN GLOSSARY

balisage waymarking

bandit d'honneur outlaw who, by tradition, has been forced into banditry after committing a vendetta murder

bastelle* Corsican pasty, usually filled with spinach and ewe's cheese

belvédère natural balcony or viewpoint

bergerie shepherds' settlement/hut

bocca* pass

brêche gap in a rocky ridge serving as a pass

buvette snack van

cala* beach

camping sauvage wild camping (ie not on a designated campsite)

canastrelli* traditional Corsican biscuits

capitainerie harbour master's office

capu peak*

castagna* chestnut

casteddu* Megalithic castle

châtaigne/iers chestnut/chestnut tree

chiostru* circular stone shelter for storing and drying chestnuts

cirque natural amphitheatre at head of valley

col pass

contrôleur ticket inspector

curé priest

département administrative region

étang lagoon

étape stage (of walk)

farina* (chestnut) flour

fiadone Corsican flan made with chestnuts and honey

flèchage waymarking

foce pass

funtana spring

gardien warden of a refuge

gérant warden of a gîte d'étape

Grande Barrière nickname for the Paglia Orba massif

Grande Randonnée French Trekking Authority's official designation for a special class of long-distance routes, all numbered separately

Hôtel de Ville town hall

lavoir village laundry tank

libre service self service (supermarket)

mairie town hall (mayor's office)

maison forestière forest hut (for use by forestry staff)

maquis* Corsican scrub

maquisard Resistance fighter in World War II

menhir standing stone

mouflon rare Corsican mountain sheep (see box p128)

navette shuttle bus

névé patch of eternal snow

ONF French national forestry service

Parc Naturel Régional Corse (PNRC) regional nature park of Corsica (see p59)

partage des eaux watershed (see p57)

passarelle (suspendu) (suspension) foot bridge

pétanque boules (French bowls)

piste unmade, dirt road

piste forestière forest track

polenda* traditional Corsican dish – a paste made from chestnut flour

polyphony/ies choral singing (see box p133)

pozzi*/pozzines high-altitude streams running through spongy turf banks

Préfet French government's top representative in Corsica

rau* stream

ravin gully

règlement de compte 'settling of scores' – a vendetta term

sac allegé 'lightened bag' – a bag-carrying service offered by some trekking companies

scandule* roof tile

séchoir drying shelter (for chestnuts)

Topoguide French trekking authority's (FFRP) official route guide, featuring topographical maps

torregiani* wardens of Genoan watch towers

torri* Genoan watchtowers

trinighellu* Corsica's diminutive train

vendetta/vinditta* feud

Note * = Corsican word

APPENDIX B: USEFUL WORDS AND PHRASES

As English is not widely spoken or understood in Corsica, you'll almost certainly have to speak French at some stage during your trek. The following list of words and phrases is designed as a practical aid, to help you converse with fellow trekkers, understand directions and weather forecasts, secure accommodation and find what you need in the towns and villages. An additional glossary, explaining the meaning of words and phrases that appear in italics in this book, appears opposite.

In the following list (m) designates a masculine noun (to be preceded by 'un' or 'le'), (f) a feminine noun (to be used with 'une' or 'la'), and (pl) a plural (to be used with 'les').

Basic words and phrases
When addressing people in French always use Monsieur for a man, Madame for a woman and Mademoiselle for a young woman. Bonjour alone is not enough.

Hello/Good morning/Good day	*Bonjour*	Excuse me	*Pardon*
Good afternoon	*Bon après midi*	How much is this please?	*C'est combien s'il vous plaît?*
Good evening/ good night	*Bonsoir/ bonne nuit*	Please	*S'il vous plaît*
Goodbye	*Au revoir*	Thank you	*Merci beaucoup/ Tiran graze**
Hi	*Salut*	today/tomorrow	*aujourd'hui/demain*
Help!	*Au secours!*	the morning/ afternoon/evening	*le matin/ l'après-midi/le soir*
How are you?	*Ça va?*	open/closed	*ouvert/fermé*
Fine thanks	*Oui ça va*	more/less	*plus/moins*
Do you speak English?	*Est-ce que vous parlez Anglais?*	hot/cold	*chaud/froid*
I don't understand	*Je ne comprends pas*		

General vocabulary

bank	*banque* (f)	telephone booth	*cabine téléphonique* (f)
post office	*poste* (f)	phone card	*télecarte*
stamp	*timbre* (m)	mobile phone	*portable* (m)
money	*argent* (m)	timetable	*horaire* (m)
grocery shop	*épicerie* (f)	methylated spirits	*alcool à bruler* (m)
supermarket	*supermarché* (m)	left-luggage office	*consigne* (f)
bakery	*boulangerie* (f)	toilet block (campsite)	*bloc sanitaire* (m)
tobacconist's	*tabac* (m)	slide film	*pellicule diapositive* (f)
launderette	*laverie automatique* (f)	cash dispenser/ATM	*distributeur (automatique) de billets* (m)
toilet	*toilettes* (pl)		
police	*gendarmes* (pl)	tourist office	*office de tourisme/syndicat d'initiative* (m)
police station	*gendarmerie* (m)		

Directions and travel

north	*nord*	(to the) right	*(à) droite*	near	*près de*
south	*sud*	behind	*derrière*	far	*loin*
east	*est*	in front of	*devant*	over	*sur*
west	*ouest*	before	*avant*	single ticket	*billet simple*
(to the) left	*(à) gauche*	after	*après*	return ticket	*billet aller-retour*
straight on	*tout droit*	under	*sous*		

Where is . . .? *Où se trouve ....?*
  the bus station *la terminal routière* or *gare routière* (f)
  the train station *la gare SNCF* (f)   the airport *l'aéroport* (m)

Where is . . .?		*Où se trouve* ....?	
the ferry terminal	*la gare maritime* (f)	the bridge	*le pont* (m)
What time does the train/bus leave?		*Il part à quelle heure, le train/bus s'il vous plaît?*	
What time does the train/bus arrive?		*Il arrive à quelle heure, le train/bus s'il vous plaît*	
Is this the road to ....?		*Est-ce que c'est la route à* .... ?	
How many kilometres to .....?		*Combien de kilomètres à* ....?	

On the trail

trekking	*randonnée* (f)	trekker	*randonneur* (m)/*randonneuse* (f)
footpath	*sentier* (m)	mule track	*chemin muletier* (m)
waymarking	*balisage* (m)	well/badly waymarked	*bien/mal fléché*
stage	*étape* (f)	slope	*pente* (f)
zigzags	*lacets* (pl)	steep	*raide*
descent	*descente* (f)	ascent	*ascension* (f)
map	*carte* (f)	compass	*boussole* (f)
rucksack	*sac à dos* (m)	head-torch	*lampe frontale* (f)
water bottle	*gourde* (f)	corkscrew	*tire bouchon* (m)
shepherds' huts	*bergeries* (f)	sleeping bag	*sac de couchage* (m)
signboard	*panneau* (m)	spring	*source* or *fontaine* (f)
slippery	*glisseux*	It's steep! (colloquial)	*Ça grimpe!*
to climb	*grimper*	to cross	*traverser* or *franchir*
to go up again	*remonter*	to go down again	*redescendre*
to follow	*suivre* or *longer*	to bear or turn (left)	*bifurquer (à gauche)*
provisions/re-provisioning	*ravitaillement* (m)		
suspension bridge	*passarelle suspendue* (f)		
pocket knife	*couteau de poche* (or *Opinel*)		
Is this the GR20 path?	*Est-ce que c'est bien le sentier GR20?*		

Landscape

mountain	*montagne* (f)	ridge	*crête* (f)
pass	*col* (m)/*bocca** (f)	valley	*vallée* (f)
summit	*cime* (f)/*sommet* (m)	river	*rivière* (f)
plateau	*plateau* (m)/*pianu** (m)	stream	*ruisseau* (m)
forest	*forêt* (f)	mountain stream	*torrent* (m)
wood	*bosquet* (m)	waterfall	*cascade* (f)
gorge or ravine	*défilé* (m)	boulder choke	*éboulis* (m)
slab	*dalle* (f)	snow patch	*névé* (f)
rock	*rocher* (m)	rocky	*rocailleux*
cliff	*falaise* (f)		

Health

blister	*ampoule* (f)	plaster	*pansement* (m)
sun cream	*crême solaire* (f)	sunstroke/sunburn	*coup de soleil* (m)
sprained ankle	*cheville tordue* (f)	knee	*genou* (m)
broken leg	*jambe cassée*	twisted leg	*jambe tordue* (f)
sore knees	*mal aux genoux* (m)	toothache	*mal aux dents* (m)
doctor	*docteur* (m)	dentist	*dentiste* (m)
toilet paper	*papier hygiénique* (m)	ear plugs	*bouches d'oreille* (f)
tampon	*tampon* (m)	condom	*préservatif* (m)
It hurts	*Ça me fait mal*		

Weather

| weather | *temps* (m) | weather forecast | *météo* (m) |
| good weather | *beau temps* (m) | bad weather | *mauvais temps* (m) |

rain	*pluie* (f)	wind	*vent/venteux*
drizzle	*crachin* (m)	strong/weak (wind)	*fort/faible*
snow	*neige* (f)	hail	*grêle* (f)
ice	*glace* (f)	fog	*brouillard* (m)
storm/stormy	*orage* (m)/*orageux*	mist	*brûme* (f)
lightning	*foudre* (f)	thunder	*tonnerre* (m)
flooding	*innondation* (f)		

Accommodation (see also pp70-3)

accommodation	*hébergement* (m)	mountain hut	*refuge* (m)
hotel	*hôtel* (m)	dormitory	*dortoire* (m)
hostel	*gîte d'étape* (m)	bivouac area	*aire de bivouac* (f)
B&B	*chambre d'hôte* (f)	restaurant/inn	*auberge* (f)
municipal campsite	*camping municipal* (m)	campsite	*le camping* (m)
bed	*lit* (m)	one night's stay	*nuitée* (f)
breakfast included	*petit déjeuner compris*	half-board	*demi-pension* (f)
warden (refuge)	*gardien(ne)*(m/f)	warden (gîte d'étape)	*gérant*
boss/proprietor	*patron(ne)* (m/f)		

I'd like to reserve ....   *Je voudrais reserver ....*
  a room for one/two/three people   *une chambre pour un(e)/deux/trois person(ne/s)*
  with/without a shower   *avec/sans douche*
  with/without washbasin   *avec/sans lavabo*
  with separate toilet   *avec WC à l'étage*
  en suite   *avec douche-WC dans la chambre*
  with a balcony   *avec balcon* (m)
Can I see the room?   *Est-ce que je peux voir la chambre?*
Do you accept credit cards?   *Est-ce vous acceptez les cartes de crédit?*

Eating and drinking

breakfast	*petit déjeuner* (m)	pepper	*poivre* (m)
dinner	*repas du soir* (m)	salt	*sel* (m)
lunch	*déjeuner* (m)/*repas du midi* (m)	Moroccan stew	*tagine*
snack	*casse croûte* (f)	morel (mushroom)	*morille* (f)
service included	*service compris*	egg	*oeuf* (m)
service not included	*service non compris*	cheese	*fromage* (m)
set menu	*le menu/menu fixe* (m)	ewe's cheese	*brocciu*
menu	*carte* (f)	warm goat's cheese	*chèvre chaud*
Corsican menu	*menu corse* (m)	biscuits	*biscuits*(pl)
meal(s) of the day	*plat(s) du jour* (m)	bread	*pain* (m)
bill	*l'addition* (f)	noodles	*nouille(s)* (f/pl)
desssert	*déssert* (m)	pasta	*les pâtse* (pl)
vegetarian	*végétarien(ne)* (m/f)	pancake shop	*crêperie* (f)
sandwich	*sandwich* (m) or *panini* (m)	fish	*poisson* (m)
meat	*viande* (f)	vegetables	*légumes* (pl)
cured meat	*charcuterie* (f)	aniseed spirit	*pastis*
liver sausage	*figatellu*	local spirit	*eau de vie*
dry sausage	*saucisson sec* (m)	jug (of wine)	*pichet* (m)
wine	*vin* (m)	milk	*lait* (m)
beer	*bière* (f)	coffee	*café* (m)
tea	*thé* (m)		

Note * = Corsican word

Numerals

1	*un/une*	16	*seize*	40	*quarante*	150	*cent-*
2	*deux*	17	*dix-sept*	50	*cinquante*		*cinquante*
3	*trois*	18	*dix-huit*	60	*soixante*	200	*deux cents*
4	*quatre*	19	*dix-neuf*	70	*soixante-dix*	300	*trois cents*
5	*cinq*	20	*vingt*	71	*soixante et*	400	*quatre cents*
6	*six*	21	*vingt et un*		*onze*	500	*cinq cents*
7	*sept*	22	*vingt-deux*	75	*soixante-*	600	*six cents*
8	*huit*	23	*vingt-trois*		*quinze*	700	*sept cents*
9	*neuf*	24	*vingt-quatre*	80	*quatre-vingts*	800	*huit cents*
10	*dix*	25	*vingt-cinq*	90	*quatre-vingt-*	900	*neuf cents*
11	*onze*	26	*vingt-six*		*dix*	1000	*mille*
12	*douze*	27	*vingt-sept*	95	*quatre-vingt-*	5000	*cinq mille*
13	*treize*	28	*vingt-huit*		*quinze*	1,000,000	
14	*quatorze*	29	*vingt-neuf*	100	*cent*		*un million*
15	*quinze*	30	*trente*				

APPENDIX C: MINIMUM IMPACT TREKKING

DOS AND DON'TS

With 17,000 or more people pouring along just the GR20 each summer, the potential impact of trekking on Corsica's natural landscape is considerable. The onus is therefore on every visitor to help preserve the island's natural environment as far as possible. There are a number of ways you can do this without making any great personal sacrifices:

Don't leave litter Everything you take with you on Corsica's trails should either be eaten or packed out and disposed of in the nearest village, where you'll always be able to find a municipal wheely-bin. This includes orange peel, which takes around six months to decompose. On the GR20 the refuges are all equipped with trash bins (emptied at great effort and expense by helicopter) which you're welcome to use.

Don't light fires Never be tempted to burn your rubbish, or anything else, or to make fires if you camp wild. Each year upwards of 15,000 hectares of forest and maquis go up in smoke in Corsica (see box p198). Some of the fires are started by careless trekkers.

Don't pick flowers However tempting it may be, leave the flora completely intact for others to enjoy.

Don't pollute water sources If there's a latrine available, use it. Never defecate within 20 metres of a water source. When washing yourself or your clothes with detergents, don't pollute streams or lakes. Carry the water at least 20 metres from its source before pouring it away.

Dispose of toilet paper hygienically In the summer months you rarely need waymarks thanks to the lines of discarded toilet paper that litter Corsica's footpaths. This is a particularly unpleasant problem along the more accessible stretches of the GR20. The best way to deal with your used toilet paper is not to bury it, but stick it in a plastic bag for hygienic disposal when you reach a refuge or village.

Never defecate in the rocks, where your faeces will attract flies and create a health hazard. If you get taken short, dig a hole in woodland soil at least 20m away from any path or stream and cover it up well afterwards.

INDEX

TRAILBLAZER GUIDES – TITLE LIST

Title	Edition
Adventure Cycle-Touring Handbook	1st edn out now
Adventure Motorcycling Handbook	5th edn out now
Australia by Rail	5th edn out now
Azerbaijan	3rd edn out now
The Blues Highway – New Orleans to Chicago	2nd edn out now
China Rail Handbook	1st edn late 2008
Coast to Coast (British Walking Guide)	3rd edn out now
Cornwall Coast Path (British Walking Guide)	2nd edn out now
Corsica Trekking – GR20	1st edn out now
Dolomites Trekking – AV1 & AV2	2nd edn out now
Inca Trail, Cusco & Machu Picchu	3rd edn out now
Indian Rail Handbook	1st edn mid 2008
Hadrian's Wall Walk (British Walking Guide)	2nd edn mid 2008
Himalaya by Bike – a route and planning guide	1st edn mid 2008
Japan by Rail	2nd edn out now
Kilimanjaro – the trekking guide (includes Mt Meru)	2nd edn out now
Mediterranean Handbook	1st edn out now
Nepal Mountaineering Guide	1st edn late 2008
New Zealand – The Great Walks	1st edn out now
North Downs Way (British Walking Guide)	1st edn out now
Norway's Arctic Highway	1st edn out now
Offa's Dyke Path (British Walking Guide)	2nd edn out now
Overlanders' Handbook – worldwide driving guide	1st edn early 2009
Pembrokeshire Coast Path (British Walking Guide)	2nd edn out now
Pennine Way (British Walking Guide)	2nd edn mid 2008
The Ridgeway (British Walking Guide)	1st edn out now
Siberian BAM Guide – rail, rivers & road	2nd edn out now
The Silk Roads – a route and planning guide	2nd edn out now
Sahara Overland – a route and planning guide	2nd edn out now
Sahara Abenteuerhandbuch (German edition)	1st edn out now
Scottish Highlands – The Hillwalking Guide	1st edn out now
South Downs Way (British Walking Guide)	2nd edn out now
South-East Asia – The Graphic Guide	1st edn out now
Tibet Overland – mountain biking & jeep touring	1st edn out now
Tour du Mont Blanc	1st edn mid 2008
Trans-Canada Rail Guide	4th edn out now
Trans-Siberian Handbook	7th edn out now
Trekking in the Annapurna Region	4th edn out now
Trekking in the Everest Region	5th edn late 2008
Trekking in Ladakh	3rd edn out now
Trekking in the Pyrenees	3rd edn out now
The Walkers' Haute Route – Mont Blanc to Matterhorn	1st edn May 2008
West Highland Way (British Walking Guide)	3rd edn mid 2008

www.trailblazer-guides.com